Praise for Ralph Blumenthal's

Stork Club

"*Stork Club* is a glistening, immaculately researched requiem for a heavyweight establishment that set inarguable precedents for all the trendy operations to come. . . . The book's incessant roll call of celebrities (accompanied by a multitude of photographs) is made even more involving by their exploits. . . . Blumenthal is quite adept at synthesizing profuse historical documentation into a lucid narrative that is remarkably breezy and easily digested." — Frank Halperin, *Philadelphia City Paper*

"A wonderful book." — Liz Smith, *New York Post*

"An evocative, well-researched book. . . . An important addition to our social history." — Pete Hamill, *New York Times Book Review*

"A highly entertaining, instructive, superbly anecdotal work that lifts the curtain on an era destined not to return." — Don Freeman, *San Diego Union-Tribune*

"Ralph Blumenthal has deftly recaptured the Stork Club's evanescent glamour. . . . He has dug up notes Billingsley made for a never-written autobiography; interviewed the proprietor's family, friends, and former employees; and ransacked appropriate archives. His accumulated data give heft to what is in effect a twin biography, of the club and its owner-manager. . . . Blumenthal's good-humored style keeps the story going." — Mike Wallace, *New York Times*

"A seductive account of the legendary night club. . . . Blumenthal tells it in a smooth and engaging way that harbors all the panache Sherman Billingsley could have hoped for." — Clay Smith, *Austin Chronicle*

"Blumenthal brings alive a period we'll never see again." — Neal Travis, *New York Post*

"A marvelous evocation of New York night life from the Depression through the mid-sixties. . . . While Blumenthal is clearly enchanted with the comings and goings at the club — as a social history of the years from Prohibition through the Vietnam War — he's not a romantic. He's not trying to create a nostalgic view of Billingsley's reign but a clearheaded, concise account of how power among organized crime, Hollywood celebrities, New York politicians, and the wealthy came together over an oversized black-and-white ashtray and a couple of martinis." — Michael Blowen, *Boston Globe*

"A generously vivid account of a rarefied segment of twentieth-century Americana, casting Gatsbyesque characters against a glittering background of show business glamour, politics, greed, and infamy. A most arresting read." — Bobby Short, entertainer

"Blumenthal was able to get to the bottom of the club's fame. . . . He weighs in on what is perhaps the most storied moment in the storied club's history, the night in the summer of 1951 when black chanteuse Josephine Baker showed up, didn't get served, and created one of the great stinks of the early Civil Rights era. . . . Blumenthal sheds new light on what really happened, the motives of those involved, and how that racist moment developed a momentum that broke the back of longtime civil-rights proponent Winchell and the club he had long championed as 'the New Yorkiest place' in the Big Apple." — Roger Moore, *Fort Worth Star-Telegram*

"A vivid portrait . . . full of anecdotes. . . . There's romance in this story — and plenty of murkier dealings, too. . . . Sherman Billingsley's own story — from Oklahoma small town to master salesman of New York glitter — is so colorful. . . . *Stork Club* is a compelling account of Billingsley's extraordinary career." — Andre Balazs, *New York Observer*

"A glorious evocation of the onetime epicenter of celebrity in all its glamour, its excess, and its idiocy. It is a story that has long needed telling, and *Stork Club* tells it with both punch and polish." — Neal Gabler, author of *Life: The Movie* and *Winchell*

STORK CLUB

STORK CLUB

RALPH BLUMENTHAL

AMERICA'S
MOST FAMOUS
NIGHTSPOT
AND THE
LOST WORLD
OF
CAFÉ SOCIETY

POSTSCRIPT BY
SHERMANE BILLINGSLEY

LITTLE, BROWN AND COMPANY
BOSTON, NEW YORK, LONDON

TO MY STORK CLUB — DEBBIE, ANNA, AND SOPHIE

Originally published in hardcover
by Little, Brown and Company, May 2000
First Back Bay paperback edition, November 2001

For information on Time Warner Trade Publishing's online publishing program,
visit www.ipublish.com

Library of Congress Cataloging-in-Publication Data
Blumenthal, Ralph.
Stork Club : America's most famous nightspot and
the lost world of café society / Ralph Blumenthal.
p. cm.
ISBN 0–316–10531–7 (hc)/0-316-10617-8 (pb)
1. Stork Club (New York, N.Y.)   2. Billingsley, Sherman.
I. Title.
TX945.5.S76B558   2000
641.5'09747'1 — dc21   99–40200
10 9 8 7 6 5 4 3 2 1
Q-MART
Book design by Iris Weinstein
Printed in the United States of America

CONTENTS

PROLOGUE

SSSssshhhhhhhh.

A flat rectangle of water slides down the rocky wall of a sudden oasis in the skyscraper canyons of Manhattan's East Fifties. The cascade erases the blaring traffic horns and soothes brown baggers, fugitive smokers fleeing their offices, and urban vagabonds with their bundles of soda cans and cardboard shelter. Spindly young trees shade the white wire chairs and round all-weather tables wobbling on the rickety cobblestones. Sandwiched between the Bank of the Philippine Islands and a gallery for children's art studies, this little tableau of peace is a perversely inappropriate monument marking a site where thrills, not tranquillity or sanity, once ruled the New York night. By the entrance, a bronze plaque dedicates this pocket park to the memory of Samuel Paley (1875–1963), the father of broadcasting pioneer William Paley. At seven-thirty each night, a guard shuts off the waterfall; at eight he locks a tall iron gate and washes down the sidewalk with a hose. It's closing time at what remains of the Stork Club.

The green canopy over the sidewalk is long gone. So is the blue-uniformed doorman, his whistle bleating. Gone too the hastily parked automobiles, whitewalls planted insolently on the sidewalk; the crowds of craning gawkers and autograph hunters; the trudging union pickets; the traffic backed up in the beams of streetlamps; lines of taxis and limousines disgorging men in black tie and silk hats, servicemen in uniform, and veiled ladies in capes and furs and seamed stockings, black stiletto heels going *tap-tap-tap* over the glistening pavement and through the heavy bronze door. . . .

Gone the solid-gold chain and the din of conviviality at the crowded bar, the rattling of ice in cocktail shakers, the pop of champagne corks and the sudden blare of rhumba music when a distant door slid open, the flare of flicked lighters and air violet with pleasurably exhaled smoke, the *clik . . . clik . . . cliiik* from whirled dials of squat black telephones at the café tables and the definitive *clunk!* when the heavy receiver dropped back on the sprocketed cradle, white-jacketed captains marching telephones around the room for important conversations, and roving photographers firing blinding barrages from silvery Speed Graphics.

Gone the mirrored, L-shaped dining room, the golden silk drapery and midnight-blue velvet, the chairs of yellow and gray satin, the crystal chandeliers, the Latin and society bands sliding into each other's places without a break in the wall of music, the colossal globed brandy snifters the size of hot-air balloons, the six-foot-square wine list that could do double duty as an air-raid shelter, silver chafing dishes piled high with shimmering flakes of ice nestling olives, cocktail onions, radishes, and two-foot-high stalks of celery flying table numbers like nautical flags flapping from the mainmast.

Gone the sanctum sanctorum of the Cub Room — the "snub room" — with its captain-guardian familiar to everyone as Saint Peter. Gone the Duke and Duchess of Windsor; J. Edgar Hoover; Frank Costello; Dorothy Kilgallen with heartthrob Johnnie Ray; Brenda Frazier, pale as the goblets of White Spiders she habitually sipped; Hemingway; Chaplin; Hitchcock; the Kennedys; the Roosevelts; the Harrimans; the shah; and, of course, Winchell, strangely bareheaded without his cocked fedora, holding court at table 50, the Royal Box, reviewing the passing parade even as the torch passed to eager successors like young Liz Smith out of Fort Worth, Texas, who thought, *Oh my God, I'm in the Stork Club!*

Gone, too, the fights, dubious attractions of what the tabloids called a café slugging season, bouts like one before the war that pitted Sidney Solomon, former proprietor of the Central Park Casino, and George White, impresario of the Broadway *Scandals* revue who was entertaining one of his chorines at the Stork. White had bought a couple of rounds, and then Solomon offered to reciprocate.

"Aren't you plastered enough?" White inquired.

"Have one anyway," Solomon said, dashing a scotch and soda into White's face before fleeing, as the band struck up one of White's tunes, "Are You Having Any Fun Yet?"

White caught up with Solomon outside the club, delivering a punch like the one he used to drop Rudy Vallee backstage three years before.

"I like a drink," White said, "but not in my face."

Tallulah Bankhead's aunt Marie and the Bankhead clan from Alabama — a Speaker of the House of Representatives, a senator, and assorted other relatives who had come to town for the World's Fair at Flushing Meadows with a detour to East Fifty-third Street — were enthralled. "I've seen two good shows and the fair," said Aunt Marie, "and now I've seen a fight at the Stork Club."

For a while it became a standard Broadway greeting to ask owner Sherman Billingsley, "Hey, Sherman, who's fighting at your place tonight?"

If there had never been a Stork Club, said café boulevardier Lucius Beebe, "mankind in his vast and urgent necessity would have invented one." More than any city on earth, he wrote in his 1946 bible of mixology, *The Stork Club Bar Book,* New York dined, drank, danced, and slept in public, supporting a vast industry of "paragraphers" and eager readers. And the paragon was the Stork Club, where day was mere prelude to the night, and life with all its tumult and industry began in earnest after dusk. It was, Beebe said, less a nightclub than a restaurant, and less a restaurant than a rendezvous of celebrities who happened to like drinking, eating, and dancing, probably in that order. Still, people came expecting a nightclub complete with floor show, and nothing Billingsley could do or say would disabuse them or keep them away.

"To millions and millions of people all over the world," Beebe wrote, "the Stork symbolizes and epitomizes the de luxe upholstery of quintessentially urban existence. It means fame; it means wealth; it means an elegant way of life among celebrated folk. The Stork is the dream of suburbia, a shrine of sophistication in the minds of countless thousands who have never seen it, the fabric and pattern of legend." If a dogfight on Main Street got greater play than war in Europe, well then, a fistfight at the Stork was more newsworthy than the atom bomb.

Why? Beebe pondered. Was it Billingsley's lavishness with favors and friendship with the press? His fortunate location? His cuisine? The occasional patronage of Mrs. Vanderbilt? But the Stork was a success in its first location on the wrong (i.e., west) side of Fifth Avenue, Beebe reflected. Other saloons feted the press. And Mrs. Vanderbilt and her ilk surely patronized other clubs. Beebe left his question unanswered.

Few, it seems, stop these days to puzzle over the irony of this quiet refuge now occupying what was once the apex of the social world, the Everest of the Society Climber. One who does is a spindly, wild-haired musician who is sometimes mistaken for Woody Allen. Don Bader is also a comic of sorts, but he thinks of himself, above all, as the last bandleader at the Stork Club.

It was somewhere under the Burger Heaven sign now painted on a wall of the Philippine bank, he realizes, that his piano once stood. And it was right there, outside on the sidewalk, where during a break one night, he encountered Errol Flynn and his blond teenage girlfriend, Beverly Aadland.

"Hullo, Mr. Flynn," he said.

The blustery, mustached Flynn looked him up and down. "What do you want?" he asked. "Money?"

Bader was mortified. "No," he replied, "I'm the orchestra leader of the Stork Club."

"Oh," said Flynn. "I thought you were a beggar."

Flynn looked Bader over again. "Take her home," he said, inclining his head disdainfully toward the pouting Beverly, who looked barely sixteen. "Get her off my hands. She's bothering me."

Beverly broke Bader's embarrassed silence. "Don't be a wise guy," she hissed to Flynn, and stalked off. Flynn merely shrugged in response.

Bader smiled weakly and headed back into the club.

As was true of so many of its staff, it was a fateful, roundabout route that had brought him to the Stork Club. A Jersey boy, living with his parents in Bradley Beach, he had come to New York on a visit in 1955 and was driving through Central Park with a buddy from NBC when his pal said, "You see the car in front of us with the *X* in the license?" It was a cream-colored Cadillac convertible with red upholstery, only the license plate didn't *have* an X in it — X *was* the license.

"Yeah," he said. "So?"

"That belongs to Sherman Billingsley."

"You're kidding," Bader said. "Sherman Billingsley of the Stork Club?" Even people living in Bradley Beach knew who Sherman Billingsley was. "Jeez, I watch him all the time on the Sunday night program. *X!* What a license!"

And that was it until two years later when Bader and his band were playing in the Rainbow Room of the Albion Hotel in Asbury Park, the Copa of the Jersey Shore. The engagement had five days left to run, and Bader and his boys had no idea what they would do next. One night a man walked up to the stage and said, "How would you like to play at the Stork Club?"

The first thing Bader thought of was the license plate, and then he laughed off the invitation as a joke.

The man returned during the break. "Look," he said, holding up a talisman that shimmered in the club's spotlights. It was a gold Stork Club compact. Bader gave him his phone number. "Ma," Bader said when he got home that night, "they want me to play in the Stork Club."

He had grimaced the first time he tried the Stork's piano. Out of tune, even shot. He complained, but Billingsley didn't want to hear about it, not from him, anyway. Billingsley had his own complaints with Bader, grumbling that the whole band was being paid when many times during their sets only one of the musicians was playing.

"Bader," he said, "you trying to screw me?"

Bader couldn't believe the conversation. Was the boss putting him on?

"No, it's a solo, see."

"They're not playing," Billingsley repeated stubbornly. "Why do they have to stop?"

At times like that you couldn't argue with Mr. B. Maybe he just felt like giving Bader a hard time. Billingsley could be like that.

But Bader could be stubborn, too. He continued protesting about the piano. It was unplayable.

Then one morning the old piano was gone. In its place was a new Baldwin, felt pads wrapping the pedals and the price tag still on it: $2,400. The Stork Club was his baby, Bader could see. Mr. B would do anything for it.

Sometimes, he thought, Mr. B seemed paranoid about people being after him, which may have been why Billingsley was such good friends with Costello and why there were microphones all over the Stork Club. Not that Mr. B ran scared.

"You know, Don, I got the guts to do anything," he told Bader one day as they sat in the club's private seventh-floor suite, where the walls were hung with photos of Billingsley's daughters. "I saw everything. I saw a guy get shot right in front of my face."

Bader shook his head in wonderment. There was no one like Mr. B.

"You know my trouble, Don?" Billingsley said. "The way you're born is the way you're going to be the rest of your life."

The Burger Heaven sign reminds him of another bad moment, the day in 1963 when he picked up the *New York Times* and saw the Stork Club advertising a hamburger and french fries for $1.99. Bader clipped the ad and showed it to the band.

"Guys," he said. "It's all over."

THE ENTRANCE TO THE STORK CLUB

STORK CLUB NIGHTS

ONE

THE WAR WAS ON THEN, the war that was just called "the War" because everyone knew what war you were talking about, and Sherman Billingsley, the blue-eyed and pink-cheeked owner of the Stork Club, was in a rage. "Look at this!" he commanded his lawyer Monroe Goldwater, the partner of Edward J. Flynn, the Bronx Democratic boss and kingmaker who had helped put Franklin Delano Roosevelt in the White House.

Goldwater looked at the photograph Billingsley was waving and couldn't make much of it. It showed the big, mop-haired writer Quentin Reynolds, whom they all knew, standing in front of a strange-looking building called the Stork Club. But it wasn't *their* Stork Club on East Fifty-third Street. Goldwater asked where it had been taken.

"In London!" Billingsley blurted.

"Well," Goldwater asked after a while, "what do you want me to do?"

Billingsley looked at him with scorn. It was enough to make him tear out his hair — he still had it then. "Have Ed see Churchill!" he shouted. The Battle of Britain could wait. Nothing drove Billingsley crazier than somebody trying to horn in on his franchise, and the war years were the best the Stork Club ever knew. He had ridden out of the Oklahoma of covered-wagon days and opened his first club as a speakeasy on West Fifty-eighth Street, when Prohibition meant that nothing was prohibited, eventually discovering — to his great surprise, he insisted — that his partners were three of the city's toughest gangsters. At a time when there seemed to be more nightspots than celebrities to fill them, he had scrounged for business with ads in the college papers offering coupons for free food and drink, and with circulars mass-mailed to the home addresses of movie stars in Hollywood. Winchell then had given the struggling speakeasy a stupendous plug, calling it "New York's New Yorkiest place on W. 58th." Other scribes, enticed by Billingsley's rich celebrity feast, quality whiskey, and endearing habit of never letting a friend pick up a check, dutifully followed: Archer Winsten,

Damon Runyon, Mark Hellinger. So many columnists and stars were on the cuff, Stork habitué Gary Stevens said years later, that the sight of an open wallet and a bill coming out would have caused a riot. But it was more than just Billingsley's largesse that captivated them. The Stork Club was a pinnacle in the landscape of attainment, an embodiment of the deluxe, a place where the door swinging open and the effusive beckoning of the maître d' told the favored, "You're home," and where tennis star Fred Perry once tipped headwaiter Victor Crotta $10,000 — and it wasn't even his biggest tip. He had once gotten twice that from another millionaire. And there at the hearth was Billingsley, a roguish, sometimes cloddish presence projecting himself as the perfect host, trying desperately to please while often riding roughshod over his astonished and intimidated minions.

The *Post*'s Leonard Lyons arrived one night with Carl Sandburg in tow. "What does he do?" Billingsley whispered.

Writer, Lyons confided. Writes books.

"Tell him," an impressed Billingsley said, "to stick in 'Stork Club' once in a while."

With an ashtray as his battle standard, Billingsley had taken on El Morocco with its distinctive blue-and-white zebra stripes (which were easily matchable after Prohibition raiders had smashed up the furniture), the "21" club with its secret cellars, and the reviled Toots Shor's, sending private detectives to secretly check on their service and prices, only to have them spy on him in return. He left no doubt about who was boss, papering the pantry with stern reminders dictated to secretaries who typed it all just the way he said it, mistakes included.

> *I WANT ALL THE EMPLOYEES, WHO ARE STUBBORN, TO KNOW THAT I OWN THE STORK CLUB AND HOW I WANT THINGS DONE, MUST BE DONE THAT WAY. I WILL NOT STAND ANYONE WHO BUCKS ME. WHEN ANYONE THINKS THEY CAN DO THINGS THEIR WAY AND NOT MINE, THEY CAN DO THEIR THINKING ELSEWHERE. EVEN IF I'M WRONG — I HAVE A RIGHT TO BE IF IT'S MY WISH. I WANT MY ORDERS CARRIED OUT.*

He signed his notices "S. B.," which left just enough space for employees to scribble an O in the middle.

As an ex-bootlegger who had made the leap to society by an intuitive sense of how to captivate the haut monde, he presided over chambers electric with possibility, irresistible attractions and interactions, a human fission of supercharged personalities crammed onto banquettes and

SHERMAN BILLINGSLEY IN HIS DOMAIN

A TYPICAL CROWD OF GAWKERS AND PATRONS OUTSIDE
THE STORK CLUB IN THE LATE 1940s

around narrow tables colliding, splitting apart, and recombining, releasing titanic bursts of energy and hilarity. He had been raided out of his first club and outgrown a second, and now here he was in his third and final Stork Club, which was the envy of a world convulsed in war. When you came in from California, when you came in from anywhere, you announced your presence by showing up at the Stork Club. The leisure class, whose only occupation was to change clothes and go out, was always in residence.

Now, in the sincerest form of flattery, imitators were cropping up all over. A spurious Stork Club had threatened to open in Chicago, too, but there one of Billingsley's faithful with good underworld connections said simply, "They don't have a Tom Dewey in Chicago. I'll take care of this. It won't open." It didn't.

Billingsley had found that even his own nephew, the son of his troublesome brother Logan, was getting into the game, opening a Stork Club in Key West, Florida. Billingsley called his friend Ernest Hemingway, who had a house there. Hemingway often came to the Stork Club and had remembered it fondly in a 1938 book of drawings, *All the Brave,* by his friend Luis Quintanilla, whose studio and paintings and frescoes were destroyed by a Fascist bombardment in Spain.

> *When you have sat at a table and been served a plate of water soup, a single fried egg and one orange after you have been working fourteen hours, you have no desire to be anywhere but where you were, nor to be doing anything but your work, but you would think, "Boy, I'll bet you could get quite a meal at The Stork tonight." Hunger is a marvelous sauce and danger of death is quite a strong wine. You keep The Stork, though, as a symbol of how well you would like to eat.*

One night in 1940, back in New York, Hemingway had grandiosely tried to pay his bar bill at the Stork with a $100,000 royalty check he had gotten for the screen rights to *For Whom the Bell Tolls*. (A hundred thousand dollars in 1940 would be $1.2 million today.) Billingsley shook his head; no way he could cash that check, not then. But if Hemingway could wait until closing time . . . Then, amazingly, Billingsley did cash it, although it is hard to imagine how, with the club then grossing — officially, anyway — by Billingsley's account, $3,500 a night. Now Billingsley needed a favor back. Could Hemingway recommend a good lawyer in Key West? There was this Stork Club there . . .

Billingsley had given a job in his club to his brother Logan's estranged son Glenn, the innocent product of an old family scandal that had ended with a killing. But Glenn had spent too much time chasing the girls, though he finally settled down and married a woman named Barbara (the Barbara Billingsley who would later star as television's June Cleaver in *Leave It to Beaver*), whom Billingsley irrationally resented for being so thoughtless as to have the same name as his middle daughter. After leaving New York, Glenn and Barbara resettled in Key West, where, Billingsley complained to Hemingway, Glenn had the nerve to open his own Stork Club.

"I'll be your lawyer," Hemingway said.

He called back an hour later. "The Key West Stork Club has changed its name to Billingsley's Cooked Goose."

But then even Billingsley's own brother Fred opened a restaurant on Park Avenue in the forties that he had the temerity to call Billingsley's. Sherman cut Fred off, too.

At *the* Stork Club, the year that would take America from peace to war had opened, as usual, with a celebrity-crammed New Year's Eve party. Perky Jinx Falkenburg, the model and actress who had appeared on Broadway with Martha Raye and Al Jolson in *Hold On to Your Hats* and was destined to become the first Miss

Rheingold, had been to the theater and, with no taxicabs to be found, walked up Eighth Avenue, parrying the halfhearted advances of woozy male revelers. Ordinarily she might have been with her regular beau, Tex McCrary, Walter Winchell's editor at the *Daily Mirror*, but Tex was off with the Canadian Air Force delivering the first Lend-Lease bomber to embattled Britain.

Jinx may have been the only one sober in the Stork that night. A few years before, she had been in Hawaii posing for Edward Steichen, taking photographs for the Hawaiian Steamship Company, when she fell through a thatched roof of the Royal Hawaiian Hotel, landing in the dining room below and badly injuring a kidney. Now, with only one good kidney, she steered clear of alcohol, although she did contribute a recipe for "Sangrita" (claret, pineapple juice, soda, and lime juice) to Beebe's *Stork Club Bar Book*.

In the hospital, as luck would have it, she had met Jolson, who had offered her the part in *Hold On to Your Hats*. Jolson, who was also at the Stork that night, was a little teary — he usually was on New Year's Eve — and the orchestra's rendition of "There's a Great Day Coming Mañana" did little to boost his mood, what with his people under attack in Germany and Hitler's panzers on the rampage in Europe, the Nazis and Reds coming to terms, and the swastika flying over the Arc de Triomphe.

Raye was there, too, her usual blustery self, making a New Year's resolution not to get married. Not that anyone had asked her, she said, but in case anyone did, she would wait awhile.

Seated nearby was Errol Flynn's wife, the tempestuous French actress Lili Damita, also in her cups, also lamenting her solitude. Flynn himself, with his secretly treasonous Nazi leanings, was en route to the Burma Road — "a helluva of a place to be," Damita remarked. "I'm sure he'd enjoy this much more than being where he is now."

New York's lieutenant governor Charles Poletti offered up a poignant prayer that 1941 would prove happier for the world than the year past had been. As for resolutions, not drinking more than two cocktails that night might be a worthy goal, but in the longer run, he said, everyone should dedicate himself to sacrifice for the defense effort in the war that would surely soon engulf America.

The year that had begun so ominously fulfilled its promise. By the end of 1941, Pearl Harbor had become a synonym for treachery and America was at war. But phony Stork Clubs notwithstanding, Billingsley was doing splendidly. The worldwide conflict had sent the cream of international society fleeing to safer shores, and now the boîtes of New York — from the Stork to the Copacabana, Le Coq Rouge, the Versailles, Café Pierre, and the Iridium Room of the St. Regis — were thronged nightly with the likes of the prince and ranee of Pudakota, the duchesse de Tallyrand, the Baron de Goldschmidt, the Baroness Koenigswasser and other assorted Rothschilds, and Princess Windisch-Grätz and her husband, Archduke Franz

Josef, great-nephew of the Hapsburg emperor. To make them feel at home, Billingsley reached to England for a new bandleader, Jack Harris, a favorite of prewar London café society.

It seemed strange, but somehow a world traumatized by financial catastrophe, global carnage, and war rationing craved the distractions and extravagance of deb parties, old cognac, balloon nights, and rhumba breakfasts. But perhaps it wasn't strange at all, for as well as having become a shining symbol of social aspiration, the Stork Club came to represent in the public imagination the home front, normalcy, and Why We Fight.

The club sat on the uptown side of Fifty-third Street, about a hundred feet east of Fifth Avenue. Inside the front door was a gold chain, real fourteen-karat gold, and beyond it a small lobby with telephone booths and the checkroom, where ladies left their minks and ermine capes and men their hats and topcoats. There were so many similar-looking fur coats that the pretty checkroom girls remembered them by name — Ethel . . . Martha . . . The girls smiled at you, and you pushed a nice tip through the slot on the counter into a locked box below. The girls got none of it, however, because the concessionaire to whom Billingsley sold the checkroom paid them straight salary and collected the tips himself. To the left as you walked in was the barroom, seventy feet long by thirty feet wide. Above the bar stretched a long mirror that allowed Billingsley to look up and keep an eye on everything and patrons to admire themselves and one another under softly flattering lights — the ultimate entertainment at the Stork Club.

Past the bar, through the thick glass door, was the main room, also paneled in mirrors, where bejeweled ladies in ankle-length dresses and clean-shaven men in evening dress, dark suits, or service uniforms and black shoes supped and sipped and slow-danced and rumbaed to music that never stopped, as Beautiful Mary of the feather-white skin snapped publicity photos. The cash registers rang to music, as Billingsley had long since discovered. The peppier the sound, the more customers drank and ate. But the entertainment was secondary. The patrons themselves, the movie stars and out-of-towners and jelly beans — the good-looking preppie kids to whom Billingsley threw open the doors — were the real attraction, his floor show.

A month after Pearl Harbor, Rita Hayworth posed in the club with boys from the army, navy, Coast Guard, and marines, and the photo made the front page of the *Daily Mirror*. Almost any night, stars like Joan Blondell, Lana Turner, Peter Lorre, Claudette Colbert, Greer Garson, and Gertrude Lawrence could be found at the bar buying drinks for servicemen.

Otherwise, the Stork Club seemed little touched by the war, except, of course, that uniforms were now acceptable as eveningwear for the 2,500

THE COATCHECK ROOM

patrons who dropped in on an average day and night for a drink or dinner. Billingsley, who was fit and hearty at forty-five (and even told everyone that he was four years younger, probably because he couldn't face being older than the twentieth century) himself had escaped military service. But he supported the fighting forces — especially in his club. "They can't be beaten for good conduct and sobriety," he wrote in a guest column for his friend Winchell. "It springs from their pride of self and pride of uniform."

By contrast, Winchell, who in 1940 had earned $800,000, making him the top-salaried American, had applied for active duty the day after Pearl Harbor and was now a lieutenant commander in the naval reserve. Despite appeals to his friend President Roosevelt to be sent overseas, however, he was deemed too valuable and was assigned instead to press duty in New York. He took his orders seriously, donning his snappy uniform and writing out his will, prepared for any contingency, including, it was said, a sneak attack on the Stork Club.

Early in the war, opening a new front, Billingsley took space west of the club and broke through a wall of the bar to create the Cub Room, as Winchell named it for no specified reason. Here in this railroad flat of an

THE BAR

annex Billingsley and Winchell and Leonard Lyons and other anointed guests could play gin rummy and socialize insulated from the nightly crush. It quickly became the most exclusive corner of the club. Billingsley later told some people he built it out of love for his flame Ethel Merman, so she would have a place to go after the theater, and others that he built it to get over Merman after they broke up and she got married.

Past the Cub Room through a canyon of slumbering vintages in dusty bottles was the Loners Room, where stag gentlemen supped and drank in a bistrolike setting of red-and-white-checker-clothed tables and macho solidarity. Up a flight of stairs was the Blessed Events Room for catered parties and the city's most exclusive barbershop, where Billingsley or Winchell or another of their inner circle could get a trim or a shave any hour of the day or night. The ladies' room, also upstairs, was decorated with silver-gray wallpaper patterned with red roses and black lace fans, and furnished with well-cushioned black-and-white-striped chairs. A counter was set with Lucien Lelong powder and perfumes, and in the stalls the toilet seats were sterilized by ultraviolet-ray devices. Nora, the attendant, crocheted ugly purses and solicited tips to light candles and pray for customers at Mass.

THE MAIN ROOM

The men had a rest room downstairs by the bar, but it was urinals only. For stalls, they had to take an elevator up to the third floor. Mr. B didn't want anyone stinking up his club.

War or no war, *Stork Club Talk,* Billingsley's intermittent love letter to his loyal patrons, insouciantly memorialized their comings and goings. *Tea dancing seems to have come back with a bang. Every afternoon the Stork Club is crowded with pretty girls and handsome gents in uniform who have popped in to do a bit of dancing to Ray Benson's music.* The issue published shortly before Christmas 1942 chronicled the safe return from an overseas mission of Lieutenant Franklin Roosevelt Jr., who had made straight for the Stork with his wife, Ethel, as did Averell Harriman, "who had just Clippered in from one of his Lend-Lease missions." The Roosevelts were joined by Bo'sun Alfred Gwynne Vanderbilt, who had inherited the family fortune from his father (lost on the German-torpedoed *Lusitania* in World War I) and traded his polo ponies for a navy career. Other columns were filled with news of Adolphe Menjou and "Georgie" Jessel, the Milton Berles (before Berle was barred for excessive table-hopping), Sam Goldwyn, Victor Mature (also now in navy blues), the Ray Bolgers and George Murphys, Gary Cooper, the Artie Shaws (announcing that *their* stork was hovering), the Michael Todds, circusmaster John Ringling North, Lincolnesque Raymond Massey, *Sun* columnist Ward Morehouse and the missus, Orson Welles, Edward G. Robinson, and Detroit Tigers slugger Hank Greenberg, who had made baseball history by refusing to play on the Jewish Day of Atonement, Yom Kippur, in 1934 and had played only three weeks of the 1941 season before becoming the first diamond star to be drafted into the army, thus dramatizing to Americans the growing seriousness of the war situation.

From somewhere in Asia, World War I flying ace Captain Eddie Rickenbacker wrote his friend Sherman to mark the end of the first year of all-out war and pray that the New Year would bear the seeds of victory. "So while we are enjoying Christmas at home," he said, "let us not forget our loved and dear ones in the four corners of the world and share with them the spirit that makes us proud and glad of our heritage, trusting that 1943, or the not too distant future, will see them home again with us — happy for the privilege of having served."

The war notwithstanding, each year Billingsley and his intimates looked over the crop of the season's debutantes, selecting a dozen for a kind of Stork Club fellowship — debs in residence — who would make the club their headquarters and receive food and drink gratis. They might

THE CUB ROOM

A PERIOD POSTCARD OF THE BLESSED EVENT ROOM

be short of pocket money now, Billingsley figured, but someday they'd be rich or famous. Besides, he often said, "The finest decoration the Stork can have is a lot of beautiful girls." They, in turn, voted one of their number "Glamour Girl" at a tea and cocktail party at the Stork.

For the 1941–42 season the winner was an eighteen-year-old diminutive blonde, Betty Cordon of Park Avenue. The following season the crown fell to Eugene O'Neill's smoldering sixteen-year-old daughter, Oona. A student at the prestigious Brearley School, a striking beauty with straight jet-black hair, a dazzling smile, dark-lashed Asiatic eyes, and a shapely figure, Oona had been showing up at the club since she was fifteen, getting her name and picture into the papers and infuriating her grave and tormented father. At the press conference announcing her selection, Oona was handed a bouquet of red roses and asked by a particularly obtuse or mischievous newsman what her father did. "He writes," she giggled. Asked what she thought of the world situation, even she spotted the trap. "Wouldn't it be silly for me, sitting here in the Stork Club, to comment on that?" As for telling her father about her honor, she thought she'd let him find out for himself. In fact, O'Neill was livid. "I would rather have one Red Cross nurse or airplane factory worker for a daughter than fifty million glamour girls — to put it mildly," he said, recalling his own father's admonition: "God deliver me from my children!" Any chance of a reconciliation vanished the following year when, at eighteen, Oona migrated to Holly-

wood and eloped with the thrice-divorced, fifty-four-year-old Charlie
Chaplin, then in the middle of a paternity suit.

As the war raged on, the Stork was ever more jammed, and *Stork
Club Talk* chronicled the revelry.

> *They're all in town this summer — the girls with
> the war jobs, the boys with the furloughs. . . . Night af-
> ter night, the Stork Club has been crowded with good-
> looking youngsters in uniform with pretty girls, with the
> women who spend their days working for the A.W.V.S.,
> the Ship's Service Commiteee, the Red Cross and such,
> with the men in essential war jobs.*

Crowding the Stork's banquettes and café tables that second sum-
mer of the war were Mary Martin, Lord Beaverbrook, the Herbert Bayard
Swopes, the Bill Hearsts, Fred Astaire, Alexander Korda and wife Merle
Oberon, George Burns and Gracie Allen, the Bing Crosbys, Claudette
Colbert, Paulette Goddard, Red Skelton, Leo Durocher, Robert Benchley,
Billy Rose, lovebirds Betty Grable and Harry James, the Ray Bolgers,
Brenda Frazier, and the Georges Jessel and Balanchine.

THE WOMEN'S LOUNGE

LIEUTENANT JOHN F. KENNEDY WITH FLO PRITCHETT

The plush precincts of the Stork made for some bizarre skirmishes against the Nazis and their sympathizers. Winchell had boycotted the club for a while after author Quentin Reynolds brought in a loathsome subject for one of his magazine pieces: Ernst (Putzi) Hanfstaengl, one of Hitler's earliest confidants and a former foreign press chief for the Nazis. Before breaking with him in 1934 and fleeing Germany three years later, the six-foot-four Hanfstaengl and his socialite wife had often played host to the crude and seething ex-Corporal Hitler, entertaining him late into the night with piano renditions of his beloved Wagner. "Certainly I used to tell him my jokes," Hanfstaengl later acknowledged, "but only to get him into the sort of mood in which I hoped he would see reason." Billingsley finally convinced Winchell that he had not known who Hanfstaengl was when Reynolds brought him in, and Winchell forgave him. Meanwhile, Winchell had somehow picked up rumors that Hitler was a homosexual, whereupon the columnist waved around a bogus telegram purporting to be from Der Führer inviting Winchell out on a date. Not surprisingly, Winchell had received death threats and so had started carrying a pistol, but one night he went into the club's men's room and emptied out the bullets for fear of being tempted into a deadly confrontation.

It was also no secret to Winchell that the Duke and Duchess of Windsor had voiced sympathies for Hitler and had been banished to the Bahamas by an embarrassed British government. Winchell had particularly little use for the duchess, calling her the "Dookess of Tookis." On their frequent trips to New York, they often stopped by the Stork, where one night Winchell pointedly snubbed them, stupefying Billingsley. They had first come to the Stork Club early one morning after the Cub Room had emptied out and Billingsley had kicked off his shoes to leaf through the newspapers. A captain came running in to say that the duke and duchess were outside, getting out of a limousine. Billingsley leapt up, searching frantically for his shoes, but shamefacedly had to welcome them in his stocking feet. They politely pretended not to notice.

By 1943, although most Americans were rationed to three pairs of shoes a year and twenty-eight ounces of meat a week, Stork Club guests could eat and drink their fill. Like other leading restaurateurs and cabaret owners, Billingsley had his connections. The club's fanciful menu, cooked in the basement kitchen and carried upstairs by the waiters, who did a delicate dance when they met someone else going down, was strictly à la carte, featuring crêpes suzette, crabmeat cocktail, broiled royal squab Casanova, chicken hamburger à la Winchell, oyster baby asparagus, and café diable. There were fresh flowers everywhere, multiplied by the omnipresent mirrors, and the signature Stork Club ashtrays, which disappeared — five dozen or more a day — into pockets and purses.

Billingsley himself kept to a modest routine, usually walking between the club and his large apartment on Park Avenue and Ninety-first Street. He took frequent massages and tanned himself under sunlamps at the New York Athletic Club, which was across the street from his first Stork Club speakeasy on West Fifty-eighth Street. From midday through the wee hours, he rarely left the club and limited himself to a simple diet largely free of heavy foods and alcohol. Smoking didn't appeal to him. For a man who trafficked in excess, he was surprisingly abstemious.

Billingsley was now grossing $1.25 million a year, more than $12 million today. The net, he said, was nobody's business. He spent $50,000 a year on redecorating and lost another $25,000 on theft and breakage. He had 200 employees serving the 374 guests who could be seated at any one time.

Amid fateful battles in the Pacific and North Africa, the military brass made the Stork a mandatory stop during home leaves. Commanders diagrammed strategies on the Stork's tablecloths, which patriotic doorman Albino Garlasco then made sure to throw in the garbage rather than risk sending to an *Asian* laundry.

After his mishap at sea in 1943, Navy Lieutenant John F. Kennedy recuperated at the Stork Club, casting a covetous eye on the vivacious Flo Pritchett, a recently divorced ex-model and fashion editor of the *Journal-American,* who also seemed to have caught the fancy of his roving-eyed father, the family patriarch Joseph P. Kennedy. Photographer Alfred Eisenstaedt of *Life* came by to shoot a picture story on the Stork as America's most famous nightclub, a lustrous black-and-white photo spread laid out between articles on the retreating Germans and FDR's obscure fourth-term running mate, a Missouri senator named Harry Truman.

These have been gala times indeed around the Stork Club as night after night chums turn up, fresh back from overseas or home on leave after months in the outposts. The January 1944 issue of *Stork Club Talk* was breathless with news. Dancer-host Billy Reardon's first anniversary at the club was toasted by the Bill Hearsts, Mrs. Douglas Fairbanks, and Alfred and George Vanderbilt's "delightful mama," Mrs. W. Averell Harriman. Superdeb Brenda Frazier on the arm of husband John "Shipwreck" Kelly met her incandescent match in Gloria Vanderbilt di Ciccio.

> *And speaking of attention, you should have seen the girls swoon when Captain Winthrop Rockefeller came in — he had a pretty gal with him, however, so swooning didn't do anybody any good. John Jacob Astor attracted a good deal of attention, too, when he dropped in after the opening of the opera complete in white tie and tails. The first of the season according to experts.*

The celebrity fine print was dizzying. Newlyweds Orson Welles and Rita Hayworth post-honeymooning in the Cub Room, publicity czar Steve

FRANK SINATRA

Hannagan romancing Ann Sheridan, Moss Hart celebrating the smash opening of *Winged Victory*, Frank Sinatra entering to female swoons, "and all the men getting even when Greer Garson arrives," and Louella Parsons and Lana Turner and Lieutenant Commander Jack Dempsey and Mr. and Mrs. Al Smith, and the entire Eddie Cantor family and Count Oleg Cassini and wife Gene Tierney and Bob Hope and Mrs. Freddy Brisson (*Rosalind Russell to YOU*) and John Gunther and, yes, Captain Eddie Rickenbacker, back safely for a respite with old pals in the Stork Club.

The war years were not completely trouble-free for the Stork Club. Mayor Fiorello H. La Guardia, the rumpled Republican-Fusion reformer who had taken over a scandal-ridden City Hall from the disgraced but still widely beloved Jimmy Walker a decade earlier, had long regarded Billingsley with suspicion. La Guardia had a priggish side, and although he wasn't much of a nightclubber, when it came to alcohol, he had stood defiantly against the folly of Prohibition. His first wife, Thea, and their baby daughter, also named Thea, had both died of tuberculosis, and his political career had been forged in enough ignominious defeats to take public service seriously. If Walker had been New York's night mayor, La Guardia was its morning man, bestirring his commissioners even before breakfast to get the jump on political hacks and deadbeats.

Shortly before the war La Guardia's resolutely anti-Tammany police commissioner Lewis J. Valentine had ordered that virtually everyone connected with a nightclub, including owners, be fingerprinted. If he expected a fight from Billingsley, he was disappointed. Billingsley said he already had had all his waiters fingerprinted and their backgrounds checked. La Guardia then ordered a ban on gin rummy in nightclubs — another crackdown that Billingsley unexpectedly applauded. "We're glad to have an excuse to cut it out," he responded. "People came in and asked for a deck of cards and kept a table six hours, buying no liquor or food. We found it necessary to turn away people who actually wanted to eat and drink."

La Guardia suspected that underworld boss Frank Costello was part-owner of the Stork Club and other clubs as well. Early in 1944 La Guardia had Commissioner of Investigations Edgar Bromberger seize the books of the city's leading clubs, ostensibly to check on the whereabouts of city employees. Soon after, La Guardia unleashed his tax accountants on the Stork, the Copacabana on East Sixtieth Street, and La Vie Parisienne on East Fifty-second Street, just as Washington burdened nightclubs with a heavy 30 percent cabaret tax (eventually lowered to 20 percent when patronage slumped and owners howled in protest). For the next six months, city auditors pored over the records. In July they turned in a hundred-page report charging that the clubs routinely overbilled patrons on tax, supposedly to cover "breakage." The clubs then paid the city the actual amount due and pocketed the difference. La Guardia called it "the kind of break the sucker never gets" and threatened to auction off the Stork Club.

On a Saturday that July, with the clubs gearing up for their usual prime weekend revelry, investigators arrived at the Stork with a court order to seize the overcharges as unpaid taxes due, plus penalties, totaling $181,000.

Billingsley was out, away on a rare weekend with his family. Without his go-ahead, employees refused to turn over anything.

"Okay, we'll close the joint down," commanded one of the officers, calling for reinforcements.

At that point Billingsley walked in. "We don't owe the city a dime," he insisted. "We've paid our sales taxes in full, month by month. And I've got records to prove it." The city agreed to a compromise. The club could stay open under the watchful eye of a custodian. Billingsley patronized him as "a nice, quiet little fellow — he's still wandering around the place."

Billingsley's lawyer, Monroe Goldwater, lambasted the raiders. "Why did they have to pick Saturday night to put on their act? They know that on the weekend we wouldn't get hold of a judge to give us a hearing. The whole thing stinks. Makes you think of the Gestapo, doesn't it?"

Billingsley quickly won a court order ousting the custodian and rallied his influential friends. Sportswriter Bill Corum used his column to attack La Guardia for targeting New York's favorite nightspot. The critic George Jean Nathan offered to pay the assessment himself. But Billingsley vowed to fight it, while carrying on his feud with city hall.

Billingsley was outside the Stork Club one day when a fire truck went racing by with La Guardia, jacket flapping, clinging to its running board. As the two men locked eyes, they simultaneously raised thumb to nose and waggled their fingers, exchanging raspberries.

The tax charge was to drag on in court for five years and ultimately cost Billingsley $100,000, although he defiantly boasted, "It was worth more publicity than we could ever get."

> *Even the foliage at the Stork is apt to conceal a celebrity, as argus-eyed star-gazers discovered the other night when they peeked behind three carefully combed fronds and found writer Ernest Hemingway, actor Monty Woolley and sculptor Jo Davidson enjoying whiskered wassail and exchanging bearded badinage in a quiet corner.*

The hirsute trio was featured in the September 1944 issue of *Stork Club Talk*, perhaps for the first and last time together anywhere. Also in residence those heady weeks after D-Day were the "amplitudinous" Alfred

THE SEPTEMBER 1944 ISSUE OF
STORK CLUB TALK

Hitchcock; "Schnozzle Durante poking his probiscus into a birthday cake with only one candle"; Winchell and daughter, Walda, sipping lemonade; former child star Jackie Cooper looking very grown-up in sailor's whites; Cesar Romero in navy blues; Anna May Wong; Bill (Hopalong Cassidy) Boyd; and Joes E. Brown and E. Lewis.

Two Air Corps fliers, Lieutenant James Braydon Savage and his captain, Philip Dower, ignored the beauties at the bar, burying their noses in photos of their B-17, christened *The Stork Club*. Savage left Billingsley a souvenir photo of the plane, emblazoned with the club's top-hatted Stork logo and the assurance that their flying *Stork Club* "visits Germany regularly with a full complement of bombs to drop as calling cards on Herr Hitler, with Uncle Sam's compliments."

Wherever GIs were planting the flag, Stork Clubs were springing up, and for once Billingsley was not objecting. From somewhere in North Africa, ten members of Headquarters Squadron, Fifth Wing (U.S.), announced the formation of the "Stork Club-a-la-Arab" consisting of two tents and an improvised awning. They were already planning a banquet in the namesake on Fifty-third Street, they wrote, "but as our plans are a bit indefinite at present, please do not regard this as an application for a reservation."

One Superfortress crew christened successive bombers *The Stork Club Boys* in commemoration of a flier's memorable visit to the club on his last night of furlough. Three separate planes carried the Stork's logo to the Japanese skies. Then came another night raid over Tokyo, as Billingsley later heard in a letter from a relative.

> *The Boys flew a brand new B-29-A. The Stork Club Boys #4 she would have been if they'd have had time to paint on the emblem. Maybe it was bad luck not having the emblem because The Boys did not come back. . . .*

Billingsley kept a supply of Tiffany-made Victory pins to decorate the crews of these Stork Club namesakes.

From Manila Sergeant George M. Kountz enclosed a well-worn Stork Club guest card he had held since 1941. "Since then," he wrote, "it has traversed a great part of the world in my possession. It has been strafed, bombed and shot at, and had been quite a little fox-holer." In New Guinea, he continued, "four other Storkers and myself formed a small club where we spent many a night in the jungle remembering the days of tails, top hats & mink — God bless them!" The card bore neatly lettered inscriptions from postings in the Canal Zone, Costa Rica, Jamaica, Cuba, Alaska, Australia, the Philippines, and New Guinea. Unfortunately, Sergeant Kountz wrote, "I was unable to take it to Tokyo, where I intended mailing it to you." However, he went on, a friend did in fact carry the card with him to Tokyo and back. Sure enough, marked triumphantly at the bottom was "TOKIO!!" Now, wrote Sergeant Kountz, all he wanted in exchange for the old card was . . . *a new one!*

In October 1944 Louis Sobol of the *Journal-American* cast his column as a letter to a soldier. He wrote of the twin shocks of the deaths of political lions Al Smith and Wendell Willkie and of the tedious parties and openings he was suffering through. The autograph hounds were becoming really pesky. He ended with a P.S.: "Sherman Billingsley's third little girl arrived just

FRANCES LANGFORD AND BOB HOPE
(SECOND AND THIRD FROM RIGHT) VISIT THE NORTH AFRICAN
WARTIME OUTPOST OF THE STORK CLUB

as I finished this letter. He says she is the most beautiful baby that was ever born."

In the months to come there was other cheering news, courtesy of *Stork Club Talk*, whose Girl of the Month for January 1945 was Billingsley's favorite home-front beauty, the former Barbara Schick, whose husband was overseas with the Canadian Black Watch Regiment. Lieutenant Robert Taylor had been spotted in the Cub Room "*STAG!*" Gary Cooper had dropped in, along with Lieutenant Commander Robert Montgomery, Beatrice Lillie, Shirley Temple, Dorothy Lamour (who years earlier had been fired as one of Billingsley's first speakeasy entertainers), U.S. Attorney General Francis Biddle, Senator Claude Pepper, Sinatra, Henry Ford II, and . . . *Helen Keller!*

With the end of the war in sight but bitter fighting surely ahead, Washington ordered a midnight nightclub curfew. The New York City Council patriotically endorsed the measure with its own bill, over the furious objections of Billingsley and other club owners. Disregarding their threats of widespread layoffs, La Guardia signed it into law, while winking at scattered transgressions. But with Billingsley flagrantly testing its limits, a citizen representing the obscure Taxpayers Union of New York City went to the police demanding his arrest. A reluctant sergeant promised to file a report.

The celebrating was stepping up now. To the Stork flocked Clark Gable, the Sam Goldwyns, Artie Shaw, Ava Gardner, Barbara Stanwyck, Mrs. Joseph P. Kennedy with her son Bobby, Busby Berkeley, Judy Garland and Vincente Minnelli, Humphrey Bogart and Lauren Bacall, Myrna Loy, Chicago mayor Ed Kelly, Fay Wray (sans Kong), Harold Lloyd, and (as *Stork Club Talk* had it) "Miss Marjorie Truman, daughter of the Vice President." Oops, sorry, Margaret.

And then, suddenly, the war was over. Two million revelers packed Times Square as the flickering news zipper proclaimed the Japanese surrender. With crowds besieging bars and liquor stores, Billingsley fortified his door with extra staff. That night only regular patrons, with reservations, were admitted.

TWO

EVERYONE AT THE STORK CLUB had a story — especially the
people who worked there. Tall and willowy at twenty-seven with
long auburn hair, a pert smile, and curvaceous figure, Emmy Lou
Sheldon was far better looking than she suspected. She had grown up in
Vermont, served as a WAC in the Army Air Corps during the war, and
ended up living with her sister in Hartford, Connecticut. On a lark, she
packed a bag and took the train to New York. She got off at Grand Central
and walked across town to Times Square. Then, struck suddenly by the
enormity of the city and what she had done, she put down her white suit-
case, perched on it, and began to cry.

"Why are you crying?"

She looked up to see a young man with dark hair and dark eyes.

"Because I have no money and no place to go."

He took her hand and, somewhat surprising herself, she let him hold
it. "Come on," he said. "We'll get a cup of coffee at Horn and Hardart's."
She told him her story. He told her that he was Henry Serabian, a Syrian
and a pool player. She had never heard of a pool player — she had never
heard of a Syrian, either — but she liked his manner. There was something
trustworthy about him, and he was nice looking.

"Did you ever see a pool hall?"

She shook her head.

"I'll take you there." They walked a few blocks and then he led her
down some stairs into a grimy building where men were playing pool. She
dropped into a chair and watched, sitting there until dark.

"You come home with me," Henry now told her. "I'll find you a job."

Surprising herself once again — she had had only a few dates and
had certainly never spent the night with anyone — she accepted. Somehow she wasn't frightened.

EMMY LOU SHELDON, AT RIGHT, WITH JIMMY DURANTE

The next day Henry bought her a white satin blouse. "Put this on," he said, "and go over to the Stork Club and ask for job as a hatcheck girl." Even in Vermont, Emmy Lou had heard of the Stork Club. She took the bus to the East Side and found the famous canopy. It looked a little scary to her.

The doorman had her wait at a round table by the door, where she nervously eyed herself in the mirrors. A few minutes later a rugged, good-looking man with a crooked grin and thinning hair sat down at her table.

"Why do you want to work at the Stork Club?"

The question caught her off guard, but she answered from the heart. "Because I heard it was the nicest place in New York City." It must have been the right answer, because Billingsley — for it was indeed he, she later learned — told her to come back at 4:30 in the same blouse, a black skirt below the knee, and black sandals. She rushed to the pool hall to tell Henry. He kissed her.

From where she worked, she could see people being admitted and many more turned away. She could also see Billingsley sitting at his regular table by the entrance, watching her and everyone else. For $28.50 a week and no tips, she stood outside the checkroom, took coats and hats, and handed them over the counter.

The celebrity parade thrilled her. She saw Sonja Henie, her radiant face framed in golden curls and her body swathed from head to toe in mink so that only the tiniest tips of her shoes stuck out. Walter Pidgeon actually addressed her as she took his coat one night and fought a sneeze from the sniffles. "Got a cold, eh?" he asked in the deep, sonorous voice she remembered from *Mrs. Miniver,* and he might as well have been asking her to elope with him.

After a few weeks Emmy Lou graduated to the attic of the checkroom. There was a trapdoor in the ceiling where the girls climbed a ladder to pass up the hats and coats, wrapped up against dust, to be stored by number. The first night she saw girls crawling among the coats, rummaging through the pockets for money, and it sickened her.

A few nights later, near closing time, after Emmy Lou had been working at the Stork Club about a month, she heard a commotion at the door. She looked over to see Henry straining against a bouncer and shouting, "I came to pick up my girl!" She tried to signal to him that she wasn't quite ready to leave yet, but Henry was in a rage, ordering her out.

Just then, as it happened, the ominous screen duo of Sydney Greenstreet and Peter Lorre loomed in the doorway. Lorre, who had a mischievous streak bordering on sadism (one night at the Stork Club he sent his perfectly fine steak back repeatedly just to get Billingsley's goat), drank in the scene and improvised, *"Doooooooooon't touch zat gerl! Youuuu cannot doooooo zat!"* Even Billingsley laughed, mortifying Emmy Lou.

Then Henry burst free, grabbed her arm, and pulled her out behind him. She barely had time to blurt, "I quit," and grab a souvenir ashtray before fleeing the Stork Club, never to return. She left Henry soon afterward and became a photographer. She would never marry.

With a staff that presented endless surprises, Billingsley came to rely on a an inner circle of friends and loyalists. His closest confidant was Steve Hannagan, a twinkle-eyed, ebony-haired Irish Hoosier who unofficially augmented the club's in-house publicity team, which included a young socialite and former John Powers model, Jeanne Lourdes Murray, who ended up marrying Alfred Gwynne Vanderbilt. Hannagan, three years Billingsley's junior, had made his reputation in his native Indiana in 1919 when he came up with the right publicity formula to make the Memorial Day auto race at the Indianapolis Motor Speedway the biggest one-day sports event in the world. Speedway developer Carl Fisher then hired Hannagan to promote a mangrove swamp he was struggling to develop into a new warm-water resort called Miami Beach. Using Miami as his girlie backdrop, Hannagan pioneered the cheesecake photo. And even bad news had its opportunities. "Flash," he cabled news associations, "Julius Fleischman dropped dead on the polo field here this afternoon. Don't forget Miami Beach dateline."

STEVE HANNAGAN AND SHERMAN

Beyond his promotional genius, Hannagan was known, too, for his unshakable integrity. When *Time* magazine asked for his report on the 1930 season in Miami Beach, he replied, frankly, that it was "lousy."

"Cancel the story," Henry Luce ordered. "Let's do one instead about an honest press agent."

Hannagan put his shrewd news sense at Billingsley's disposal. When Hemingway gave Warden Lewis E. Lawes of Sing Sing a shove one night at the Stork Club, knocking him to the floor, Hannagan assuaged Billingsley's fears of repercussions. One fight a year was good publicity, he insisted, "providing the names of the fighters are big names."

On Hannagan's advice the Stork Club stayed open in summer, unlike its rivals, thereby winning faithful new patronage. Billingsley also kept the Stork open Sunday nights, when other clubs typically went dark. He hired a regular club photographer, Chic Farmer, a former radio singer, to immortalize his guests, and a suave professional dancer, Billy Reardon, sometime partner of Irene Castle, to double as club host and escort.

Encouraged by Hannagan, Billingsley lured pretty girls to the club with free champagne and trinkets, a virtual cornucopia of pins, cosmetics, lucky pennies, and souvenir storks destined to become prize collectibles in decades to come. Hannagan, a big fan of gifts, once interrupted a conversation with a guest in the Cub Room to order an assistant: "Send bow ties to the United States Senate!"

Hannagan even gave Billingsley a gift — a platinum ring with a cabo-chon sapphire.

Another member of Billingsley's inner circle was the Irish tenor Mor-ton Downey, who was married to the actress Barbara Bennett, sister of ac-tresses Joan and Constance. The sleekly groomed Downey had gotten his start with the Paul Whiteman jazz orchestra; entertained for Ziegfeld, Cole Porter, and the Duke of Windsor; and by the early thirties was making an astonishing $12,000 a week in radio and theatrical engagements, a fortune that would enable him to acquire the Cape Cod estate that President John F. Kennedy would borrow for his summer White House thirty years later.

Billingsley, too, was awash in cash. In the bank one day, depositing proceeds in the vault, he was entranced by a seductive fragrance. It wasn't a bank smell, the smell of money. It was a *woman's* smell. As it happened, a French perfume importer who was storing some product in his safe-deposit box had broken a bottle. Nothing would do but for Billingsley to acquire the distributorship to the perfume, Sortilege, akin to the classic fragrance Joy, jasmine-scented with accents of the rare Bulgarian rose. He persuaded Hannagan and Downey to become his partners and soon added a fourth, Arthur Godfrey, a ukulele-playing radio announcer with a folksy

GREGORY PAVLIDES AND THE FAMOUS GOLD CHAIN

manner and raunchy sense of humor — he liked to plug his Bayer aspirin sponsor as "bare-ass prin." They called their perfume business Cigogne — "stork" in French.

Billingsley's longtime maître d' and future guardian of the gold chain, hired four days after he opened his first speakeasy, was a slender, wavy-haired Greek, Gregory Pavlides. He had come to the United States at eighteen in 1924 from Constantinople, Turkey, where some of his brothers and sisters had starved to death and a great-grandmother had been devoured by wolves. As a youth Gregory and his father dug graves for Armenians whose throats had been slit by the Turks. He had then made his way to New York, where he worked in the Deauville Club on Park Avenue and Fifty-ninth Street before moving to the new Stork Club, then a speakeasy on West Fifty-eighth Street, where Billingsley started him off in the men's room. Gregory, ten years younger than Billingsley, told his new boss a cautionary story. At the Deauville, owner Charlie Hanson didn't bother to mingle with his customers, leaving that to his headwaiter. Inside of a year, the head-waiter owned the Deauville, and Hanson was working for him. Billingsley got the point. He was bullheaded, certainly, but he was usually ready to listen to a sensible idea and learn something, as he informed his staff in one of his famous memos:

> ANY SUGGESTIONS YOU CAN MAKE FOR PRIVATE PARTIES OR FUNCTIONS FOR THE NEW PRIVATE ROOMS YOU WILL BE DOING A LOT OF GOOD FOR ALL OF US. DON'T FAIL TO GIVE ME ANY IDEAS YOU MAY HAVE.

He had compelling reasons to trust Gregory. Billingsley was putting money into the safe one night when Gregory saw that he had left a pile of $5,000 behind, which he immediately pointed out to his boss, who acted surprised. Later Gregory decided that the incident had been deliberate: Billingsley had been testing him.

Billingsley's first line of defense at the door was a rugged Italian with the mouth-filling name of Albino Garlasco. At his interview he had assured Billingsley that he knew all the tough characters of the gangster era.

"Okay," Billingsley said, "you'll be the doorman. Keep out everybody you know."

Albino, who blew his whistle so piercingly that people complained to Mayor La Guardia, had also been with Billingsley since the speakeasy days. He had come to New York from Fubine, Italy, near Torino, in 1900 at the age of fifteen with three gold coins sewn into his overcoat and his mother's warning ringing in his ears: *You are not to sell the gold coins unless you are dying!* Because she figured he would need some looking after in New York, she arranged for a friend, Luisa Leone, to come and cook for him. After Albino married and no longer needed Luisa's tending, he encouraged her to open a restaurant, which she did, calling it Mama Leone's.

Albino's wife, Elvira, knew D. W. Griffith and dreamed of becoming an actress, but she came to share her husband's passion for motor cars and auto racing. In April 1920 he entered a Cadillac in the race at Havana's Oriental Park, with Elvira, her cropped hair hidden under a leather helmet, in the copilot's seat. They won, assuring the marque a proud place in automotive history. Cadillac scored it as a milestone in its campaign for recognition.

Albino's brother Frank, meanwhile, had also come over from Italy and was making his mark in nightclubs, launching the Lido, Trocadero, Place Pigalle, Ted Lewis', Dansant, and the Jungle. Frank employed the dancing team of Fred Astaire and his sister Adele, and actor-gangster George Raft, and hired perhaps the first in-house cabaret photographer, Jerome Zerbe, before losing interest in the nightlife scene and decamping for Lake Como. It was through Frank that Albino had gotten work in 1931 as a doorman at the newly opened El Morocco. Still, they struggled through the Depression, and Elvira had to take in sewing. Then one day the following year Frank came home with good news. "Elvira, I got a job at the Stork Club."

As doorman, Albino also became Billingsley's de facto bodyguard. He asked Billingsley why he kept so close to the buildings when he walked down the street.

"Albino," Billingsley said, "I come from rumrunner country. If a car comes around the corner, I have to have a doorway to duck into."

To the portals one evening in November 1945 came a character Damon Runyon was to portray as "a glowering heavy-set chap who was immediately spotted as an old time starker from the lower East Side." Above his open shirt, deep scars lined his face, and on each arm he had a woman. He was not immediately identified, but he was Farvel Kovalick, an extortionist and strongarm man for the racketeers controlling the fur industry, gangsters like Louis Buchalter, alias Lepke, executed in the electric chair two years before, and Benjamin "Bugsy" Siegel, for whom Kovalick served as chauffeur and whose estranged wife, Esther, in fact, was one of the women on his arm.

The three were turned away. This made Kovalick very unhappy, and he let everyone know it. Billingsley was summoned, assessed the trio, and echoed the call. Kovalick then turned his rage on Billingsley, warning, as Runyon had it: "This is the second time you have given me that reservation business when I know there is plenty of room inside. I'll be back again, and next time if you don't let me in, I'll leave you here." This, Runyon explained, was underworld patois meaning *demise,* "unnice talk to be issuing at the portals of the Stork where it might fall on the ears of some of our leading society folks and cause them to shudder."

YETTA GOLOVE

Billingsley called the police. Kovalick's two companions prevailed upon him to leave, which he did, with a parting shot: "I'll show you how to handle such things."

Albino was also on the door one night before the war when F. Scott Fitzgerald came staggering out of the Stork Club. Albino offered to call him a cab or drive him home, but Fitzgerald wouldn't hear of it and demanded his car. After a brief scuffle, Fitzgerald flung himself behind the wheel, lurching forward and driving over Albino's foot.

Albino survived and also got his son, Albino Jr., a job at the club. Although the boy was still a few weeks shy of eighteen and couldn't legally drink, Billingsley put him on the bar, where, chafing under Billingsley's staff strictures, he helped himself to eighty-year-old Napoleon brandy and popped open bottles of Piper-Heidsieck, draining the premier champagne through a straw. He was soon moved to the dining room staff.

Upstairs in the seventh floor business office and telephone exchange toiled Yetta Golove, a robust young woman with long brown hair and a good figure. Yetta, who lived with her Russian Jewish immigrant mother in a tenement on Simpson Street in the Bronx, had been working in a small real estate office for seven dollars a week when she saw an article in *Cosmopolitan* on the Stork Club. On a whim, she wrote Billingsley for a job. To her surprise he hired her as one of six girls who went through the *Social Register* and celebrity listings compiling names and addresses for Stork Club invitations. It paid eighteen dollars a week and was not bad work.

Shortly after she started at eighteen in 1940, he made a little play for her. She ignored it, letting him know that she didn't consider such services part of the job. To her relief, he didn't force his attention, but instead promoted her to the bar cash register. She knew she had done the right thing when one day she saw Billingsley put his hand on the buttocks of a thin, muscular checkroom girl, who hauled off and whacked him, sending him flying over the desk. Perhaps wary of Yetta's independence, too, he soon moved her to the switchboard, the nerve center of the club, where he eavesdropped on staff and guest conversations. It was a sensitive location, as he made clear in one of his inimitable staff notices.

> FOR ANY REASON WHATSOEVER:
> NO ONE IS TO GO INTO THE SWITCH-
> BOARD ROOM BOTHERING THE TELEPHONE
> OPERATORS. THERE ARE NO EXCEPTIONS
> TO THIS. I MOVED THE SWITCHBOARD UP TO
> THE SEVENTH FLOOR AWAY FROM EVERY-
> THING SO THAT THE BUSINESS THAT IS
> TRANSACTED OVER THE SWITCHBOARD
> STAYS THERE. I DON'T WANT ANYONE
> * WITHOUT EXCEPTION * TO GO INTO THE
> TELEPHONE ROOM, LISTEN TO THE CON-
> VERSATIONS AND OVERHEAR WHAT IS BE-
> ING SAID. THE ONLY PERSONS THAT ARE TO
> GO INTO THE SWITCHBOARD ROOM ARE
> MYSELF, THE TELEPHONE OPERATORS, OR
> THOSE THAT I SEND ON SOME ERRAND.
> TAKE THIS SERIOUSLY.

Whenever he had to be away from the club, he usually called Yetta to ask, "Who's in the house?"

One night she reported, "J. Edgar Hoover is here."

"With Mrs. Hoover?" Billingsley asked.

Yetta was taken aback. "I didn't know he was married."

"Don't be stupid," he said. "I mean Clyde Tolson."

Once she grew accustomed to his style, they got along. Billingsley urged her to change her name to the more continental Yvette. She told him to forget it; if it was too Jewish for his taste, that was his problem. He never brought it up again. It was strange, Yetta thought, that while anyone could become a target of his casual slurs, person to person he seemed to get along with almost everyone.

Greeks were laughable, he said, for the way they jammed their hats down on their head, but Gregory was obviously a favorite. Billingsley would malign Italians and Jews, even though the club was full of them. There she was, there was Garlasco and Winchell and Jolson, there was Billingsley's lawyer, Monroe Goldwater, and there were all the Jewish comics and Hollywood moguls who crowded the club each night. And what about the kosher chicken and liver Billingsley insisted on buying for his kitchen and the Chinese chef he hired to prepare his Chinese menu? Blacks, though, were another story, and one she couldn't explain away. When they were admitted to the club at all, they were usually exiled up-stairs to the Blessed Events Room. Homosexuals likewise made Billingsley queasy. If anything, Yetta decided, Billingsley was probably an equal oppor-tunity bigot. No one could meet his standards but himself.

But standing up to him helped, she found. Billingsley himself had implied as much in one of his notes to employees.

> I APPRECIATE "ACTION" MEN MUCH
> MORE THAN I DO "YES" MEN.
> A WORD TO THE WISE IS SUFFICIENT.

So the next time he yelled at her on the phone, Yetta just held up the heavy receiver and, as if losing her grip, let it drop to the floor. There it lay, his curses smoking out of the earpiece until she finally picked it up and heard him rail, "You broke my fucking eardrum!"

THREE

"WHY DO PEOPLE COME HERE, Daddy?" Billingsley's little daughter Jacqueline had asked him years earlier at the club. He insisted he didn't know, and added, "A lot of times I want to get away for ninety days and figure that out for myself." But then he said that New York was no different from his hometown of Anadarko, Oklahoma, where all the kids congregated at Baird's candy store because they knew that was where all the other kids were. Only at the Stork, he told Jackie, "The out-of-towners come to see the natives, who come to see each other."

For pampered youth, admission to the Stork Club had become a rite of passage. Mary Ellin Berlin had been taken to the club by her father, Irving Berlin, on her nineteenth birthday in November 1945 — their visit made the cover of *Stork Club Talk* — but going there on a date for the first time was a privileged entrée into café society and adulthood, a milestone akin to the first pair of high heels or the first cigarette.

As soon as he got out of the air force, entertainer Peter Lind Hayes took his wife and partner, Mary Healy, to the Stork Club. They headed back to the Cub Room and were gaping at Leonard Lyons sitting by the door at table 50 with Orson Welles when a headwaiter gave them the once-over and shook his head. "No," he said, dooming them to expulsion. At that moment Lyons looked up. "Oh, let them in," he said. Billingsley, who was nearby, assented. He soon learned that Peter's mother was Grace Hayes, the jazz singer he had heard in his early days in New York, and from then on, Peter and Mary were welcomed with open arms. Billingsley once forgot his name and called him Joe, so Peter became known as Joe, as did Mary, and they in turn called Billingsley Joe.

If the war had been good for nightclubs' business, peace was even better. Couples separated for years had a lot of celebrating to catch up on, and defense jobs, wartime shortages, and the postwar boom left people with plenty of unspent money. One count put the number of nightclubs in

New York City in May 1945 at eleven hundred, perhaps more than one-tenth of the nation's total, and the number of patron visits a year at 2.5 million — five times the number in 1939. In a guest column that Billingsley contributed to the *Herald Tribune* in 1945, he reported that 200 million Americans a year visited nightclubs, with up to 3 million patrons expected to welcome New Year's Eve 1945.

When he had moved his post-Prohibition Stork Club into the East Fifty-third Street Physicians and Surgeons Building in 1934, the doctors had protested the arrival of a nightclub. As the Stork's fame spread, though, they had dropped their objections, eventually bragging to patients that they were in "the Stork Club Building." But Billingsley had never forgotten the affront and in October 1945 quietly contracted to buy the seven-story building for $300,000 cash.

Money was no problem. With the Stork more popular than ever, Paramount had paid him $100,000 to call a new movie *The Stork Club,* to shoot some scenes at the club, and to copy parts of the interior for its Hollywood set. Apart from these elements, the film, starring a winsomely dizzy Betty Hutton, leprechaunish Barry Fitzgerald, droll Robert Benchley essentially playing himself, and a somber Bill Goodwin as Billingsley, mythologized the real Stork. It was framed around the Cinderella fable of a big-hearted hatcheck girl who saves the life of an old man whom she takes to be a bum but who is really an eccentric millionaire. He showers her with lavish gifts, alarming her suspicious bandleader boyfriend, although in the end, of course, it all gets sorted out happily, complete with music, including a catchy Hoagy Carmichael ditty, "Doctor, Lawyer, Indian Chief," belted out by Miss Hutton. Goodwin's Billingsley was laughably pious, the nightclub owner as statesman and kindly uncle, stern but unfailingly fair and impeccably correct. The film was produced and written by the veteran Tin Pan Alley tunesmith B. G. (Buddy) DeSylva, who had collaborated for years with George Gershwin and Irving Berlin and had written "California, Here I Come" with Al Jolson and Joseph Meyer in 1924. *The Stork Club* premiered in December 1945 to the musical accompaniment of Woody Herman and his orchestra at the ornate Paramount movie palace on Forty-third Street in Times Square.

But just as Billingsley was preparing to leave for the gala premiere in Hollywood, word came that DeSylva had died. The parties were canceled.

The following April, shortly before seven o'clock on a Saturday morning after the last guest had left, a porter was sweeping the sidewalk and the night watchman was in the basement when two men in blue overcoats ran through the open door and hurled three

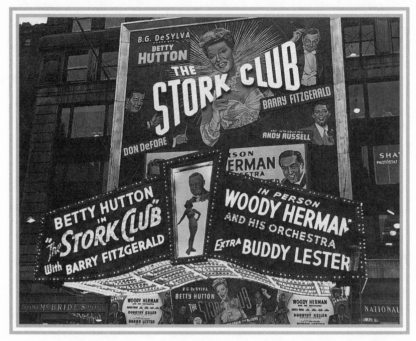

THE MARQUEE ADVERTISING HAL WALKER'S 1945 FILM
THE STORK CLUB

makeshift stink bombs, lightbulbs filled with a sulfurous liquid and stoppered with a cork. A choking rotten-egg stench wafted through the club.

While another club owner might have called the police. Billingsley telephoned his pal Hoover. The FBI's special agent in charge in New York, E. E. Conroy, visited the Stork Club himself to take Billingsley's statement and assigned two of his best agents to work the case.

There was no shortage of suspects. Racketeers had long been making moves on nightclubs, Billingsley told the agents, although he could point to no specific recent threats. He did recall a union boss who years before had tried to organize the waiters and slip a Mickey Finn into the soup. But he didn't think there was much union sympathy around, not with waiters already averaging up to $200 a week in wages and tips.

Then Billingsley remembered the threat from the hoodlum with the two babes. He thought his name was Little Farvel. Runyon had written a story, "The Brighter Side," about the incident. He might remember who and when it was.

When the agents came back, they had a photo of Kovalick and now Billingsley could say, yes, he was the one turned away. The Bureau found that the Protective Fur Dressers Corporation had employed Kovalick and

Lepke as enforcers and had used similar stink bombs to intimidate furriers who refused to maintain prices and business rules demanded by the racket. The connection to Kovalick seemed persuasive, although the two men who threw the stink bombs remained unidentified. Two months and hundreds of man-hours after entering the case, the FBI closed it down, unresolved.

Hoover was happy enough to put the FBI at Billingsley's disposal. After all, a crime had been committed, although not necessarily a federal one. He and Tolson had long been regular patrons of the Stork. In that same June 1946, they were among the luminaries who converged on the club before Joe Louis and the brash light heavyweight Billy Conn faced off in a celebrated rematch at Yankee Stadium. Five years earlier, in a vastly different world, Conn had nearly managed to dethrone the Brown Bomber, but had made a bad mistake in trying to slug it out with the champ. Now, with the war over for a year and both boxers out of the army, they were meeting again. Someone suggested that Conn might have an advantage in speed and footwork, but Louis dismissed the prospect with a riposte that would long survive him: "He can run, but he can't hide."

Before the bout it was mayhem at the Stork Club. All the Cub Room regulars demanded their regular tables. Roosevelt adviser Jim Farley and his wife sought table 50, the Royal Box, where Winchell usually presided. Theater critic George Jean Nathan of *The Smart Set* and *The American Mercury* wanted his favorite table by the door. President Roosevelt's second son, Elliott, and his latest wife, actress Faye Emerson, needed to have

STORK CLUB STAR BETTY HUTTON IN A STILL FROM THE FILM

table 51, next to the Farleys. Henry Ford II had to have space for his large party, which included Hoover and Tolson. Upstairs in the Blessed Events Room, financier Bernard Baruch was hosting Russia's dour Andrei Gromyko and members of the United Nations. They were rushing through cocktails to make the fight and wanted to return afterward for supper.

Billingsley was running around trying to please them all, but at least he would soon have more space. In March 1946 he had broken the news to the fifty or so doctors and dentists, dental suppliers, and architects in the Stork Building, sending them legal notice that they had up to three months to vacate. They all protested, but he was unsympathetic. Sure, he conceded, the lawyers' eviction notices sounded tough, but what did people expect from lawyers? "We are not trying to work a hardship," he told the press, "but we need the building for the club and intend to occupy the whole building." He said that he planned to expand quarters for his staff of 250, add dining and banquet rooms, and create his own bakery and laundry.

A few weeks after the Louis-Conn bout a letter addressed simply "Stork Club New York" turned up in a packet of mail left by the postman. Crudely printed on a page torn from a stenography pad, it ordered Billingsley to leave $3,000 at a drop in Ozone Park, Queens. IF YOU DON'T WE'LL TELL THE *REAL* STORY.

Once again Billingsley called the FBI. Hoover, who happened to be in New York, was alerted by his office, but not quickly enough. "Hereafter when I am in New York City," he complained, "it is desired that you advise me direct on matters of this type in which I am interested."

The FBI chief took a personal hand in the investigation, but before agents could make much progress, a second letter arrived. This one warned Billingsley that the nursemaid for his middle daughter, Barbara, was going around saying that she was in love with him and trying to enlist Barbara as her ally. There were enough specific details in its claims to shake up Billingsley; the writer clearly knew a lot about the family. The Billingsleys did have a nursemaid known as Mamie, a tall and slender red-head who had been with them for ten years and indeed did seem to have eyes for Billingsley. She once told Barbara that if her mother tried to fire her, the girl should threaten to throw herself down the stairs.

At the time, Billingsley's wife, Hazel, was in the grip of a pervasive depression, exacerbated, no doubt, by her husband's chronic infidelity. She and Sherman seemed to share few intimacies any longer — at least their daughters saw little evidence of affection. Shermane had been only nine days old when her mother placed her in the care of her own live-in nurse-maid named Nellie, and except for Thursdays, Nellie's day off, Hazel spent almost no time with the little girl. It was Nellie who brought Shermane down every afternoon to the Stork Club, where Sherman snatched her up delightedly and carried her outside into the sunlight for a few minutes of

tanning rays. Summers, a time for families to be together, meant long sep-
arations, as Billingsley packed Hazel and the girls off to Lake Placid while
he stayed in town with his club and his women. When he did visit, he
made sure to prepare in advance a trunkful of prewritten postcards to his
customers promising, "Hope to see you when I return," which he would
mail home from the local post office as soon as he arrived.

Although the FBI had trouble finding any criminal wrongdoing in the
letter about Barbara's nursemaid, Hoover ordered a check of the six Royal
typewriters at the Stork Club. The FBI laboratory sought a forensic link
between that letter, the demand for the $3,000, and the stink-bombing,
but came up clueless.

Agents scrutinized 400 Stork Club employee records for handwriting
matches, but again to no avail. Others converged on John Adams High
School, within blocks of the Ozone Park drop, looking for handwriting
matches among the 4,500 students. Still other agents scoured 400 payroll
checks at a nearby business. Selective Service files were searched and local
stores canvassed for the type of stenographer pads with pages similar to that
used in the extortion note. Agents even screened nearby P.S. 108, but the
kindergarteners through sixth-graders there were dismissed as unlikely
suspects. The investigation was closed inconclusively in December 1946.

A seat at the Stork Club was also ominously empty. For
some time, Damon Runyon had been battling cancer
of the larynx. Runyon, who had come to Broadway via Manhattan — Manhattan, Kansas, that is — and humanized Times Square's faceless bookies
and touts and loan sharks in stories that became the basis of *Guys and Dolls,*
had long been a regular denizen of the Stork, swapping yarns with Winchell
and Billingsley at table 50 while assiduously teetotaling. Now estranged from
his second wife and son and daughter, he lived alone in a hotel as his life
ebbed. Finally he could only breathe through a tube in his throat and carried
on conversations by writing on a pad. On the nights Runyon could drag himself to the Cub Room, Billingsley ordered a ban on smoking. Bill Harbach,
whose father, Otto, had partnered with Jerome Kern in 1933 to write the
lyrics to "Smoke Gets in Your Eyes," sat with Runyon on one of those smoke-
less nights and asked him when he would like to have lived, if he could pick
any time. Runyon scrawled his answer on a napkin. *"NOW!"*

It was not widely known, but Runyon had started writing a book
about Billingsley. He called it *The Saga of "Mr. B.," of the Stork Club,* and it
was full of the Runyonisms for which he had become justly renowned.

> . . . *Glamor is Sherman Billingsley's chief stock*
> *in trade. The liquor that he sells is largely incidental*

SHERMAN WITH DAMON RUNYON (LEFT)
AND WALTER WINCHELL (CENTER)

to the more than a million dollars gross business that
he does annually in the Stork Club. So is the food.
What he really sells there is atmosphere — the atmosphere of New York glitter and sophistication, of which
this former Oklahoma small town fellow has come to
be regarded as the master salesman of all time. However, I must say the food is excellent. Also, as I am informed, the liquor . . .

While he was still in his teens he was riding the
bleak western roads through the dark of night with
loads of liquor for the relief of the thirsty in the dry dis-
tricts, as a friend of mine who was once in the same
game used to mock-heroically phrase it, though of
course it was against the disapproval of John Law and
really not a nice thing to do. It was what they called
rum running.

Nearly all of us have regrets for youthful indis-
cretions and Sherman Billingsley probably is sorry
that he ever disregarded Uncle Samuel's regulations
concerning liquor. But he was young and it was under
the high excitement that youth craves and I would not
be surprised if there are times when, as he sits in the

*lush elegance of his Stork Club, absently nodding to
the passing celebrities, he sees beyond the lights and
the gay crowd the lone reaches of some dark and
muddy road in the back country of Iowa or Nebraska
and hears above the oompah of the rhumba band only
the steady hum of his motor as he crouches above the
steering wheel driving furiously through the night . . .*

*I find it almost impossible to reconcile his gentle
personality with the facts of his early career but of
course every man changes when responsibility takes
him by the elbow and starts directing his steps. . . .*

He was up to Billingsley's bootlegging days (in a Detroit "fairly free of
gunfire") when he wrote on page fourteen, *"to be continued."*

Runyon died on December 10, 1946, leaving enough of the typescript
to serve as a future cover story in *Cosmopolitan.* Eight days after his crema-
tion, by his request, Eddie Rickenbacker, the fighter ace and founder of
Eastern Air Lines, and John F. Gill, Eastern's chief pilot, took the funerary
urn aboard a twin-engine plane and, several thousand feet above Times
Square, tipped the ashes over Broadway. The Sunday after Runyon's death,
with Hoover's participation, the Damon Runyon Memorial Fund for Cancer Research was established at the Stork Club. Billingsley contributed
the first $5,000. Winchell, down in Miami Beach, passed the hat among
the bookies.

FOUR

I N THE SPRING OF 1947 the Chefs, Cooks, Pastry Cooks and Assistants Union, Local 89, of the American Federation of Labor renewed decade-old efforts to organize the largely Puerto Rican kitchen workers.

Billingsley went on the offensive. One fired employee told the New York State Labor Relations Board that Billingsley had threatened his kitchen workers. Another employee who joined the union testified that Billingsley had branded him a company spy, "a skunk, a lousy stool pigeon," and had him followed to and from his home, and even into the men's room.

As the organizing efforts intensified, Billingsley called a meeting to remind his staff: "I give you ties, whiskey, cigarettes, money, a lot of things." In fact, the labor strife did tend to overshadow the genuinely paternal relationship Billingsley had long enjoyed with many of his workers. He provided every Stork Club employee a free $1,000 life insurance policy and announced in one of his staff memos:

> IF WE ARE EVER UNFORTUNATE TO
> HAVE TO SEND AN EMPLOYEE TO THE HOS-
> PITAL, I WANT THEM TO GO TO THE ROO-
> SEVELT HOSPITAL WHICH IS THE BEST AND
> I HAVE CONNECTIONS WHEREBY I CAN GET
> THE BEST FOR US.

He also assured them that

> ANY ONE OF YOU MAY COME TALK TO
> ME IF YOU HAVE ANY COMPLAINTS OR
> DIFFICULTIES THAT YOU WISH ME TO
> STRAIGHTEN FOR YOU OR YOU CAN WRITE
> TO ME IF YOU RATHER.

When he fined employees — as he did for such infractions as bringing in a relative as a customer — whatever amount was docked was matched by him and went into an employee-benefits fund. If anyone on staff needed something, he often said, he or she should just ask, and Billingsley would grant it. And often, in fact, he did. What he couldn't stomach, he said, was anyone's stealing from him. But then, typically, he undermined his own generosity, boasting, "You know I got twenty million dollars to buy the union and everybody else if I have to. If I don't succeed in buying it out, I'll close the place." He later laughed off the claim. "I never had one million dollars," he said, noting that he was wearing a fifty-dollar suit and a gift tie. He *used to have* three thousand ties, he said, but was down to his last fifteen hundred, having given the rest away. Taking up Billingsley's cause, Winchell, in his column, warned: "A world-renowned smart spot boss is thinking of closing for the first time in his long career, rather than submit to a threat of unionizing. Pays the highest wage of anyone. 200 workers may be looking for jobs if he gets sore enough."

In fact, the whole affair was a reprise of the uproar in the summer of 1937 when rumors spread through the Stork Club that Billingsley had hired a new headwaiter and crew in upstate Saratoga Springs so he could fire the existing staff. Many panicked; thirteen waiters hurriedly signed union cards. Billingsley did fire them anyway, claiming they were unkempt, dishonest, and disruptive, although judges later questioned why, if that was true, they had worked there for so long.

Billingsley's opinion of the unions had been formed indelibly in the thirties when Dutch Schultz and Tammany district leader Jimmy Hines had terrorized the restaurant industry with the corrupt waiters union Local 16 and the Metropolitan Restaurant and Cafeteria Association, which despite its name was nothing more than a multimillion-dollar shakedown racket. Restaurant and club owners either joined it and got a sticker to put up in their window or faced stink bombs, labor trouble, vandalism, or violence. Legitimate union organizers found themselves at the wrong end of lead pipes and pistols wielded by Schultz's labor enforcer, Big Julie Martin. Even Runyon's enfabled Lindy's paid off rather than suffer the consequences.

Now, in the spring of 1947, a world war and seven years later, Schultz was long dead and Hines was in jail, but Billingsley was still having labor trouble. He called the workers he fired "a bunch of racketeers" and vowed never to let the union in. Instead, he organized a company union, the Stork Club Restaurant Employes (sic) Association.

That May the New York City Hotel Employees and Restaurant Employees Union scheduled a representation election in the club. The night before the vote, Billingsley threw the kitchen staff a party as lavish as any he had held for his Glamour Girl debs. Workers sipped champagne as Billingsley exhorted them to stay out of the union, promising higher wages and a five-day week. One dishwasher recalled the affair as "dreamlike" and entrancing, while another remembered, "We were called upstairs and offered drinks, cigarettes, and ties." He sat at a table marked "Reserved" and remarked, "I never saw anything so pretty." Another worker was less starstruck. "Everybody was drunk. It looked like a crazy house," he told the state labor board as Billingsley sat in the audience chewing mints and toying with a gold tie clip inscribed SHERM FROM MORT.

In his defense Billingsley described the affair as "just a meeting." "Naturally we served a few drinks," he said. "We believe in giving our help a drink or a cigar or carfare home when they need it. We have been doing it for seventeen years. We believe it is one reason our food is so good."

The union lost the election, charging Billingsley with vote-tampering. At the least, Billingsley had arranged transportation to the polls, as a note to doorman Albino Garlasco suggested: *Please Albino — Better bring Chico to vote again tomorrow same as you did today and of course you will take him home tonight.*

After the vote against the union Billingsley threw the workers another party. This time, a dishwasher said, Billingsley handed him a hundred dollars. Another dishwasher, he said, got five hundred, and the other employees each got a folded banknote.

THE STORK CLUB STAFF POSES FOR A GROUP PORTRAIT
ON ITS WAY TO A COMPANY PICNIC.

Billingsley ridiculed the charges of payoffs. "Who would give a dishwasher that kind of money?"

Then a dishwasher testified that the night before the labor hearing, Billingsley handed him a hundred dollars in the club and the next morning sent five hundred more to his home.

Suddenly the inquiry developed criminal overtones. Dewey's successor, Manhattan district attorney Frank S. Hogan, opened a grand jury investigation.

Billingsley waived immunity and took the stand. Meanwhile, the dishwasher, under cross-examination, had to admit that the roll was not exactly untouched. He had made change for someone, trading a twenty for two tens. And maître d' Gregory Pavlides testified that the dishwasher had asked for the money so that he could take his wife and child to Puerto Rico.

The grand jury voted no indictment. "I wasn't worried," Billingsley told the press. "I didn't lose an inch of sleep."

But the state hearings ground on, resuming after the holidays in January 1948. With tensions high, Billingsley and the union's lawyer, the petite and sharp-tongued Vera M. Boudin, went at each other in the corridors, trading what the *Daily News* gleefully headlined 1ST RATE BILLINGS-GATE.

Spotting Billingsley talking to a reporter, she muttered in a stage whisper, "What's that racketeer got to say?"

"I'll sue you for that," he said, taunting her. "You defend the Communists."

"I'd rather defend them than you."

"Did you take down the picture of Stalin in your office?" Billingsley countered.

"I'd rather get my orders from Stalin than from Hitler." Boudin pronounced him "a very arrogant specimen of the illegitimate male."

Billingsley rushed to take the bait. "I wouldn't have my wife doing this kind of work, shooting her mouth off before a bunch of men."

The reporters scratched furiously in their pads.

"You'd better print it," Billingsley said, "before the Commies take over."

Within two weeks, however, a truce was negotiated. Billingsley would take back "without discrimination" three of the eight kitchen workers he had fired in May (the five remaining had found other jobs) and pay back wages to seven of the eight, as one worker dropped his dismissal claim. The dishwasher who had received the five hundred dollars was one of those who returned, and as part of the agreement he was allowed to keep Billingsley's money. In all, the settlement cost Billingsley more than $5,700. But it was hardly the end.

FIVE

EAGER TO RECONNECT with his public after the long union ordeal, Billingsley gave an interview to *Good Housekeeping,* in which he counseled women (but not men) in an article titled "How to Behave in a Night Club":

> *Don't give reasons when going to the Ladies' Lounge. Omit the coy remarks. Simply excuse yourself. . . .*
>
> *Don't become overfriendly with musicians. It isn't considered nice. . . .*
>
> *Don't talk to strangers at adjoining tables. And don't be too friendly ever with people you know but who are not part of your party. Particularly, don't flirt — it is embarrassing to your escort. . . .*
>
> *Don't table-hop, no matter how well you know the other guests. It often looks show-offy, and it's almost always annoying. . . .*
>
> *Don't accept notes sent to your table by strangers, and never give your name, address or telephone number to anyone to whom you have not been properly introduced. . . .*
>
> *Don't engage in conversation with waiters. Don't give your order to a waiter — give it to your escort; he, not you, is supposed to do the ordering. . . .*
>
> *Don't hold conversations with cab drivers while going to or from nightclubs.*

Billingsley's relationship with Yetta was not nearly so genteel. Once he flippantly speculated aloud on her underwear, for which she cut him dead with a withering glare. If now and then he reached out and touched her hand or arm, she'd pretend to swoon, pulling back. "Ooooh, Billingsley touched me. Can I frame this?" Even he would laugh.

By 1948 Billingsley had added publicity duties to her secretarial and switchboard work. He raised her salary to $100 a week while warning her never to talk to a rival nightclub. And on the rare occasions he risked a short vacation or other absence from the Stork, he felt confident leaving Yetta in charge.

She shopped for and distributed many of the gifts of clothing and accessories that Billingsley showered on patrons: shirts and ties from Sulka and gold cigarette lighters from Cartier and Tiffany, benificence that offended her sense of proportion and rectitude. Why should Hoover of all people accept such presents? Yetta also knew when Billingsley hit on the checkroom girls and when his wife, Hazel, called up the club in desperate tears. She knew when an overamorous deb and her beau were caught *in flagrante delicto* in a Stork Club phone booth. Jack Kennedy's assignations, too, were open secrets. There were nights when the hyperactive young war hero waited in his car to drive home one or another of the Stork Club beauties, including a girl who, among other favors, cooked him steak dinners. Billingsley, as sharp-eyed as Yetta, spotted him outside one night and couldn't resist asking, "Having steak tonight?"

Yetta also discovered that Billingsley had bugged the place. She already knew that he kept an eye on employees through two-way mirrors. Clubgoers saw their own reflections in them, but Billingsley could see out through the dark glass. From her work on the switchboard, Yetta also already knew that Billingsley listened in on staff and customer phone calls, but one day she saw strange new tubes running behind her desk from the ceiling down the wall to the floor. She sought out day manager Ed Wynne.

"What the hell is that?" she asked, pointing to the tubes.

Wynne put a finger to his lips. "Sshhhh," he said, raising an eyebrow.

Was the bugging the handiwork of John G. (Steve) Broady, a hulking ex-cowboy from the Mojave Desert, who worked undercover for celebrity clients like the Astors and Rockefellers and was even then wiretapping City Hall to gather evidence against political enemies? Billingsley never said, and Broady, who was to be shot dead in a Thailand hotel, would take his secret to the grave.

Yetta ran a few tests. Alone in her office, she loudly cursed out Billingsley. Sure enough, later that day he chewed her out for her remarks. Her office had to be bugged.

Now it was her turn to blow up. "What the hell do you think? I spend time talking to myself?" She had him there. She took the occasion to demand her own private phone line; there was no way she was going to call through the switchboard, not with him listening in.

G od only knew all the things Billingsley was up to, Yetta thought. Was Cigogne blending its own perfume, importing just the base from France? After Billingsley had taken over the whole building from the doctors, she heard that the Sortilege bottles were being filled upstairs on the seventh floor. *What are they pouring in there?* she once asked an employee, horrified by the presumably joking answer: *urine.*

Billingsley had put Yetta on nights, starting at eight and finishing up at four in the morning, so she could be around during the busy hours. She was nervous afterward about taking the subway home to the Bronx, so she would walk over to Hanson's drugstore near the Taft Hotel on Seventh Avenue to have breakfast and wait for the morning rush to start. It wasn't all tedious — she had met the love of her life in Hanson's, a bookie named Tony Ferruccio. But her schedule finally wore her down, and she complained to Billingsley.

He shook his head in dismay. "After all I've done for you."

That set her off. "What the hell did you ever do for me? You're on Park Avenue. I'm in a tenement on Simpson Street."

Chastened, he came up with an apartment for her in an old brownstone that he and his perfume partners Downey and Godfrey had bought as an investment across from the Drake Hotel on Park Avenue at Fifty-sixth Street. It was a cramped fifth-floor walk-up — one room with a bathroom and a closet converted into a galley kitchen — which he gave Yetta for $50 a month.

As New Year's approached, Hazel prevailed upon her husband to spend the holiday with the family in Florida. He was hesitant but agreed as long as Yetta could work. But Yetta already had plans. Billingsley was incredulous. How could she have plans?

She told him that she and friends had reservations at the Riviera nightclub in Fort Lee, New Jersey.

"*New Jersey!*" Billingsley was incensed. Why not the Stork Club? Yetta could bring her mother.

Yetta looked at him with dismay. Her mother was a simple Russian immigrant who spoke only Yiddish and wore housedresses and no makeup. Did she sound like the Stork Club type? Plus, she was kosher. What would Billingsley do? Kosher a ham for her? Yetta kept her plans in New Jersey.

She did have her allies at the club, including Frank Carro, who had become Billingsley's shadow when Gregory was moved to the gold chain. Frank was a second-generation Stork Club staffer, having joined his father, Carlo, in Billingsley's service.

Carlo had come to America from Italy in 1930, finding his way to a job in Billingsley's speakeasy on West Fifty-eighth Street. His baby son, Frank, was supposed to follow him with other family members, but they delayed and were then trapped by Mussolini's war mobilization. Carlo became one of Billingsley's favorites after serving him a steak one day at the club. Billingsley thought the meat was tough. He called Carlo back to taste it. Carlo cut himself a slice, chewed thoughtfully, and said, "It's good enough for me. It's good enough for you."

When twenty-one-year-old Frank finally got to join his father in America after the war, Billingsley gave him a job, too, calling him "Junior," in deference to Carlo.

As shadow, the first thing Frank had to learn was Billingsley's body language — the silent signals of a hand on his tie or on his earlobe that directed perfume to one table, orchids to another, and Stork Club suspenders to a third. That accomplished, Frank was amused to see, Billingsley then sometimes retreated to tote up what he had given away and how he might recoup the expense from a table of tourists. Later he could gloat about it. "I gave away a hundred dollars and made two hundred."

But the code system had its limitations, as Lucius Beebe noted in his *Stork Club Bar Book*:

> The very first night the new order went into effect all hell broke loose at the Stork. The Master absent-mindedly spilled salt, fiddled with the ash tray or waved his napkin to illustrate a conversational point and right away notorious drunks were plied with ardent waters gratis, old friends of the establishment and celebrated names had their hats pushed over their ears and were being urged into the outer darkness and the Cub Room was peopled with folk of no consequence whatsoever.

Frank also learned what not to do, as Billingsley reminded the staff in one of his postings:

> TO ALL EMPLOYEES:
> PLEASE, PLEASE, WHEN YOU WANT TO SPEAK TO ME WHEN I AM SITTING WITH SOMEONE WRITE IT ON A SMALL PIECE OF PAPER, FOLD IT AND HAND IT TO ME. DON'T START TAKING LOUD TO ME IN FRONT OF PEOPLE SO THAT THEY CAN HEAR WHAT

*YOU HAVE TO SAY. NOW GOD DAM IT I'VE
REQUESTED THIS SEVERAL TIMES BEFORE
AND A LOT OF YOU JUST WON'T COOPER-
ATE. IF I AM ALONE YOU CAN SPEAK TO ME
BUT WHEN I AM SITTING WITH PEOPLE
WRITE IT ON A SMALL PIECE OF PAPER NO
MATTER WHAT IT IS AND HAND IT TO ME.*

Waiters were to take their orders from him, Billingsley demanded, not the customers:

*IN OTHER WORDS IF I SHOULD SAY
BRING A BOTTLE OF SCOTCH TO THE
TABLE AND THE PEOPLE AT THE TABLE SAY
"OH, NO. DON'T DO THAT." IN A CASE LIKE
THIS, DON'T PAY ANY ATTENTION TO WHAT-
EVER THE PEOPLE AT THE TABLE SAY —
JUST GO AHEAD AND BRING IT AS PER MY
INSTRUCTIONS.*

Waiters were also letting customers walk off with the ashtrays.

*I HAVE BEEN INFORMED THAT ONE
WAITER HAS TOLD THE PEOPLE TO SLIP
THE ASHTRAY IN THEIR POCKET. I THINK
THIS IS ILL TREATMENT.*

If necessary, Billingsley said, waiters who noticed a missing ashtray, vase, peppermill, or anything else were to start looking under the table and say, "Oh, gee, I will have to pay for whatever is missing," until the thief was shamed enough to surrender the pilfered object. Naturally, Billingsley said, "If they are high-class, steady customers, don't do anything." But in truth, he kind of liked the idea that his ashtrays were prized trophies on coffee tables across America.

In one week alone, Billingsley tallied, he lost 212 pieces of silverware at a cost of $71.32.

"I am the king," Billingsley told Frank more than once. If he wanted a cup of tea, Frank saw, he thought little of intercepting a waiter laden with hot platters. Faced with the choice of obeying his boss or catering to his table, the waiter didn't hesitate: he ran to do Billingsley's bidding.

Sometimes Billingsley rang for tea and toast to be brought up to his seventh-floor suite. When the waiter arrived, he might find Billingsley in bed with his latest conquest, as if he were determined to live up to a reputation he felt compelled to uphold. One flustered waiter, told to help himself to a five-dollar tip from Billingsley's pants over a chair, stormed out, muttering, "What am I, a whore?"

On his rounds through the club, Billingsley tested his staff by scooping up blank customer checks from a waiter's station. "I guarantee they'll never know," he said, winking to Frank. He knew all the ways his staff cheated him, including dropping counterfeit food and drink checks on the tables. Anything customers paid on these went directly into the workers' pockets.

Billingsley was also aware when waiters or bartenders sneaked off to down the drinks they were supposedly rushing to a table on priority-treatment vouchers called "speedies," or when they conspired with the cooks for illicit meals.

> ### MEN IN CHARGE OF KITCHEN
> I JUST WANT YOU TO KNOW THAT I AM
> TOLD WHEN YOU GIVE THE EMPLOYEES
> FOOD THAT THEY ARE NOT SUPPOSED TO
> GET, SUCH AS TWO LARGE STUFFED SAND-
> WICHES, VEAL CUTLETS, ROAST BEEF,
> TURKEY, LARGE ICE CREAMS, ETC., ETC.,
> TO CAMERA GIRLS CIGARETTE AND
> CHECKROOM GIRLS AND OFFICE GIRLS.
> PLEASE CUT IT OUT NOW!

And that went likewise for untouched food orders that never made it back to the kitchen.

Always on edge, Billingsley regularly took tranquilizers, "nerve pills," as he called them. When the bottles were delivered from the pharmacy, it was Frank's job to shake out the pills and count them, to make sure Billingsley wasn't getting cheated.

"Junior, let's go for a walk," Billingsley said one day. He opened a desk drawer. "Here," he said, handing Frank a pistol, "you carry this."

Frank pulled back, appalled.

"It's all right," Billingsley said. "You work for me."

Frank shook his head. No way. What if he got picked up by the cops?

Billingsley exploded. "You guinea bastard —"

Frank snapped, "Don't you *ever* call me that!"

Billingsley shrugged. Okay, they could forget about the gun.

Oh, he was a strange one, Frank thought. After *South Pacific* opened on Broadway in 1949, Ezio Pinza often came in after the show for a bowl of spaghetti with tomato sauce. His choice irked Billingsley, who took pride in his grandiose menu. "That fucking guinea bastard," he complained to Frank. "Why doesn't he go to a pasta place?"

But Billingsley seemed eager to hire Italians. He had recently taken on George Amodio, a twenty-four-year-old New Jerseyan who had worked for Joseph (Newsboy) Moriarty, the longtime gambling boss of Hudson County. George began as a busboy, the only non-Filipino on a cleanup staff of fourteen, and soon was encouraged to bring in his brother, Tony. Billingsley quickly moved George into an important new niche, as deliveryman. In his Stork Club Ford panel truck, George distributed cases of wine and liquor and other gifts all over town, including to the apartment of Joseph P. Kennedy, whose association with Billingsley went back to the bootlegging days. Kennedy was properly appreciative. "Dear Sherm," Kennedy wrote from Palm Beach after Christmas 1949, "I have known a great many men in business during my life and I will say there are many of them I wished to succeed because I thought they were smart and on the level, and because I was personally attracted to them, I was pulling at all times for their success in whatever field they tried. In that small group I certainly place you. You have made graciousness an art and generosity a habit."

Recipients showed their gratitude in various ways. One day, armed with two cases of champagne, George knocked on Tallulah Bankhead's door. "Dahling," she cooed, "come in — what'll you have?" When George entered the room, he saw that she was stark naked, as were some of the other men and women with her. He declined her hospitality. Not long before, he had delivered cases of whiskey to the Park Avenue apartment that Ann Sheridan shared with Steve Hannagan. She, too, had opened the door naked. What was it with these people?

Billingsley also hired a new photographer, an attractive hatcheck girl named Lillian Camp who had worked at Billy Rose's Diamond Horseshoe. One night Billingsley told her to photograph a table of Coca-Cola executives. As she raised her Speed Graphic, one of the men objected. "No pictures," he said, waving her off.

She reported back to Billingsley. "I want a picture," he insisted.

She went back to the table and took the shots.

When one of the men jumped up and tried to wrest away the camera, she realized the problem: the table was set with cocktails, and not a Coca-Cola bottle in sight. They struggled and then suddenly someone was by her side, fighting off her assailant. To her amazement, she saw that it was Frank Sinatra. The man backed off.

Flustered and mumbling her gratitude, she retreated with her pictures, never to forget her savior.

One night not long after her brawl with the Coca-Cola executives, Lillian Camp was summoned upstairs to Billingsley's private quarters. "Bring your camera," he said. Nervously, she obeyed.

He was sitting down with his back to her when she entered. "Don't tell anyone," he began.

"All right," she said.

"Shoot." He pointed to the back of his head.

His receding hair was noticeably sparse on his crown. Dutifully, she shot off a number of plates. "Develop them and bring them back," he ordered.

When she did, he leafed through the damp prints, frowning deeply. Clearly he hated growing old.

Tallulah, who kept a country estate in Bedford, New York, in Westchester County, had introduced Billingsley to her neighbor, Benny Goodman, and in January 1949 he bought Goodman's forty-acre Pound Ridge Farm for $100,000, although today the prime land would be worth millions. It was Billingsley's dream to relive his rustic Oklahoma childhood and supply the Stork Club with fresh milk, eggs, and produce from his farm.

A quarter mile off a main road, Pound Ridge Farm included a modern four-bedroom colonial main house with a three-car garage, pool, and two tennis courts. Grandly, he planted beds of flowers and orchards of peach, pear, and apple trees and built chicken coops out of empty champagne crates, of which he had truckloads. He sped his harvest to the club in a truck marked STORK CLUB FARM and bought a Nash with reclining seats so he could nap while his driver ferried him back and forth on weekends. And as if to make up for his absences, he ardently filmed spool after spool of home movies of the girls riding horses, running through the sprinklers, and splashing in the pool.

Relaxed for once, he patrolled his domain in cowboy garb with a Western hat or a handkerchief knotted at the corners to protect his balding crown from the sun. He drove a tractor and milked cows. He also fired shotguns, rifles, and pistols and taught his girls to shoot.

The week they took possession, twelve-year-old Barbara was stretching out for a sunbath on the diving board when she reached down for what she thought was a piece of rope. Nearsighted but forbidden by her father to wear glasses — Billingsley refused to acknowledge any imperfection that would compromise the beauty of his girls — she was about to

SHERMAN PLAYING THE GENTLEMAN FARMER
AT HIS HOME IN BEDFORD, NEW YORK

grab it when she jerked back her hand with a scream that brought everyone running. The "rope" was a copperhead. The farm, it turned out, harbored several varieties of poisonous snakes. The girls were outfitted with cowboy boots and were forbidden to roam.

Billingsley mentioned the snake problem to Hoover one night at the club, and the FBI boss had some suggestions. He thought Welsh terriers might be antisnake dogs. When Detroit city officials wanted to reclaim a swampy island overrun with snakes, Hoover remembered, they released pigs, which made short work of the snakes. Billingsley quickly bought himself a pig.

Hazel rarely confronted her husband, but this time she put her foot down: no pig, an ultimatum that grew firmer after Barbara smuggled the animal into the house. Billingsley capitulated — he had little choice, as it happened, since pigs were illegal on the property — and settled for the Welsh terriers, which seemed to work equally well. Soon he was also raising boxers and poodles, in part as a favor to Barbara's headmistress at the Spence School, who supported a Seeing Eye dog charity that sought female boxer puppies for the blind. The venture proved successful, and soon Billingsley was breeding poodle and terrier puppies to give as gifts at the Stork Club. He was extremely attached to his dogs. One day he came upon the veterinarian cropping their ears and tails for a more pleasing appearance. "Christ!" he exploded. "Don't you ever, ever let that happen again, or I'll cut your ears and tail, too!"

He also let one of his dogs, named Boy, roam free on the seventh floor of the club. A sign warned, ANY GOD DAM SON OF A BITCH WHO HITS OR KICKS THIS DOG I WILL HIT OR KICK RIGHT BACK. S. B.

Hazel was uneasy. Somehow, she felt, the farm might be a jinx that would set off an avalanche of troubles.

SHERMAN, AT RIGHT, AT ABOUT AGE EIGHTEEN,
WITH HIS BROTHER ORA

BOOT-
LEGGING
DAYS

SIX

I T ALL STARTED, Billingsley liked to say, with a little red wagon on a hot summer day in Anadarko, Oklahoma, about the time the Oklahoma Territory became a state. That was in 1907. The wagon was a rare and wonderful gift from his brother Logan. Until then Logan, fourteen years older than Sherman with three other boys and two girls in between them, had never bothered much with him, the baby of the family, although Sherman had always idolized him, especially now that Logan was already a married man with a son of his own. That he had gone to jail for killing his future wife's father only added to his mystique. He stood six feet tall, straight as a poker, with wavy black hair, fair skin, and an icy nerve seemingly impervious to fear.

Sherman played happily with the red wagon until Logan took him to their barn, where he uncovered a barrel of beer bottles. He lined the bottom of the wagon with the beer, smoothed a blanket on top, sat his baby son, Glenn, on the blanket, and told Sherman to sell the beer to the Indians who lived in the woods on the edge of town. They were forbidden alcohol, there being enough trouble with the settlers without getting the Indians drunk and riled up.

Sherman collected fifty cents a bottle, keeping the empties for resale to the saloons. And that was his start as a bootlegger, although real bootleggers, he later found out, smuggled bottles for the Indians tucked into their boots.

But the legacy of the Billingsleys began long before that. . . .

A ducal Saxon family named Billing that settled on a piece of untilled ground called a ley must have carried the name into England before the Norman Conquest, and a small village of Billingsley later sprang up in Shropshire County west of Birmingham. By Shakespeare's time, a Sir Henry Billingsley had been elected mayor of

London, and later a Colonel Francis Billingsley of Bridgnorth near Billingsley died defending the crown against Cromwell's Roundheads.

The first Billingsleys to arrive in the New World were three English brothers — John, James, and Francis — who sailed from Holland to Virginia in 1649, followed the next year by two other brothers, Thomas and William.

Sherman's forebear Francis; his wife, Ann; and their son, John, settled on two hundred acres on the west side of Chesapeake Bay in Maryland. But after his brother William was struck and killed by a swinging boom on his sloop in Virginia, Francis moved his family there to help his sister-in-law. Later they returned to Maryland, where in 1668 a William Kay was indicted for criminal assault and attempted rape of Ann. Francis served in the House of Delegates of the colonial Maryland General Assembly and as a commissioner of Calvert County, surveying and purchasing town lands and ports (including Billingsley Manor, a 430-acre estate in Prince Georges County, acquired for public recreation in the 1990s).

Francis's great-grandson, William, died in 1745 at the age of fifty-four, bequeathing his sons William and James "my two negroes Sambo and Ben." James, who married and moved to North Carolina before the American Revolution, became a patriot, resisting mounting harassment by Tory neighbors. In April 1776, when he was fifty, they invaded his home and hanged him from a tree. His widow, Elizabeth, moved to Tennessee and Kentucky and then back to Tennessee, where she died in 1839 at the age of 113.

James's great-grandson George McCreary Billingsley, born in 1820 in Tennessee, tried to join the Union forces in the Civil War but was caught and imprisoned by the Rebels. A fierce figure with a scraggly mountain-man beard, he married four times, outliving three of his wives and fathering twenty-five children, the last born several months after his death at eighty-four in 1904. His eleventh child, and first with his second wife, was Sherman's father, Robert W. Billingsley, born on July 18, 1864, in Claiborne County, Tennessee.

A strapping farmer with large, powerful hands; thick ebony hair; deep-set, restless eyes; and prominent jaw, Robert married at eighteen in 1882. His slightly older bride was a neighbor, Emily Collingsworth, petite and dark haired, with firm-set lips and lively birdlike eyes, whose family also went back generations in the American wilderness. By the end of the year, their first child, Logan, was born, and soon afterward they moved just over the state line to a farm on the Cumberland River in Middlesboro, Kentucky. Horses grazed on the famed bluegrass, and the fields sprouted tobacco, cotton, corn, and grain. By now a generation had passed since the Civil War, yet many freed slaves, with nowhere else to go, continued to live with their long-time masters. The Billingsleys had four, among them Nappy George Coates, then in his thirties. The family had been good to him, he said, and if the Lord had seen fit to give him to the Billingsleys, that's where he'd stay.

A BILLINGSLEY FAMILY PORTRAIT. SHERMAN IS AT THE CENTER
OF THE FRONT ROW, BETWEEN HIS PARENTS AND BROTHER LOGAN.

Robert and Emily had a second son, Robert Jr.; a daughter, Charlotte, or
Lottie; another boy, Ora; and then another boy, Frederich, losing two babies in
between. By the time Fred was born in June 1892, Robert was hearing reports
that more of the Oklahoma Territory would be opening up for settlement.

The pressure to expand west had been building fast. In 1870 the population of the United States was 38.5 million; twenty years later it had almost
doubled, to 63 million. The West was growing even faster. In the same period,
the population of Kansas and Texas, which sandwiched the Indian Territory,
had more than tripled, making the Indian lands too tempting to resist. Land-
hungry boomers had been eyeing them since the aftermath of the Civil War,
and it took army troops to keep them at bay. In 1889 President Benjamin
Harrison proclaimed them open for settlement, and at the signal passed
along the border by soldiers firing their pistols, the rush was on. Fifty thousand settlers poured in on foot and horseback, staking claims. A second
run for newly opened land took place in 1891, attracting another twenty
thousand settlers, some of whom were trampled in the crush. A third
opening, of Cheyenne and Arapaho lands, was set for the following year.

The news, which quickly found its way to Kentucky, left Robert eager
to join the rush, as his son Fred later recounted.

The farm was hurriedly put up for sale, Mommie (as the family
called Emily) keeping only her most precious possessions, her Haviland

and English bone china, and her sewing kit. Robert constructed four large Conestoga wagons, buying steel for the axles and hewing oak and hickory for the planking, which could serve later as the floor of their new home or barn. The lead wagon was their traveling home, laid out for housekeeping with day-to-day provisions. The second wagon was crammed with lumber, tools, nails, guns, and ammunition. The third carried the furniture. The last wagon bore as much of the precious Kentucky seed as could be loaded aboard and the staples: smoked meats, flour, salt, sugar, coffee, and three barrels of Robert Billingsley's mellowest Kentucky bourbon whiskey.

In early summer 1892 the family set out for the West, accompanied by their four former slaves, now farmhands, including Nappy Coates. Battling the mountainous terrain, the wagon train managed no more than fifteen miles a day. They foraged for wild grapes and berries, squirrels, wild turkeys, and doves. And almost any morning an inquisitive deer could be dropped with the long-barreled Kentucky rifle or one of the new Springfields.

They forded the Mississippi near the Missouri-Arkansas border, where they met throngs of other travelers, cattlemen, drifters, carpetbaggers, gamblers, and families of homesteaders like themselves, everyone talking about Oklahoma. The whole country, it seemed, was on the march west.

At Little Rock they made camp a mile north of the city, venturing in to gape at the drunks and gamblers and saloon girls. Robert sensed an opportunity. He may have looked like a rube, but long nights alone playing solitaire had honed his cardsharp skills. He could deal cards from the cen-

SHERMAN'S FIRST HOME, WHERE HE IS ALSO BELIEVED
TO HAVE BEEN BORN

ter of the deck or off the top or bottom. To him, it wasn't cheating, just cutting down the odds. Playing poker in Little Rock, he put his gifts to use.

They made Oklahoma by September. With his sizable grubstake, Robert filed claim on a 160-acre homestead in Enid, a onetime stagecoach stop called Skeleton in the Cherokee Strip north of Oklahoma City.

He cleared his own roads into the land. He cut down trees and hauled the logs by mule to a sawmill to be cut into planks for a simple L-shaped house. Having acquired enough training to consider himself an engineer, he dug a well and a storm cellar for refuge from cyclones. To keep out wolves, coyotes, and foxes, he strung barbed wire around the house and poultry pens, grain sheds, and fields, but snakes, possums, squirrels, and rabbits overran the farm, which he grandly named Gracemont. Soon he was raising horses, mules, cows, pigs, sheep, goats, turkeys, and chickens, butchering for himself the meat the family needed for the table.

Robert and Emily had a sixth child, Pearl, in 1894 and two years later, a seventh and their last, John Sherman Billingsley.

It was wild and unforgiving country, Sherman later recounted. Summers were hot, winters were frigid, and heavy winds blew year-round. Fierce hawks and buzzards threatened the livestock and the children. Robert fought off a pack of wildcats, killing two of them with his sickle. Cattle rustlers stole a dozen of Robert's horses, and he set out alone and retrieved them. But it was also a bucolic life, lived by the light of pig-tallow candles and the rhythms of nature.

Sherman was too young to have his own bed, so at dusk he was given a glass of warm milk to put him to sleep. Whoever in the family turned in first would pick him up and carry him along. He dressed in denim overalls, blue shirts, and a fifteen-cent straw hat with a shoestring for a hatband. Summers he went barefoot, winters he wore ankle shoes, long johns, long stockings, and a sweater.

Nineteen hundred was a census year, the twelfth decennial counting of the population in farm kitchens and squalid tenements. In June enumerator William J. Cameron plied his route in Garfield County, Oklahoma, making the Billingsley family in North Enid his thirty-eighth stop and recording his findings in quill pen on a large ledger schedule. The list started with Robert, described as a mechanical engineer (Cameron had some trouble with the word *mechanical*) and ended with Sherman, age four, born in March 1896. (So much for Sherman's later insistence that he was born in 1900.) But there was one anomaly in the Billingsley family census: seventeen-year-old Logan had vanished. In his place, listed as the firstborn child, was "Lola," age sixteen. Was the family already trying to cover Logan's renegade tracks?

In 1901 the government opened three new counties to the south for grants by lottery. Nearly 170,000 applicants registered, and 6,500 lucky names were drawn from a box on a rotating wheel, Robert's among them.

Moving the family south by wagon to Caddo County, he filed a claim eight miles outside Anadarko on prairie land encircled on three sides by a low horseshoe mountain. The woods were full of black walnut trees and fruit trees of peaches, apples, pears, plums, and cherries, and the soil could be coaxed to yield cotton, corn, sugarcane, sweet Irish potatoes, tomatoes, beans, lettuce, turnips, peas, cucumbers, cantaloupes, and watermelons. Sherman did his share of the chores, milking cows, collecting eggs, chopping kindling, and mowing the grass, and earned his first pay picking cotton at a penny a pound. He also had the job of ringing the dinner bell atop the butte to summon the family and hired hands to dinner, which they ate at a long wooden table set with fried chicken, hot biscuits, hominy, beans, turnips, potatoes, milk, and pies.

Sherman sold the *Saturday Evening Post* every week and was awarded a prize of a rubber stamp with his name and address on it. Thrilled to see his name in print, he stamped it all over town. He delivered milk, picked wild plums for five cents a quart, and sold fish he had caught in the Washita River for five and ten cents apiece. He hunted squirrels, rabbits, possums, and other game to sell, and raised pigeons and chickens to sell the eggs and squabs. On Saturdays he delivered handbills for the small merchants for twenty-five cents, catching the farmers on the edge of town as they came in to sell their produce. He picked up junk in burlap bags. He washed dishes for a Mexican chili parlor in exchange for a ten-cent dish of chili. An old man who ran a soda factory paid him a bottle of strawberry pop to shoo flies off him while he read his mail and the papers.

And then in June of 1904 their lives were upended.

Sherman's father, who had been to Anadarko with Logan, came riding his horse very fast up the sand road to the farmhouse. He hollered to brother Robert to hitch the four horses up to the three-seated buggy and to get Mommie; they all had to return to Anadarko immediately. Sherman and young Robert sat in the center buggy seat, their parents in the front. His father drove the horses so fast that the backseat dropped off. They stopped at Dr. Curley's office in town, and everyone but Sherman went in, leaving him to wonder what was going on. Soon his brother led their mother out, crying as if her heart would break. Robert drove them back to the farm, leaving their father behind in Anadarko. Lottie finally told him what had happened: Logan had shot and killed a man, the father of Chloe Wheatley, who accused Logan of getting her pregnant.

Logan refused to marry Chloe, enraging her father. When Robert and Logan went into Anadarko one day for some grain, Andrew Wheatley was waiting with two large knives. Logan ran, with Wheatley in close pursuit. Robert started after Wheatley, who saw him and whirled, raising his knives over Robert's back. Logan drew a snub-nosed .45 double-barrel pistol and shot Wheatley through the heart.

Logan was now being held for homicide in the county jail, and Robert moved the family into Anadarko so they could bring him food and work on his case. Years later Sherman still remembered the stinging smell of the jail's disinfectant.

Anadarko was a typical frontier town of sand roads and plank sidewalks, with a candy store, bank, saloon, hardware store, pawnshop, drugstore, grocery, clothing store, hotel, blacksmithy, lumberyard, post office, school, and courthouse. The Billingsley house itself was primitive, without running water, electricity, or gas. Sherman chopped the wood for the stove, and the family bathed in a tin washtub with stove-heated water. Mommie seemed to turn into an old woman overnight, and Lottie took over the household. Robert, who was too busy on Logan's case to work, sold his farm to pay lawyers and keep the family alive. After years of big farm meals, they struggled against starvation. Mommie cooked two gallons of vegetable soup with a ten-cent soup bone. Sherman made do with the simplest of treats, bread sprinkled with brown sugar and a few drops of water to keep the wind from blowing the sugar away. His toys were makeshift, a pig's bladder for a football, a stuffed sock or melon for a baseball, and a tree limb for a bat. A schoolmate who lived next door to a tennis court invited Sherman to play tennis, but because a racket cost three dollars, Sherman was out of luck. On Christmas Eve he hung up his stocking with high hopes, only to find it the next morning tied in hard knots around lumps of coal, his brother Fred's idea of a joke.

Robert's first enterprise in Anadarko was the soda concession at the county ballpark. One hot summer day, during a doubleheader, he hiked his price from a nickel to a dime and took in a hundred dollars, becoming the talk of the town. He ended up buying a cigar store and confectionery, and after school Sherman sometimes sold sodas at the fountain.

Logan went to trial and was convicted. He appealed on grounds of self-defense, won a new trial, and in twenty minutes was acquitted. Chloe had her baby, and she and Logan married. Logan ran the confectionery and made a home for Chloe and their son, Glenn.

In early 1906 the Billingsleys' second child, nineteen-year-old Robert, fell ill with influenza and died. Following so soon upon Logan's homicide case, the shock was too much for Mommie, who suffered a breakdown. Robert and Sherman hitched up the buggy and drove her to Mineral Wells, Texas, to recuperate. She later returned to Anadarko, but she was never the same. The house rang with bitter arguments, and once, in a fury, his father seized Sherman and held a gun to his head.

In 1912, with only bad memories of Anadarko, Robert moved the family again, this time sixty miles northeast to Oklahoma City, capital of the new state. The covered-wagon days were over. This time they traveled by train, with Sherman put in the boxcar to watch their furniture, cow, and dog.

SHERMAN AT AGE NINE

Robert found a large house and pursued opportunities in building and real estate. Ora opened a tailor shop in outlying Packingtown. Fred took a job as a stenographer. Lottie found work as a clerk and cashier. Sherman went to school and, goggle-eyed, explored the streets of Oklahoma City. The buildings were tall and new, and the streets freshly paved and thronged with fortune hunters drawn by the free land and oil that had begun to gush in response to the growing demand from the booming automobile industry. There were three busy hotels, the Kinkade, the Lee Huckins, and the Skirvin, each conveniently close to gambling houses and brothels, run by madams who combed the countryside for girls from poor farm families. Sherman met whores, opium smokers, gamblers, bank robbers, and legions of bootleggers and witnessed regular shoot-outs in the center of town, with the man left standing usually set free on grounds of self-defense. Prostitutes showed up in court once a week, paid a fine, and underwent examination for venereal disease. Gamblers likewise reported regularly, paid their penalty, and went back to business. The city thrived on vice. The gambling halls were thronged with bar girls pushing drinks on the players so they could be more easily fleeced in crooked games. The gambling houses, in turn, often would be held up by armed robbers who knew that the gamblers couldn't complain.

Sherman delivered a morning paper at dawn for two dollars a week, often then losing the pay in a slot machine by a food wagon at the end of the paper route. He mowed lawns for a quarter, worked in a candy factory for three dollars a week, and hawked soda pop at five cents a bottle out of a

LOTTIE WITH SHERMAN, AT AGE TEN

stand he bought for five dollars. He had trouble recouping his investment. Maybe it was the location, but he figured he had to be running the most unfamous drinking spot in the world.

Logan worked for a while in the Indian service and enrolled at the University of Oklahoma, but it wasn't long before he was back in the bootlegging trade. The new state was officially dry, but people were free to have a gallon a month shipped in for their personal consumption. Logan went around buying up these allotments for resale by the pint or by the drink.

He opened a whiskey-selling gambling house called the Night and Day Drugstore on West Grand Avenue. Sherman and Fred hung out there, selling sundries, soft drinks, and whiskey. For the fifth grade, his parents had put Sherman in a small private school for two dollars a week, but he found that as long as he delivered the tuition money, the schoolmaster didn't care whether he attended or not. Sherman was more interested in seeing how the liquor and gambling joints were run. Posted behind heavy doors reinforced with steel bars and a peephole for screening visitors, lookouts kept watch for the local lawmen. If they spotted a raiding party arriving with sledgehammers, they sounded the alarm and hid the roulette wheels and liquor. Sherman liked to hang around the tables, where winners sometimes gave him their loud neckties or threw him loose change. But witnessing their cheating ways and the tricks of the house, he swore off gambling.

Now the law began to catch up with Logan. In February 1912 he was sentenced to thirty days in jail for operating a gambling house. In March he was again convicted and sentenced to sixty days. In November he was convicted of selling alcohol and received another ninety days.

By then, however, he was long gone, decamping for Texas, where Sherman joined him until things cooled down. When Sherman returned to Oklahoma City, he and Fred went into business, buying the Lyric Pharmacy for $500 and soon moving it to a prime location across from the Skirvin Hotel, owned by the family of Perle Mesta. They stored their whiskey in a rented house a few blocks away and moved it into the drugstore a few quarts at a time. There they poured it into medicine bottles stoppered with medicinal corks and hid it among the dozens of authentic nostrum containers lined up over the prescription counter.

Business quickly boomed. Sherman made expeditions to Fort Worth, Texas, where he bought a dozen suitcases, filled them up with bottles of legal whiskey, and paid off the Pullman conductors to help him on and off the train. That scheme lasted until the night a conductor stole the suitcases.

Looking for a safer system, Sherman and Fred bought a big Lozier automobile and started ferrying in carloads on nighttime runs over the sand and mud roads from Wichita Falls, Texas. Logan, meanwhile, had moved to Charleston, West Virginia — he and Chloe had since divorced — and Sherman and Fred soon joined him there, running a gambling house over a liquor-dispensing cigar store. They had to leave in a hurry, though, after Logan cracked a billiard cue over a man's head, nearly killing him.

Then, with Washington State about to go dry in 1914, it was on to Seattle. Attired in suits, white shirts and ties, and almost identical white hats tilted rakishly back on their heads, the four Billingsley brothers climbed aboard a Union Pacific train, posing defiantly on the balcony of the caboose by a sign that anyone who knew them might have taken as a threat: LEAVING ST. LOUIS BOUND FOR THE WEST.

But under his fancy clothes, eighteen-year-old Sherman was still a rube. He was no sooner in Seattle than he eagerly bought a watch and rings from a man on the street who claimed that they were solid gold and that he needed to sell them cheap to visit his sick mother in Chicago. Spotting his first seafood in a restaurant window, he turned away queasily from the mountains of lobsters, crabs, shrimp, and other shellfish. How could anyone eat things like that?

With their father, Robert, coming out to join them for a time, they opened up the Stewart Street Pharmacy and quickly ran through the alcohol supply they had shipped out. Logan secured a medicinal permit to obtain a case of alcohol, erased the number 1 on the form with ink eradicator, and filled in 1,000. It was that simple.

But again they fell afoul of the law when Sherman was charged with selling a drink to an undercover agent. The Billingsleys hired an ex–district attorney, George F. Vanderveer, for the defense. He told Sherman to dress

LEAVING ST. LOUIS, BOUND FOR THE WEST

UNION PACIFIC

WABASH

THE BILLINGSLEY BOYS HEAD WEST TO SEEK
THEIR FORTUNE. FROM LEFT: FRED, LOGAN,
SHERMAN, ORA

plainly and neatly in the most oversize shirt and suit his brothers could find
and to sit in court looking forlorn. He was to be excessively polite, not to
volunteer any testimony, and if he got into a tight spot, just to look at the
prosecutor and say, "Well, what would you do?" Vanderveer knew Sherman
would be chastised by the judge, but it would make the prosecutor mad
and give Sherman time to figure out his answer.

For his summation, Vanderveer offered an impassioned plea for the
poor young country boy from Oklahoma. As he spoke, tears started stream-
ing from his eyes, and he dropped his head and strode out of the courtroom
to compose himself. The jury went out and returned quickly. Not guilty.

Sherman soon packed his things and headed home for a while to visit
his parents and, as it turned out, to take a wife.

He had known Iva Dee Risk since high school in Oklahoma City
(even though he would later always maintain that he had never gone beyond the fourth grade). Iva Dee, known as Dee Dee, a short and perky

farm girl with wavy brown hair and soulful dark eyes, was eighteen and Sherman nineteen when they eloped in April 1915. Her enraged parents disowned the young couple, who ended up moving in with the Billingsleys.

In Seattle, meanwhile, Logan, Fred, and Ora were running the city's largest bootlegging ring. But they were battling an influential rival, an ex-detective with powerful connections to city hall.

On the night of July 25, 1916, two police agents knocked on the door of the Billingsleys' liquor warehouse, most likely to pick up some whiskey. A Japanese watchman panicked and shot at them, and the two agents returned his fire. All three died, a bloodbath that set off a civic furor. Mayor Hiram C. Gill ordered the Billingsleys arrested.

Sherman was still out of town, and Logan fled to San Francisco. But in December 1916 he was seized on a fugitive warrant and sent back to Seattle. Facing years in prison on liquor charges, Logan offered the government a tantalizing prize. He could flip. In March 1917, in a deal with prosecutors that shook Seattle to its foundations, Logan and Fred showed up in federal court to plead guilty to conspiracy to violate the liquor laws and testify for the people against the mayor and his administration in the most sensational court case the Pacific Northwest had ever seen.

Logan's testimony was riveting. The previous August 30, a month after the killings at the warehouse, he withdrew $4,000 in hundred-dollar bills from his hotel safe-deposit box and delivered it to Mayor Gill in his city hall office.

In exchange, Logan testified, the mayor returned to him seized records of the Billingsleys' whiskey-smuggling business. Logan also swore he had paid off the sheriff, the chief of police, and four policemen with ten dollars a whiskey barrel in protection money.

And then, after four rancorous weeks, the case went to the twelve-man jury.

The deliberations consumed the night. By 7:30 the next morning, March 31, 1917, the verdict was in: not guilty.

The jurors did not tarry to explain, but one panelist stopped long enough to say, "I believe there was infamous lying from witnesses on both sides throughout the trial."

Even when they put themselves on the right side of the law, nobody believed the Billingsleys.

Logan sent his mother in Oklahoma City a postcard saying, "Everything went all right in Seattle." In what may have been a code, the two-cent stamp was affixed upside down.

For their previous guilty pleas, Ora was sentenced to thirty days in prison, Fred to six months, and Logan to thirteen months. Logan alone appealed, staving off the sentence for a year, but ultimately he lost and entered the McNeil Island penitentiary in May of 1918.

SEVEN

S HERMAN ALONE ESCAPED the debacle. With Nebraska about to go dry, he and Dee Dee moved to Omaha, opening a large cigar store and arranging to drive in whiskey from the nearest wet town, St. Joseph, Missouri. He bought some large Paige touring cars, had heavy springs installed, and removed all the extra seats so he could pack in forty cases of whiskey, which he would wrap in heavy black paper and cover up with black canvas to make the back of the car look like empty black space.

Michigan went dry next, then Ohio, opening further opportunities for the Billingsleys. With wet Toledo just sixty miles from dry Detroit, free-flowing traffic in liquor was inevitable, especially since the two cities were conveniently connected by hourly trolley service and the Dixie Highway, U.S. Route 25, commonly known as Avenue de Booze and Rummers Highway. Ingenious amateurs subdivided their automobile fuel tanks to carry liquor as well as gasoline, and secreted whiskey in hot-water bottles, dolls, and even falsies. But they were bit players.

By the end of 1917 Sherman and Dee Dee reunited with his brothers, now out of jail, in Detroit. They opened a liquor storehouse and the usual cigar store and grocery fronts, supplying notorious Black Hand gangs, thirty-five Detroit hotels and restaurants, and the city's elite: bankers, socialites, businessmen, and politicians. A $10 case of whiskey bought in Toledo could be sold for $75 in Detroit. Such were the persuasive economics.

In early 1918 Logan returned to Seattle to sort out his legal problems, while Sherman watched the business in Detroit, sending for his parents to help out. It was a fateful visit for Robert, who, after all the hardships he bore in migrating to Oklahoma and carving out a homestead in the Indian Territory, was run over and killed in May by a streetcar. Sherman, Fred, Ora, and Mommie accompanied his body to Anadarko for burial. They cabled Lottie in El Reno, Oklahoma, to break the news to Pearl ("use precaution") and meet them at the train station. THIS IS TERRIBLE BUT MUST BE STRONG WE ARE COMPELLED TO DEPEND UPON YOU MAMA IS STANDING IT WELL.

Afterward, back in Michigan, Sherman's luck also ran out.

He and Ora had gone into business with a stranger who had come to them with a scheme to slip liquor from Toledo into Detroit by bribing state troopers to relax their blockades. Guided by their new partner, William B. Chase, the brothers drove twenty-two missions without a hitch. Then, on the night of September 18, 1918, as Chase halted their five-car convoy at a narrow bridge at Adrian, Michigan, to pay off the troopers, the bushes by the roadside were suddenly illuminated by the headlights of twenty-five waiting police cruisers. Troopers rushed up with guns. After the arrests, they posed proudly with the seized cars and booty, 1,500 quarts of high-grade whiskey, worth up to $150,000 today, memorializing what became known in the history of Michigan rumrunning as "the capture and arrest of the Billingsley gang."

The operation had been a sting all along; a Kentucky whiskey salesman miffed at the Billingsleys for buying elsewhere had set them up. The authorities had recruited Chase, an ambitious chemist eager to make his mark by nailing the Billingsleys, who were considered by Michigan authorities to be the largest whiskey runners in the country.

Sherman was indicted on twenty-three counts, one for each smuggling trip — "enough charges," he worried, "to keep us in jail forever if convicted." His fears were well founded. At their trial, the prosecutor announced, "We have not been able to find any one of them in the last twelve years that has ever done an honest day's work."

Chase was the star witness, insisting that he had not shared in the bootlegging profits. Sherman's lawyer, George Vanderveer, who had represented him in Seattle, offered an entrapment defense, arguing that Chase had manipulated the Billingsleys. The jury came in with its verdict on January 24, 1919 — guilty on five counts. Ora got two years and six months, and Sherman fifteen months in the U.S. penitentiary in Leavenworth, and each was fined $5,000.

Sherman, though, got a measure of revenge, telling a Justice Department lawyer that Chase had lied about keeping some of the money and had smuggled whiskey himself from Milwaukee into Grand Rapids in furniture crates — a tip that ultimately drew a confession from Chase and landed him also in Leavenworth on his own eighteen-month sentence.

Billingsley appealed but lost. He was relentless, however, lobbying prosecutors for a pardon and even getting every member of the jury to sign a petition calling the conviction unjust. When that failed, he started on the witnesses, getting them to sign petitions that reached as far as President Warren G. Harding's White House.

He was soon visited by Harding crony Howard Mannington, from Harding's hometown of Marion, Ohio, who offered Billingsley a pardon for $25,000. He laughed it off as a scam.

Logan by now was in another jail outside Seattle, where he grew weary of waiting for a pardon. So he escaped.

It was well plotted. Tire tracks of Fred's car were later found nearby.

Within a month Logan was arrested as a fugitive in Toledo, Ohio. He was released on $750 bail and fled, heading for Detroit, where a case of Canadian whiskey from Windsor, Ontario, bought for five dollars could be resold for $150. The cargoes, a thousand cases at a time, ostensibly bound for Nassau or Cuba, were routed through the Detroit railyards, where yardmasters well paid by Logan diverted them to quiet sidings for off-loading. Then Logan left for the Caribbean to see about other rumrunning ventures. He was gone a long time, and his syndicate partners started getting suspicious.

Sherman, with Dee Dee, had returned to his grocery stores in Detroit, but he couldn't go anywhere in town without running into Logan's partners, who were asking menacing questions. After finally hearing from Logan, who was in New York, Sherman headed there to warn him about his dangerously nervous partners. He expected to stay a few hours; instead, he ended up staying more than forty years.

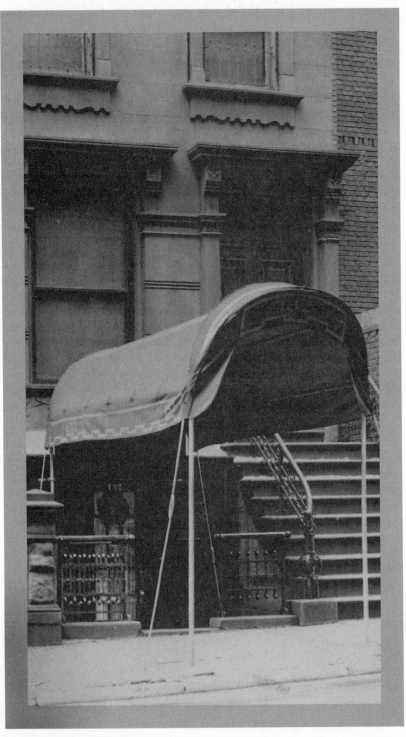

THE ORIGINAL STORK CLUB ON WEST FIFTY-EIGHTH STREET

SPEAKEASY
DAYS

EIGHT

O N   A N   E A R LY - S P R I N G   M O R N I N G   when legal alcohol was already a fond and fading memory and the twenties were just beginning to roar, John Sherman Billingsley — in *his* roaring twenties — stepped off a train from Detroit in Grand Central Terminal. It is easy to picture him the way he appeared so often in early photographs, smartly turned out in a white shirt with high rounded collar, necktie, and a dark vested suit. Under a wide-brimmed hat, rakishly tilted back off his high forehead, his dark glossy hair was combed straight back, accentuating his great, squarish head and long jaw, prominent cheekbones, and deep-chiseled eyes, the legacy, no doubt, of some Indian forebears in the nearly three centuries of Billingsleys in the American wilderness. His carriage suggested that he was pleased with himself, although he always thought Logan with his ramrod bearing and coal-black wavy hair was the one with the real looks.

Outside the dark, vaulted terminal he passed up the lumbering trolleys, wheezing double-decker buses, and honking taxis — although there was surely enough money in his pocket — and walked downtown, eager to take the measure of the strange and noisy new metropolis, flashy Gotham in May 1920 at the dawn of the Jazz Age. At Twenty-seventh Street, across from Stanford White's Moorish towered palace of Madison Square Garden, he checked the address of an apartment hotel with striped awnings and went in.

The city that swallowed him up was a hedonist's paradise, the world capital of excess, escapism, and showmanship, where the ravages of the world war were being drowned in bootleg whiskey, theatrics, fast music, and sex. Broadway blazed with the light of incandescent constellations, spectaculars that stitched the night sky with glowing tributes to White Rock water and Wrigley's spearmint chewing gum, toothbrushes, underwear, shoes, laxatives, automobiles, cigarettes, thread — totems of an exuberant new era of consumerism and electronic mass communications. For the first time more Americans lived in cities than in the countryside. Public amusement was displacing manufacturing as the city's primary industry. New York's theaters, show halls, and motion picture houses could seat 2 million people — the equivalent of nearly half the city's population. "Don't give the people what they want," preached impresario Roxy Rothafel, whose gaudy film palaces were lending movie playhouses a generic brand name, "give 'em something better!"

The freshly consolidated city of five boroughs had become a gourmand's paradise. To evade curfew laws, entrepreneurs bought up the names and charters of antiquated societies and reopened them as membership clubs imbued with the cachet of privacy and exclusivity — the first nightclubs. The great age of media was dawning, its signposts everywhere. Newsstands were laden with raffish dailies and weeklies in a babel of immigrant tongues, book clubs flourished, and listeners were amazed by the first experiments with a revolution called radio.

A social revolution was brewing, too. On a cold February night in 1919, an astute little bonbon of a society writer, Maury Paul, about to join the Hearst organization as its Cholly Knickerbocker columnist in the *New York American*, had been nibbling pâté and keeping toasty in the Ritz-Carlton Hotel when he scanned the room and was struck by the heterogeneous assemblage. Socialites from Newport, Southampton, and Tuxedo Park, old guard, wild youth, were all gaily commingling — *in public*. In the old days, Paul reflected, they would have been entertaining at home; now they were stepping out. He gave the phenomenon an indelible name: *café society*.

As the bootlegging Billingsley brothers descended on an unsuspecting New York, the nation was four months into the debacle that would become risibly known as the Noble Experiment. Prohibitionists like Dr. Henry Louis Smith, president of Washington and Lee University, saw America entering a utopian age of well-being and spiritual enlightenment, "the longest and most effective step forward in the uplift of the human race ever taken by any civilized nation."

Prohibition was the most radical aim of the temperance movement, which sprang up at about the same time as the antislavery abolitionists. Both were strongly female-based, and both called Americans to a higher standard of morality and idealism. If slavery could be outlawed, prohibitionists preached, so could the rum and whiskey that consumed men's paychecks in saloons and brothels while their wives and children begged for food. As a pragmatist, Lincoln favored temperance over abolition for alcohol. But spearheaded by Carry Nation and her furious hatchet, zealotry was on the march, mobilizing a powerful new force, a nativist antipathy toward the foreign tide that was pouring into America — 25 million immigrants between 1885 and 1924. The newcomers were disdained as whiskey-drinking Irish, wine-drinking Italians, beer-drinking Germans. Censorious WASPs, capitalist princes like the Fords, Rockefellers, and du Ponts, made their stand.

By 1912, as the Billingsleys were building their bootlegging empire in Oklahoma City, nine states, encompassing half the population, had gone dry. Four years later the number had risen to nineteen. In 1919 Congress — swayed by the anti-immigrant forces, hatred for the German kaiser and his humbled nation of brewers, and the simplistic vision of a new Eden cleansed of alcoholism and its evils — voted a nationwide prohibition law, the Volstead Act, barring the sale (although not the consumption) of drinks containing more than .5 percent alcohol. President Woodrow Wilson vetoed the legislation, but with the national momentum becoming overwhelming, Congress overrode him, and the act became law on October 26, 1919. Drinkers lamented with a rueful ditty: "How are you going to wet your whistle / when the whole darn world goes dry?" But the Volstead Act was only the beginning. A proposed constitutional amendment had been making its way through the state houses. Utah's passage put it over the top, chiseling the ban into the nation's bedrock charter as of January 17, 1920. That Saturday morning, on a front page black with banner headlines reporting the reopening of Allied trade with the reviled Bolsheviks, the *New York Times* wryly mourned a mythic figure:

JOHN BARLEYCORN
DIED PEACEFULLY
AT THE TOLL OF 12

It seemed, at first, simple enough. The night before, the redoubtable Colonel Daniel L. Porter, supervisor of Internal Revenue agents for the New York district, had rejected plans for any last-minute raids on newly illegal saloons, taverns, beer joints, and liquor suppliers, as he did not anticipate any trouble. At six foot two and a crack shot with rifle and pistol, he was not a man to cross. As an army veteran who had trained for his job battling moonshiners around military camps in the South, Porter knew his enemy. New York, he and his agents vowed, was about to go as dry as the Painted Desert of Arizona. Sportingly, he promised not to interfere with any farewell toasts by mourners preparing to lay their dear, departed bottles to rest in black-draped caskets. No, the colonel insisted, New Yorkers were not about to defy Prohibition — not with his one hundred agents on alert. Plus, of course, the entire New York City gendarmerie, fifteen thousand strong. How they and their national counterparts were to seal off eighteen thousand miles of American coastline did not seem a critical question at the time.

Prohibition's first frigid night passed with surprising cheer and good humor. Sultry Helen Morgan, dressed for the occasion in black velvet, sat on her club's bar and gamely toasted the anticipated return of legal alcohol. Uptown at Columbus Circle, Reisenweber's dance hall staged a funeral ball. At Maxim's the waiters came dressed as pallbearers. William B. Masterson, better known as Bat, the legendary Dodge City sheriff and gunfighter who had taken to writing a boxing column for the *Morning Telegraph* in Hell's Kitchen, turned up at Shanley's up the block from the *New York Times* on Forty-third Street, ordering a steak and a cup of tea. The racketeer Arnold Rothstein (soon to be charged with fixing the 1919 World Series) spent the night playing cards. Filthy Phil, renowned downtown for his vile mouth, found a friend in City Hall Park, and together they hunted up a secretive dive with strong libation.

In the ice-clogged Hudson River off West Ninety-fourth Street, divers from a wrecking company worked frantically to recover a huge cargo of suddenly contraband whiskey, destined for Nassau in the British West Indies, that had been aboard a barge when it sprang a leak and sank. Elsewhere, a mere two arrests and the confiscation of five hundred cases of whiskey marked the dawn of Prohibition in New York. Police guarded millions of dollars' worth of liquor trapped on the piers awaiting safe transport, ostensibly to Havana and other sanctuaries. In Coney Island the brothers Razio and Eusebio Paciello were arrested in their café after four detectives swore that they had been served glasses of claret and a search of the cellar turned up a barrel of wine, and 204 quarts and three demijohns of whiskey.

Some of Porter's men were busy that Saturday guarding the five hundred cases of seized whiskey, while others hunted for twelve men suspected of removing the liquor from a bonded warehouse just before the onset of Prohibition. The revenue boss had another good reason for optimism that morning. Waiting for him at his office was a long line of men looking for jobs as federal agents. Maybe, Porter said, he'd hire 150 of them; possibly, he could use them.

An army of half a million — as New York's doughty mayor Fiorello La Guardia would later tell President Franklin Roosevelt — might have been more like it.

NINE

SNAZZILY REOUTFITTED IN NAVY BLAZER, straw boater, and white ducks, and complete with hip flask, the newly arrived Sherman did the town, escorted by Ora as they made the rounds of the vaudeville houses and film palaces of Times Square. It didn't take Sherman long to assess the opportunities. If the rest of the country laughed at Prohibition, New York was convulsed in hysterics. You couldn't find a drink — not unless you walked ten feet in any direction. If you owned a drugstore, Sherman knew from happy experience around the country, you practically owned a wholesale liquor business, and if you owned a dozen drugstores, well then, you had a dozen wholesale liquor businesses. Besides Dee Dee, all he had waiting for him in Detroit was his inconvenient liquor conviction. He called his wife with orders to sell his grocery and candy-store fronts in Detroit, send his belongings east, and follow. They were moving to New York.

By his second day in town, leaving the bustle of Manhattan to explore the Bronx frontier, Sherman found a room to rent on a quiet ten-acre estate near the corner of Tremont and Sedgwick Avenues, where the land climbed steeply from the east bank of the Harlem River. Between the estate and the river ran the long straightaway of Cedar Avenue, and it was here, facing the river at 177th Street, that he found a small drugstore that would do fine.

Henry Cook's Morris Heights Pharmacy was for sale for $5,000 or, if he could pay it off within a month, $4,500. He borrowed the money from Logan, who was already making a name for himself in Bronx real estate, and plunged into business. He and Logan also found a house for their widowed mother on nearby University Avenue, and she soon came from Detroit to join them.

At first Sherman was the toast of the neighborhood. But after hundreds of cases of whiskey were loaded in, letters of complaint started to circulate, as Sherman found when a sympathetic resident slipped him a sampling. He wasted no time pasting the letters up in the window, which effectively stopped them.

Up the hill was the Morris Heights precinct station house, where Sherman dropped in to introduce himself to Captain Jim Brody. If, Sherman offered, he could be helpful to the commander and his men in any way, if there were any *medicinal supplies* they might ever require, he would be only too pleased to be of service.

Business boomed. It was amazing how many pharmaceuticals the people of Morris Heights consumed. With money pouring in faster than he ever imagined, Sherman roamed the Bronx, Brooklyn, and Harlem, hunting up marginal new drugstores to buy and often bringing in the pharmacists as one-quarter partners.

Despite all Sherman's efforts, his Detroit conviction refused to go away. His lawyers advised him that there was only one way to avoid going to prison: to actually go in. It sounded crazy, but unless he was in custody, they couldn't make a habeas corpus case for his release. So he asked the U.S. marshal in Detroit to jail him. The marshal refused.

Next Billingsley tried the sheriff, who was also resistant but then came up with an idea. Because he lived in a corner of the jail compound, he suggested, "You can come over and stay in my house."

At night they played cards, and no matter how hard he tried to lose, Sherman kept winning. It couldn't go on. The only thing left to do was to finally enter Leavenworth.

Interrupting his promising bootlegging career in New York, he became a prisoner in Kansas at the end of February 1922.

Time hung heavy on his hands. The clocks seemed not to move. And yet, he realized he had it pretty good. He slept in the hospital and had his meals in the bakery — some of the best food of his life.

Best of all, now that he was in, he had a chance to get out.

On May 2, 1922, after Sherman and Ora had spent several months in Leavenworth, the district court in Kansas overturned the sentence, ruling that they had been improperly given misdemeanor terms for felony convictions. They were ordered released.

Leavenworth's warden appealed, but in December 1923 the circuit court of appeals upheld the reversal, ruling that the Billingsleys had been properly sprung.

But Sherman was still worried that he could be resentenced and returned to prison. He carried his appeal to the legendary Mabel Walker Willebrandt — "Prohibition Portia," as Al Smith called her — the deputy attorney general and commander of national Prohibition enforcement, a vivacious protofeminist and single divorcée who, somewhat scandalously for the time, had adopted a baby girl. Billingsley's lawyer beseeched her to order the U.S. attorney in Kansas to drop the case once and for all, and she did.

From then on, as far as Billingsley was concerned, he had never been convicted.

TEN

O N A N A U G U S T N I G H T I N 1 9 2 2, just months after his release
from Leavenworth, Billingsley dined with a beauteous Ziegfeld
showgirl, Billee Stanfield, at the hilltop Hunter Island Inn on the
Bronx shore. Driving out after midnight, he had eased his car into low for the
descent and didn't see the officer waving him down, or so he later claimed.

The sharp report of a shot echoed in the night, and he heard a bullet
hit the car. Now he did stop. The policeman ticketed him for speeding.

The next morning he found that the bullet had tunneled through the
frame an inch above the rear windshield, in a direct line with his head.

In court Billingsley was indignant. The owner of the Billingsley
Holding Corporation ought to be able to drive down a city street after dark
without being shot at. He told the magistrate that he and his wife(!) came
under fire after he refused to buy tickets for the police field-day games.

The story made the papers. Dee Dee had every right to rage, but it
was Logan who complained. *He* was the head of the Billingsley Holding
Corporation, not Sherman. The *New York Times* obligingly ran a small cor-
rection the next day.

Billingsley relished the playboy life. Leaving Dee Dee at home, he
prowled the cabarets and cafés, nightclubs and Broadway shows, jazz-
blown Harlem, and Fifty-second Street, lined with speakeasies. He became a regular at hot spots like the Plantation Club, Billy La Hiff's Tavern,
Dinty Moore's, and, of course, the *Follies* at the New Amsterdam on West
Forty-second Street. He had a particular soft spot for Ziegfeld's beauties,
deliciously robotic creatures in their peacock feathers who filed up and
down the theater's grand staircases, flitting among the glittering screens
and panels with a girlish purity and hauteur that drove audiences wild.
Ziegfeld himself had choreographed the girls' special walk, a kind of erect,
sliding step, as if they were making their way across a tightrope, trying to
keep their large hats from falling off.

SHERMAN WITH DEE DEE ON A TRIP TO FLORIDA

Billingsley haunted the stage door, hoping to catch glimpses of the celestial creatures before they stepped into the liveried chariots of stooped, white-whiskered gentlemen in black fur-collared coats. If he was lucky, he might hand a girl a bouquet or press a bauble into her hands or exchange glances or even a whispered word or two about a rendezvous another time, another day.

Fancying himself a Broadway Romeo, a big spender and big tipper, he was at first shy around the chorines, but soon he won dates with starlets and headliners like Louise Brooks, Blossom Seeley, Marilyn Miller, Nell Brinkley, Ann Pennington, and Helen Morgan. Eager to curry favor, he opened new drugstores around the homes and apartments of showgirls he courted, flamboyantly naming the businesses after them.

There wasn't much left to their marriage, but Dee Dee stuck by him. They had tried repeatedly to have children, but Dee Dee couldn't get pregnant. In 1924 they traveled to Miami to visit Logan, who was expanding into Florida real estate. Logan had a new wife he had met in the offices of the *Miami Herald,* twenty-one-year-old Hattie Mae Key, a police lieutenant's daughter descended from Francis Scott Key.

They all posed gaily for photos — Dee Dee, demure in cloche hat, floppy-collared blouse, and a cryptic smile; Sherman, dashing in knickers, white shirt, and plaid tie, a cigar and an expression of smoldering, almost painful intensity. They golfed, swam, lolled on the beach, and sailed, partying on deck with mischievously hoisted cocktails.

But back in New York Sherman kept chasing showgirls. One time he told Dee Dee that he was going out of town, but as luck would have it, she and her sister Blanche were driving through the city when they spotted Sherman in his Cadillac with a young woman.

"*Oh my God! It's Sherman!*" gasped Dee Dee, giving chase. A policeman pulled her over for speeding.

"That's my husband!" she protested.

Perhaps guiltily, he was especially generous, buying Dee Dee nice clothes and giving her all the money she wanted — a good provider but a lousy husband, as Blanche liked to say. He was so brazen about it that Blanche had to laugh. He once dug into the backseat of his car to retrieve cultured pearls spilled from some girl's broken necklace, restringing them and presenting them to Blanche as a gift.

One evening Billingsley met four Ziegfeld girls in Loft's and bought them sodas and candy before driving them to the theater, taking down their names and phone numbers. The next day he called the one he liked best, driving out to Brooklyn to pick her up. But when she opened the door, he realized that she wasn't the one he had had in mind. He had gotten mixed up.

Later he sorted it out. The girl he had intended to call was Hazel Donnelly, a soulful-eyed gamin with flaming red hair and ivory skin whose picture he had recognized from the "Beautiful Women" section in *Redbook* magazine. She was a dancer in the popular rags-to-riches musical *Sally* and had studied with Russian ballet maestro Sergei Diaghilev. She had also performed in the 1923 and 1924 productions of *George White's Scandals,* a Parisian-style showgirl revue with music by George Gershwin. A souvenir picture album of the scantily clad nymphs in erotic poses included a head shot of Miss Donnelly with White's assurance that he had canvassed the entire nation for such beauties. She was also featured in the *Morning Telegraph,* with a fey caption "Scandals always are interesting in our set, as we say along Broadway, but they're doubly so when they involve so personable a figure as the comely Miss Donnelly."

Billingsley eventually tracked her down to an apartment only two blocks away from his on Morris Avenue in the Bronx. He called and sent notes and flowers, but she ignored him, her sister Marion always claiming that she was out.

Hazel had dreams of becoming a prima ballerina, or at least a schoolteacher, a future far more palatable to her conservative Irish Protestant parents than a stage career, let alone what she might look forward to with a married suitor. Billingsley couldn't expect much sympathy from her father, a police captain and Jimmy Walker protégé with his eye on command of the Bronx.

Sherman tried his usual moves. Learning that she took the Jerome Avenue el each day at 167th Street, he bought a drugstore close by and put

HAZEL DONNELLY'S PUBLICITY
SHOT, AS FEATURED IN
REDBOOK MAGAZINE

his name in its window in flashing lights, hoping she would see it and think
he was a big shot. Hazel skirted the place but her sisters went in, and
Billingsley plied them with candy and soda. From them he learned that
Hazel had left the cast of *Sally* and was rehearsing for the *Follies*.

Then his break came. When she finally dropped in one afternoon, he
confessed his admiration. He succeeded in charming her, and she let him
drive her downtown.

By August 1925 Billingsley, already described in the papers as "a
wealthy Bronx builder," divorced Dee Dee in Mexico and married Hazel.
Dee Dee refused to recognize the shuffle and hired a private eye to shadow
Billingsley and gather evidence for a desertion action.

Weeks later Dee Dee and her detective were following a car with Sherman and Logan when the four tangled outside the Hotel Alamac on the West
Side, the detective later charging that he was assaulted by the Billingsleys.
Both brothers were arrested. Logan was released, but Sherman was held
on bail. By October Dee Dee was suing to overturn the Mexican divorce
decree, relenting only when he agreed to pay her $200 a month.

ELEVEN

WITH HIS DRUGSTORE ENTERPRISES FLOURISHING, Billingsley got an order to deliver ten barrels of whiskey to the Ritz Inn in Yonkers. He drove up first in his Cadillac to check out the place.

It was a corner saloon on a trolley line across from a cemetery and park. After talking with a polished young Italian behind the bar, Billingsley called his warehouse and instructed one of his partners, Fred Armour, to send the barrels with two of his black drivers, Jim Martin and Harry Shaw. They arrived at sundown, loaded the whiskey into the basement, and went back up to the bar to collect.

The young Italian had disappeared, and in his place stood a gang of small, tough-looking men who reminded Sherman of the Black Hands he had encountered in Detroit.

Billingsley told Martin to see if he had left his watch in the basement. Martin got the message and went downstairs. No watch, he said. The ten barrels had disappeared, he whispered. So had Billingsley's Cadillac.

Armour started arguing with the little killers, who grabbed his arm, trying to pull him into the back room. Billingsley, Martin, and Shaw reached for Armour's other arm to yank him out the front door. Suddenly the dinky little streetcar clanged up, stopping outside the front door. With that diversion, Armour broke free, and the four of them dashed through the door to freedom.

The police later found Billingsley's Cadillac several blocks away. They told him that a few weeks before, some soldiers from Mitchell Field, Long Island, had delivered a truckload of bootleg whiskey to the Ritz Inn. Their bodies were later found in front of the cemetery.

Clearly, the bootlegging game was turning deadly. Stickup teams ran rampant, confident that their whiskey-selling victims would never go to the authorities. Scams were commonplace, often lethal. Amateur chemists bungled the redistillation of wood alcohol, cooking up poison concoctions that blinded and killed. At best, the homemade liquor was a worthless, watery syrup colored and flavored by the shavings of oak barrels that had once held whiskey. Gangster-controlled breweries fielded armadas of trucks that crisscrossed the city, setting off mob wars whenever they trespassed into another gang's territory. The city was rife with graft, bribery, shakedowns, double-crosses, sabotage, assaults, and murders. One way or another, one in ten New Yorkers in 1925 had a criminal record.

Some of the new players were particularly violent. The dapper Owney Madden, widely known as "the Killer," a nickname he loathed, was back on the street, paroled from Sing Sing in 1923 after eight years of a ten-to-fifteen-year sentence for instigating the murder of a rival who had made two mistakes: he had tried to take over Madden's gang, and he had tried to steal Madden's girl.

Madden's crony, William Vincent Dwyer, a mild-mannered sportsman and fight promoter who operated out of a midtown hotel suite, was commanding a twenty-ship rumrunning navy out of New York Harbor. They called him Big Bill — not for his height or weight, but for his business heft.

In the summer of 1925 a Customs guard who was undercover in a speakeasy learned of an incoming liquor shipment aboard the steamer *Augusta*. The vessel was soon stopped in the Hudson, yielding thousands of cases of liquor traceable to Dwyer. The seizure — the greatest roundup in the history of Prohibition — netted sixty codefendants, including thirteen Coast Guardsmen accused of taking bribes to protect the shipments and sometimes transporting the liquor to shore. One of the sixty was known at the time as Francesco Castiglia, but he would soon Americanize his name to Frank Costello.

Dwyer, who was also charged with the deaths of twelve rumrunners who went to the bottom in an unseaworthy tug, was convicted and sentenced to two years in prison and a $10,000 fine. Yet he served little more than a year before winning parole on grounds of illness, returning to his home in Queens in August 1928.

Costello's trial ended in a hung jury.

For his trouble, meanwhile, the Customs guard credited with breaking the rum ring, Edward Starace, was bludgeoned by assailants who carved two crosses in his face with a razor blade.

Joining Madden and Dwyer was an equally disreputable partner, George Jean De Mange, known as Frenchy, who had once been Madden's rival in the Hell's Kitchen gangs but had joined him in supplying liquor to the nightclubs and speakeasies that were springing up all over town.

Even a Billingsley was out of his league.

As early as 1923, only three years into Prohibition, the New York legislature had surrendered to the inevitable, repealing the two-year-old Mullan-Gage Act, which funded state and local enforcement efforts, and joining four other states in tossing the problem back to the federal government.

Everyone seemed to know where to get a drink — everyone, that is, except the authorities who made a fine pretense of stumbling around in search of the obvious. Still, it was one thing to spot a place operating, another to get evidence to padlock it. It was also hard to keep agents honest when the sale of a single doctored liquor permit could double a man's yearly salary. One uncorrupted dry squad commander ordered his agents to hold up their hands; anyone wearing a pinkie ring was deemed ipso facto crooked and was fired.

There were other exceptions, none perhaps so lionized as "Prohibition Agent No. 1," Izzy Einstein. Built like a fireplug, fiercely honest, and relentlessly self-promotional, Izzy showed how the job could be done. He collected evidence in a funnel and bottle he had taped under his jacket and devised ever more ingenious ploys to counter the equally devious schemes of the law-defying.

But even at a record seventy-one arrests a day, he couldn't keep up. Moreover, he had trod on too many well-connected toes. He was offered a transfer to Chicago; by refusing, he courted dismissal. By 1926 Izzy was no longer bizzy.

Other crusaders also scored intermittent success. New York's hard-nosed Prohibition administrator, Major Chester P. Mills, staged an elaborate sting using a phony real estate business on Broadway as a front. Agents squiring unsuspecting young actresses in a month's partying spree gained entry to dozens of establishments in the sprawling wet zone of the West Forties and Fifties. The trap was sprung just before Christmas 1926, when raiders descended on the clubs of singer Helen Morgan and Mary Louise Cecilia Guinan, widely known as Texas, a former cowgirl and vaudeville queen who was the reigning hostess of the nightclub scene and liked to douse her fingers with perfume so that anyone who shook hands with her carried away a haunting reminder of her presence.

They also crashed a mysterious basement social club on West Fifty-first Street called Billingsley's. If it was Sherman's, he never owned up to it afterward. His first nightclub venture, he always said, was the Stork, at least two years in the future. Anyway, the charges never made it into federal court.

Clearly, the raiders were fighting a losing war; as Will Rogers so wittily put it: "Prohibition is better than no liquor at all." Society matrons filled their telephone books with page after page of speakeasy listings: *Coq Rouge. Chez Robert. Peacock. Buddy's. Mario's. The Park Avenue. The New Yorker. Moriarty's. The Gallant Fox. Tony's. Maison Felix. Tree Club. Zelli's.*

Joe Madden. Gus's. Jimmy's. Jack & Charley. Club Seville. Joe's. Dick's. Leon & Eddie's. The Follies Club. The Simplon Club. . . .

Partygivers were never more than a phone call away from deliveries by bootleggers brazen enough to put out brochures with their price lists and assurances of unadulterated quality. Penrod's offered a free quart of Bacardi rum with each five-dollar purchase and a free quart of scotch for every ten.

Families brewed their own intoxicants, too, earnestly exchanging handwritten recipes for homemade rum, gin, anisette, and kümmel. Edmund Wilson compiled a lexicon of words and phrases that had sprung up to denote advancing levels of intoxication, from the milder *squiffy, oiled,* and *edged,* through *spifflicated* and *ossified,* to the ultimate *fried to the hat.*

The widespread lawlessness had also changed the nature of the bootlegging industry. Entrepreneurs like the Billingsleys, as professional as they were, could no longer compete with the likes of Madden, Dwyer, and De Mange, as Sherman recognized after his close call in Yonkers. It seemed like a good time to find a new calling, especially now that he and Hazel had a daughter, Jacqueline, born on Easter Sunday 1926 in Hollywood, where the couple had gone on a trip. Logan had been prospering in Bronx real estate, and Sherman was tempted to follow his lead. He obtained his own real estate license and put it to work, brokering some of his drugstore deals himself, making leases with his pharmacist quarter-partners and using the commissions to start fixing up the properties. He applied for a government permit to purchase medicinal alcohol, which he then sold to other bootleggers for money to finish renovations.

He was soon prosperous enough to buy the entire ten-acre estate at Tremont and Sedgwick Avenues where he had first rented a room on his arrival in the city. Remembering the times his landlady, suspicious of his real business interests, had threatened him with eviction, he closed title, then rang her bell. "It is your turn to move," he said. "I own this house now."

He was kidding, he assured her; she could stay on. But he proceeded to develop the property, building a crescent he named Billingsley Terrace, where he based his Billingsley Realty Company in a redbrick town house overlooking the Cedar Avenue location of his first drugstore.

Now he was fast making a name in real estate, riding a wave of development in the Bronx as Irish, Jewish, and German immigrants poured in. He bought and sold quickly, and often with other people's money. Once, when the market turned soft and he was stuck with vacant lots he couldn't sell, he traded them to contractors for construction work on a big new garage at 170th Street and Inwood Avenue in the shadow of the Jerome Avenue el in the Bronx. Proudly he called it the Sherman Garage.

One day, as he told it, who should turn up in his real estate office but two gamblers from Oklahoma, men who had thrown him red ties and loose change at the gambling tables when he was a teenager in Oklahoma City. The pair, Carl Henninger and John Patton, had married sisters from Oklahoma, and told him they had come to New York with their wives to open a restaurant. Where should they locate?

He found them a spot at 132 West Fifty-eighth Street, down the block from the New York Athletic Club. The building, whose owner was listed as an Annie Dolan, was a double-width Greek revival town house about midway on the south side of Fifty-eighth Street as it sloped gently down from Seventh to Sixth Avenue. A pair of stone stairways trimmed with ironwork marched from the sidewalk to the building's raised entrances, and between them a few steps led down to a basement level. For a commission, Billingsley worked out a twenty-one-year lease on the property.

But when he asked Henninger and Patton to sign it, they surprised him by insisting that he become their partner. He had little to lose, he figured; his commission would more than pay for his investment.

And that, he liked to say, was the beginning of the Stork Club. Why Stork? Maybe somebody had left a little toy stork on the bar. He never really did remember how they picked the name, any more than he remembered precisely when they opened, or exactly how he suddenly ended up with a new set of partners.

TWELVE

BY THE WATERSHED YEAR OF 1929, when the Roaring Twenties turned into a scream of anguish, the Stork Club was up and running on three floors of the West Fifty-eighth Street town house. It opened for lunch and stayed open until 2:30 A.M. Upstairs, guests danced to trios, and downstairs there was Hawaiian music, then enjoying a vogue in the city. Billingsley also brought in Tito Guízar and a Spanish quartet, and a popular jazz combo, Red McKenzie and his Mound City Blue Blowers. McKenzie mimicked a kazoo on a comb and tissue paper, and other musicians played an actual kazoo, sax, and guitar. Eddie Condon sometimes joined the group on guitar.

Help came cheap. Waiters and busboys were available for a dollar a day, but the tips were so good that many were actually willing to pay for their jobs. Concessionaires would advance thousands of dollars just to get the hatcheck — sometimes enough to cover the entire cost of opening a place.

Billingsley barred prostitutes, gamblers, and other undesirables. He banished cuspidors as crude, put down a carpet, and selected a softer decor that he thought would appeal to ladies. Eventually, too, he ran an awning from the basement entrance to the curb. It was unmarked except for the address, but it was, nevertheless, a canopy, which few speakeasies in New York could boast. Proud of his liquor brands, Billingsley lined up the bottles behind the bar so his patrons, accustomed to being served out of pitchers from under the sink, could see what they were drinking. But some of his customers were so used to rotgut, they thought his drinks tasted funny.

In the profusion of speakeasies that covered the West Fifties, the Stork struggled to find a niche. Partners Henninger and Patton proved to be useless as businessmen. The club hemorrhaged money, and Billingsley had to dig into his own pocket to meet expenses. He had just about decided to let the place die a natural death when, by his later account, a kind of miracle occurred.

HAZEL AND SHERMAN, EARLY IN
THEIR RELATIONSHIP

A West Virginia gambler who owned a casino in Havana and was leaving for three months in Europe came in and asked them to hold $10,000 for him until he returned. They used the money to keep the doors open. When they heard that he would be back soon, they panicked: the money was gone. As luck would have it, Helen Morgan then dropped in and reserved the house for a week to give a cast party for a movie she had made. Her bill just covered their debt to the gambler.

If this anecdote seems inherently dubious, over the years Billingsley himself offered varying versions of the events. In a 1940 article in *Family Circle*, Helen Morgan is said to have stepped in with barely $2,000 for a cast party — "a lifesaver, as I was wondering where I was going to get $1,800 I needed to keep the place going." Four years later *The American Mercury* put Miss Morgan's largesse at $3,000.

More likely is that Billingsley's savior was actually Frank Costello, then parlaying his lowly rumrunning into a legendary criminal career as a gambling czar and prime minister of the underworld. A velvet-fisted ruler who knew that "hunger will make a monkey eat red pepper," as he would say, Costello was a shrewd student of human nature — one of the savvier crimelords ever to run the mob — and he could easily have discerned Billingsley's potential. Billingsley's middle daughter, Barbara, wrote years later that it was Costello who had given her father $100,000 to hold for him while he left the country for a time. Billingsley spent the money to keep the club going and just managed to recoup it when Costello returned. Thirty years later he told Costello the truth.

"Costello laughed," Barbara recounted. "He had figured that's what Dad would do. It was his way of doing Dad a favor. Dad was left with his mouth open."

Whatever the truth, by Billingsley's account, Henninger and Patton were growing increasingly disillusioned with the faltering club, and their wives were homesick. Billingsley wouldn't buy them out, so they found a man named Thomas Healy who acquired their interest for $10,000 with the understanding that Sherman would run the place and would hold 70 percent of the ownership. Healy wanted only 30 percent. At the time the division seemed strange.

Billingsley continued to struggle to keep the club alive. He asked customers for names of their friends and sent them cards and letters inviting them to come in and have a drink on the house. He also walked the neighborhood copying names from mailboxes, office buildings, and stores. Some nights, with not a patron in the house, he sat disconsolately on the second floor counting the cars passing outside and betting with himself that one out of a hundred would stop, dropping off a customer. Sometimes he dozed off during the count. One night, awakened by the doorbell, he ran downstairs expectantly, only to find the cop on the beat, eager for some refreshment.

When customers did turn up, Billingsley remembered Gregory's advice from the Deauville and made sure to welcome them personally. On one particular evening when two newcomers entered, he greeted them effusively, remembering too late another piece of advice from his lawyer — never to admit ownership. If the two were revenue agents, he realized, they had him good. He nervously poured them drinks on the house. They turned out be automobile men, owners of the nearby Duesenberg dealership. And not for the last time, his generosity paid off, for the two satisfied patrons eagerly spread the word about a speakeasy that served free drinks.

Billingsley's luck began to turn, and not a moment too soon.

The break came, he liked to recount, when Heywood Broun, the rumpled liberal conscience of the *World,* was on his way to a wake for a friend and absentmindedly mistook the dismally empty Stork Club for a funeral home.

Broun walked in, put his hat down, and headed back to pay his respects to the body, only instead of a corpse he found a bar. He had a few drinks, liked the place, and came back often with celebrity friends.

Because raids remained a constant threat, Billingsley issued numbered membership cards, keeping track of their owners, because cardholders in trouble with the law were known to buy their freedom with their speakeasy cards. Prohibition agents would then scratch off the number to conceal their source. But Billingsley pasted two cards together, hiding the identification number inside. Now when he was presented with a suspect card, he could peel it apart to determine where it came from. He was amazed at how many so-called friends were working with the agents.

His hospitality extended to the deputy chief police inspector and Manhattan borough commander, James S. Bolan, a bachelor career officer bearing the Tammany seal of approval and a man so cold, wrote the *Herald Tribune*'s Stanley Walker, "that he sweats icicles." Bolan had come to New York from Massachusetts and had been named to the force by Commissioner Theodore Roosevelt in 1896 — the year Billingsley was born — over objections by police examiners that Bolan had once owned a tavern. Put in charge of the raucous entertainment district in the 1920s, he became known as a scourge of vice, shutting down gambling dens and even arresting the cast of Mae West's risqué Broadway show *Sex*. The sole blot on Bolan's record was a fine of fifteen days' pay for a certain laxity in targeting saloons. (He had yet to meet a ferocious prosecutor named Thomas E. Dewey, under whose relentless cross-examination Bolan would feebly insist that he had never heard of a gangster named Dutch Schultz.)

Billingsley also played host to Bolan's cousin, who headed the Prohibition agents in New York. Both men dropped in regularly but separately at the Stork, seeking anonymity in private rooms on the third floor. Billingsley lived in hope that they would bump into each other sometime, thereby realizing how amazingly discreet he was.

The stock market crash in October 1929 and the era of misery it ushered in spelled doom for many speakeasies and businesses, among them Logan's real estate empire in the Bronx. But the Stork Club hung on, striving to capitalize on the same yearnings for fantasy and escape that yielded during this period 110 million movie admissions a week, out of a population of 130 million. And then lightning struck — what Billingsley called his "blessed event." Texas Guinan persuaded her friend Walter Winchell, a former vaudeville entertainer himself who was well on his way to becoming the most powerful and feared journalist in America, to give "a country boy from Oklahoma" a plug. Guinan introduced them, and in September 1930 Winchell's influential column in the *Daily Mirror* memorably anointed Billingsley's speakeasy as "New York's New Yorkiest place on W. 58th." Winchell cited with approval the Stork Club's policy of not admitting unescorted ladies after 6:00 P.M., thereby "keeping wives from suddenly startling husbands who have weak hearts." Winchell repeated the plug several weeks later on his WABC radio show, announcing, "The New Yorkiest spot in New York is the Stork Club on West Fifty-eighth Street, which entices the well-knowns from all divisions nightly."

SHERMAN IN NEW YORK CITY IN
THE EARLY 1930S

In an era when New York seemed to pulsate at the center of the universe, "New Yorkiest" had to be the ultimate tribute. Almost overnight, Billingsley found, he was banking $10,000 a week and playing host to the likes of Marilyn Miller, Helen Morgan, Earl Carroll, Harry K. Thaw, Ed Wynn, Peggy Hopkins Joyce, Fanny Brice, and the great Ziegfeld himself, who was soon to go bankrupt. Texas dropped in, too, as if to witness the miracle she had wrought, and Winchell himself started making the club the hangout that would become his virtually exclusive lair for decades to come.

Soon Billingsley felt secure enough to move his family from Billingsley Terrace in the Bronx to an apartment on West Fifty-eighth Street, a few doors from the club.

And then he got some bad news. His new partner, Healy, admitted to being just a front. Billingsley's real partners, he confessed, were Owney Madden, Big Bill Dwyer, and Frenchy De Mange, sometimes called "Le Mange" or, simply, "the Frog." Healy did not quite say that he had sold out to them or that he had bought out Henninger and Patton for them, but it was Billingsley's reasonable deduction. If they held 30 percent, it was probably 10 percent each for Owney, Frenchy, and Dwyer. Call them "the boys," Healy instructed Billingsley. In fact, he said, the boys were already on their way over to say hello.

THIRTEEN

INEVITABLY ENOUGH, Prohibition had brought gangsters and night-clubs together. Horse-faced taxi hoodlum Larry Fay, who had once hit a hundred-to-one shot on a nag with a swastika on its blanket and so had adopted the twisted cross as his good-luck symbol many years before it was taken up by the Nazis, opened a club he called El Fey in 1923 and took on Texas Guinan as his partner. Jack "Legs" Diamond was a not-so-silent partner in Hymie Cohen's Hotsy Totsy Club, where on the unlucky night of Friday, July 13, 1929, an outbreak of gunfire left two bodies on the floor, after which the depopulation of the Hotsy Totsy began in earnest. The cashier vanished. The bar waiter was murdered. The bartender was shot. The hatcheck girl disappeared. Three witnesses were killed. Finally, Cohen himself contrived to vanish.

Did the truth about the identity of Billingsley's new partners come as the shock he portrayed? Or did he have good reason to suspect that the abrupt departure (if not also arrival) of Henninger and Patton masked some underworld scheme? Had Billingsley partnered with racketeers far earlier than he was willing to acknowledge? Who can say? But whatever the circumstances, this particular trio came with particularly heavy baggage.

After what he called his "little vacation" in the Atlanta federal penitentiary for running the country's largest liquor-smuggling fleet, Dwyer returned to New York, miraculously recovered from the severe illness that gained him an early release and still in possession, it was whispered, of much of his fortune. Since the mid-twenties, he had managed to freely operate the Phoenix Cereal Beverage Company, a five-story, block-long brewery on Tenth Avenue between Twenty-fifth and Twenty-sixth Streets from which drivers the likes of gangster-turned-actor

George Raft conveyed oceans of beer designated "Madden's Number One" to the city's illicit saloons and eateries.

Dwyer's partner in this business was Owney Madden. Madden had been born in England, where he worked as a child actor, and came to New York when he was eleven. He settled with his parents in the West Side slum known as Hell's Kitchen, where he headed the notorious Gopher (pronounced GOO-fer) Gang, which terrorized neighborhood merchants and saloonkeepers. In 1912 he took a dozen slugs in a dance hall, winning distinction as Clay Pigeon of the Underworld, a title he came to share with the frequently shot Legs Diamond. Madden recovered from his wounds, and within a week of the fireplay three of the shooters were dead. In 1915 he went to Sing Sing for ten to twenty years for instigating the barroom murder of the unfortunate Patsy Doyle, who had tangled with Madden over a girl. Now known as Owney the Killer, he was out in 1923 after serving less than eight years, resuming a lucrative career in the rackets, including laundries, bootlegging, and speakeasies. It was Larry Fay of the El Fey Club who interested Madden in the nightclub game, prompting him to open a place called the Cotton Club in Harlem.

Madden was perfectly cast as a gangster, said editor Stanley Walker of the *Herald Tribune*. He wasn't fleshy like Al Capone but looked rather like "the lean, hard and catlike gentlemen who act such parts on the stage." In fact, he said, "If a theatrical manager had put Owney on the stage, to act the part of Owney Madden, the critics would have said that it was just a little too perfect for honest realism." It wasn't just that Madden actually said "dese," "dem," "dose," and "youse," which he did, it was his look and attitude, which led one police sergeant to call him "that little banty rooster out of hell." His beaky profile was falconlike. His hair was shiny black, his eyes blue. It was said that they saw everything.

The third partner of the unsavory trio, Frenchy had been a member of the fearsome Hudson Dusters, deadly rivals of Madden's Gophers in Hell's Kitchen. Arrested thirteen times by 1930 — twice on murder charges — he had spent little time in jail, a feat largely attributable to his politically well-connected Greenwich Village family. In 1915, the same year Madden went up for manslaughter, Frenchy was surprised by cops on the Bowery as he cracked a jeweler's safe containing a fortune in diamonds. He hurled himself through a plate-glass window and fled. After the host of a party he had attended on East Seventh Street was found stabbed to death, Frenchy was indicted for the killing but somehow never went to trial. In 1916 he and his mob were protecting a gambling game in Brooklyn when one of the gamblers was shot to death. Frenchy was charged with that killing, too, but again escaped trial. And when he and two sidekicks were arrested in a multimillion-dollar mail robbery, his partners wisely took the heat themselves rather than snitch on him.

TOP: GEORGE JEAN
"FRENCHY" DE MANGE

CENTER: OWNEY MADDEN

BOTTOM: WILLIAM V.
"BIG BILL" DWYER

Well before Prohibition Frenchy had migrated to Broadway, where he met Larry Fay, who was then in the process of seizing control of the city's newly motorized taxi fleet. It was Fay who reintroduced him to his old Hell's Kitchen nemesis Madden, brokering peace between them and cementing a potent alliance. Among their schemes with Dwyer was conniving a fight career for Primo Carnera, a giant but clownish Italian circus strongman touted as a champion boxer. The duped Carnera went on to earn his handlers millions in cooked bouts until he was nearly killed in the ring by a genuine slugger, Max Baer, an episode later recounted in the Budd Schulberg novel and movie *The Harder They Fall*. Carnera had a pithy reaction to the knockout punch that floored him: "Hully Jees!"

For all his cunning, Frenchy was hardly a mastermind. At the legendary organized crime conclave in Atlantic City in 1929, he was picked to present a gift to Madden. With everyone looking on, he asked Madden for his wristwatch. Surprised, Madden removed it from his wrist and handed it over. Frenchy dropped it on the floor and stamped on it. Before Madden could react, Frenchy then said: "Gee, Owney, I'm sorry I broke your watch, but here's another one for you."

And then Billingsley looked up, and there they were — Dwyer, Madden, and Frenchy, entering the Stork Club. Billingsley barely noticed Dwyer — so busy was he staring at Madden and Frenchy. Madden — wiry, unsmiling, and pale — said little and seemed to mean what he said. But it was the oversize Frenchy, topping six feet and easily two hundred pounds, who riveted his attention. He saw why the cops called him the Frog — his arms and legs seemed too long for his body.

His hands were like steel claws, long fingers with dirty nails, and his head was huge with graying hair that grew out of the center of his forehead just over his long eyebrows. His black eyes were small and sunk deep in his head. He had a large, flat nose, big lips, and prominent cheekbones.

Frenchy did the talking. He said that they didn't want anything in writing and that they would protect him. "You'll have no trouble from any of the boys or anyone else from now on, just call us if anyone bothers you, and from now on your liquor will cost you fifteen dollars a case less than you've been paying. We will tell you who to buy from."

Then they were gone.

Dazed, Billingsley grabbed a handful of cigars from the bar and walked up and down the block trying to figure out what had happened. The first thing he decided was that he didn't want to handle any cash, and he insisted they put in their own money man. Frenchy agreed.

It didn't take Billingsley long to catch their man stealing, and he complained to Frenchy.

"So, let him steal a little," Frenchy replied. "As long as he doesn't steal too much."

On top of that, Billingsley realized, his liquor was now costing him fifteen dollars *more* a case.

Their guarantee of protection was a laugh, too. When some thugs got rowdy in the club one night, Frenchy promised to take care of it. Soon four of his men arrived, led by George Raft, who talked quietly to the troublemakers until they got up and left. Billingsley found out later that the whole affair had been staged.

But Frenchy's menace was clear. Whenever a bullet-riddled corpse turned up, Frenchy said, "He must have done something wrong."

Frenchy gave him other headaches. When he learned that Billingsley was a member of the posh Wingfoot Country Club in Westchester, he began to press him for an invitation to play golf there. But Frenchy's picture had been in the paper, and the mortification of trying to sneak him in was more than Billingsley was willing to face.

Frenchy often showed up at the Stork wanting $20,000 or $30,000 for Dwyer. Billingsley asked where he was supposed to find the money. Frenchy thought it was simple. "Can't we take it out of the club?"

Other times he sought jobs or free meals for his pals, or pressured Billingsley to buy club provisions and services from connected suppliers like Madden's Hydrox Laundry and Dry Cleaning. To make matters still worse, Frenchy started showing up at the Stork Club with a favorite girl, who started giving Billingsley the eye. Uh-oh, he didn't need trouble like that.

Madden, by contrast, seemed easy to get along with. He didn't ask for anything. He wasn't much for light banter, but he was civil enough and didn't try to con him. Billingsley didn't mind Dwyer, either, who didn't act as much a racketeer as a gambler and fixer. He could fix just about anything. It was Frenchy he had to get away from.

But if Billingsley was dismayed by his partners, he continued to agree to front for them as they expanded their nightclub empire. Officially, the clubs were to be his, but he didn't delude himself about who was really in charge.

Soon, in addition to the Stork, he was running the Napoleon Club, the Park Avenue Club, the Zone Club, Zellies Club, the Five O'Clock, the Pavilion Royal, the L.I. Club, even Texas Guinan's Club and Helen Morgan's Club.

In lighter moments, Madden twitted him, saying Billingsley was crazy to have gotten mixed up with them. "You should have ducked us some way or other. You just wait long enough and you'll find out what I mean."

In fact, Billingsley didn't have to wait very long at all. Legs Diamond took a fancy to the Stork Club and tried to muscle in until they persuaded him otherwise. He shifted his sights to Leon and Eddie's Fifty-second

Street club, and then to the European Club on West Fifty-third Street, which resisted his advances until a bomb went off in the front doorway.

Not long afterward, stickup men cleaned out the safe of the partners' Park Avenue Club before lunch. Frenchy then smashed down the door of a rooming house on West Fifty-seventh Street and came away with the name of one of the robbers. That night he went on a manhunt and returned with all the club's money. He didn't say how he did it, but it couldn't have been pretty.

After raiding agents converged one night on their Napoleon Club on West Fifty-sixth Street, Billingsley rushed over and managed to convince them, no doubt with some tangible incentive, that they were making a mistake. He was hardly back at the Stork when the manager of the Park Avenue Club called to say that it was being raided, and by the same agents. Angry at the betrayal, Billingsley summoned Frenchy and his boys to more persuasively convince them anew that they were picking on the wrong clubs.

But agents continued to drop in, both on and off duty, with wives, girlfriends, and cronies. Often they left so drunk that they dropped their gift bottles on the sidewalk.

At the Five O'Clock on West Fifty-fourth Street, Billingsley was in charge of a $75-a-week inside bouncer, a strapping, happy-go-lucky former shirt and underwear salesman born Bernard Shor, but known since childhood as Toots. Now and then Shor was able to augment his income by selling a $30 case of contraband whiskey, but what made him happiest, he liked to say, was "meetin' all the celebrities — Cagney, Crosby, Eddie Dowling, all those guys" attracted by Madden and his partners. This was the life, he loved it, as he never tired of saying in almost daily postcards to his sisters in Philly. Ziegfeld's was just down the street, loaded with all those girls, and then there were Earl Carroll's girls, and George White's and . . .

Billingsley didn't like Shor, and the feeling was mutual. Billingsley fired him again and again, but Shor always got Madden or Frenchy to re-hire him. Billingsley finally had his way, and Shor got another job through Texas's brother Tommy as host at the Napoleon Club. One night Shor flattened a Prohibition agent and had to lay low in Atlantic City before moving on to other speakeasies that were not under the control of Billingsley and his backers.

Then the Stork Club itself was threatened. Whether because of heat from the police or in hopes of finding a more reputable tenant, the building's owner, presumably the Annie Dolan of record, sought to break Billingsley's twenty-one-year lease. Judge John Sullivan, who was to hear the eviction case, and district leader Andy Keating were promptly invited to the Stork Club. Billingsley won the lawsuit.

FOURTEEN

VINCENT COLL, a dimpled, blue-eyed maniac whose chiseled features were found to uncannily match those of the statute of Civic Virtue in City Hall Park, was twenty-two with a criminal record far longer than the sawed-off tommy gun he spoke through. Like Frenchy and Madden, Coll was a child of Hell's Kitchen who apprenticed in burglary and robbery before graduating to murder. Among his victims, it was said, were one of his girlfriends, May Smith, a pretty dance hall hostess, and her new lover, Carmine Barelli, an ex-con and one of Coll's boyhood chums. One night in February 1930, at 170th Street and Inwood Avenue in the Bronx, a gunman leapt out of a car, shot Barelli dead, and then chased down the screaming May, pumping two bullets into her neck and shoulder, explaining, "You saw this and you'll have to go, too." By bizarre coincidence the executions took place right outside Billingsley's Sherman Garage.

Early in his short career, Coll, along with his brother Peter, had attached himself to Dutch Schultz, who had seized control of New York's beer racket, along with its restaurant labor unions. Cover-boy Coll and the perpetually disheveled and broken-nosed Schultz, with his lank hair and dead eyes, made an incongruous pair but were kindred spirits, sadistic and homicidally flash-tempered. When they had a falling-out, it was bound to get ugly.

Coll had been getting $150 a week as a triggerman for Schultz. Now he announced that he wanted a piece of the action, a partnership in the firm. The Dutchman refused. The Colls walked out to form their own organization. Then a lot of dying started. Ten of Schultz's henchmen were the first to go, followed by six of Coll's gang, including Peter. That cost Schultz three more of his own men.

Next, Coll, turning on Madden's mob, hit upon a popular, if brazen, scheme. With the economy sinking fast in June of 1931, kidnapping had become one of America's few growth industries. Two thousand professional kidnappers were estimated to be at work around the country, with one gang in the Midwest said to be reaping ransom payments of $150,000 a month. But only sixty-five kidnappers had been convicted. Coll clearly wasn't worried.

He called Frenchy one night and arranged to meet him in the far West Fifties near Eleventh Avenue. Frenchy set off with his girl, a driver, and a couple of flunkies in his big bulletproof Cadillac.

Coll's car drove up fast and cut off Frenchy, forcing his vehicle onto the curb and over the sidewalk. Coll pointed a machine gun at Frenchy and ordered him out of the backseat. Frenchy's girl shielded him, screaming that Coll would have to shoot her, too, but Frenchy made her let him get out. Then they drove off with him.

Frenchy's boys and the girl rushed to Texas Guinan's club on Seventh Avenue and Fifty-fourth, where they blurted out the news to Billingsley and Texas. They tried to figure out whether it was the end of Frenchy or merely a kidnapping. Billingsley was particularly distraught; Frenchy was supposed to be protecting *him!*

Shaken, he drove back and forth in the rain over the Fifty-ninth Street Bridge trying to figure out what to do. He went back to Guinan's club, but there was no news.

Coll, as it emerged, held Frenchy in a hideout on Riverside Drive before transferring him to a cottage in Westchester while negotiations dragged on. The ransom seesawed between $10,000 and $35,000. Madden wanted to deliver the money personally, but wiser heads argued that it would precipitate a slaughter. They finally sent their accountant, Bill Gallagher, who was directed to a cigar store in Harlem for further instructions. Phone calls then dispatched him to a series of other locations and finally to 135th Street and Riverside Drive, where Coll and his men were waiting in a car with Frenchy. The money changed hands, and Frenchy was freed.

But he was never the same afterward. He mumbled denials that he had ever been kidnapped. Strangely, he seemed mortified by Coll's breach of etiquette and shameful poor taste.

Coll, however, continued his provocations. Bursting into Madden's Cotton Club one night, he shot up the place with a tommy gun. Later, in one of Madden's other places on the West Side, he angrily riddled a picture of Madden with gunfire.

Billingsley was spooked. He stuck close to home, venturing out only for breakfast with Texas after the clubs closed. One morning before dawn they were in Reuben's on Madison Avenue and Fifty-eighth Street when a friend of Frenchy's ran in.

"I've been looking all over for you. Frenchy sent me to find you. Coll is trying to snatch you like everyone else, and tonight is the night he expects to do it, so be careful."

The informer fled. Texas pushed away her uneaten scrambled egg and left, too.

Billingsley sat there alone, facing two cold platters. He had a hard time swallowing. He pushed away the food and walked out.

There were four of them waiting. One said, "Don't look at us, just get in the backseat of that car and don't make any mistakes."

The car traveled downtown one or two blocks and turned east and then uptown in the direction of Harlem. After some time it pulled into a garage.

He was ordered out, up a flight of stairs, and into a room with a big chair that faced a wall covered with grisly newspaper and magazine photos of murder victims. A voice ordered him not to turn around. Someone searched him for a gun — he wasn't carrying one — and told him that he could use a bathroom if he needed and that he could have food, drinks, and cigarettes if he wanted. He asked for cigarettes and a cup of coffee, which were handed to him over a shoulder.

Time dragged, and he thought he spent the whole day there and then the night and another day. There were sounds of confusion. The phone rang often. Although he hadn't slept at all, he was wide-awake when someone ordered him out and down the steps. The lights were so dim that he could barely find his way. Once again he was shoved into the backseat of a car.

At Broadway and 125th Street the vehicle slowed down and he was told to jump out.

He went sprawling. When he looked up, all he could see was a whirl of winking red taillights of receding cars.

His reappearance at the Stork Club caused an uproar. But Frenchy had big news, too: Coll had been arrested in a drugstore on Lexington Avenue and Fifty-eighth Street while waiting to collect the ransom for Billingsley. The police may have followed him there. Whatever the reason, Billingsley had been ordered released.

Coll was out of jail in a day or two, promising peace. But the war went on.

July 28, 1931, was a blisteringly hot day. In the lengthening afternoon shadows of the Italian tenements lining East 107th Street, children romped on the stoops. Just after 6:00 P.M., a large green touring car cruised west from Second Avenue toward the black latticework of the Third Avenue el. As it passed the middle of the block, alongside the Helmar Social Club, where Joey Rao, Schultz's numbers king in Harlem, had been spotted earlier, the snouts of a machine gun and sawed-off shotgun poked through the open widows of the touring car, spitting torrents of lead. When the smoke cleared, Rao and his bodyguards were nowhere to be seen, but five children lay writhing on the sidewalk, one of them, five-year-old Michael Vengalli, about to die from a bullet though his gut.

The slaughter of the innocents outraged all New York. The police department and newspapers put up a $30,000 reward kitty for information; the *Daily News* offered $5,000 for the capture of the killers "dead or alive." Police Commissioner Edward P. Mulrooney issued shoot-to-kill orders: "Draw first and give it to 'em!" Mayor Jimmy Walker, more accustomed to leading on the dance floor than leading manhunts, rallied the citizenry: "Drive these dogs out of the community!" The police quickly suspected Coll. But the trail had gone cold.

Then came a break. In early October one of Schultz's men was gunned down in the Bronx. An electrician working in a nearby manhole stuck his head up in time to catch the license number of the killers' car. A cop happened across the very same car the next day. The clues led to Coll. By now disguised with blackened hair, a mustache, and spectacles, he was tracked to the Cornish Arms Hotel on West Twenty-third Street, where he was arrested October 4 with his intended, Lottie.

The murder trial later that year began badly for Coll, with one of the young victims describing how she was shot. "I felt a pain in my shoulder and I put my hand up and I felt it was wet. I looked and I saw blood." She saw a passing car, she testified, but she couldn't see who was in it. That was left to the people's star witness, George Brecht, a blond and husky Missourian, who said he had witnessed the shooting and gotten a look at the men in the car — among them, as he pointed out in the courtroom, Coll. But the gangster's superb counsel, Samuel S. Leibowitz (later to head the appeal of the Scottsboro Boys in Alabama and to ascend to the bench in New York State Supreme Court) had received a tip about Brecht and done some investigating of his own. In cross-examination he established that Brecht had once before claimed to have seen killers fleeing a murder scene, that his testimony had been discredited and the defendants acquitted. The state's case collapsed. Coll was freed, and he and Lottie celebrated with nuptials.

It was the final straw for Billingsley; he wanted out. He sent for Frenchy, who arrived with a few of his boys.

"Look," Billingsley said, "this gets worse and worse. A year of this has aged me ten years. You only paid Healy ten thousand dollars for your interest and you have taken many times that amount out."

Frenchy looked at him with scorn. "We didn't pay ten thousand dollars for an interest in the business. We paid ten for a thirty percent interest in everything you do for the rest of your life."

FIFTEEN

O N A COLD DECEMBER NIGHT IN 1931, Sherman Billingsley sat in his Stork Club, chatting with customers and seeing to the holiday preparations. For all his partner trouble and the bleakness of the Depression, he was surviving. That year alone, nearly 2,300 banks had failed and a million autoworkers had been laid off, swelling the ranks of the nation's unemployed to 8 million, double the number of the year before. A lot of speakeasies had gone bust, too.

Mirrors reflected the sleek black decor set off with silver adornments. Just inside the lobby, a festive basket packed with bottles of fine wine was on prominent display. A sign said a hundred dollars would take it away. It was three days before Christmas. The country was winding up its twelfth year of Prohibition.

Billingsley didn't seem particularly worried about a raid. He had a bell at the entrance for the doorman to ring in the event of any surprise visitors. The extra few minutes of warning would be enough time for bartenders and waiters to dump incriminating bottles and glasses through trapdoors. Then, too, he had gotten to know many of the Prohibition agents, some of whom were even patrons of the Stork. He kept on good terms with Inspector Bolan — soon to be named police commissioner — and his cousin, who continued to drink in separate rooms and never did run into each other. Of course, he had to stay alert. There had been the big pre-Christmas sweep of 1926 targeting Texas's and Helen Morgan's clubs and dozens of other places in the sprawling Broadway wet zone known as the Roaring Forties. Another big roundup in the summer of 1928 had again netted Texas and Miss Morgan despite the protestations of both women that they were merely entertainers. Texas felt particularly aggrieved, her astrologer and the spirit voices of dead Broadwayites whom she had called up in a séance at her club the night before having failed to tip her off to the raid.

Still, Billingsley felt he had little to fear from the law, as long as the premises remained peaceable. Which was not always the case.

The year before, the Stork had hit the headlines when Johnny Weismuller, Hollywood's future Tarzan of the Apes, tangled with a navy lieutenant. Weismuller, in sunglasses, was dancing with a lady not his wife. The navy man, Cameron Winslow Jr., sat at a table by the dance floor, smoking a cigarette. Every time Weismuller whirled his partner past Winslow's table, the lieutenant extended his cigarette provocatively, or so Weismuller claimed. Weismuller suggested that he stop. Winslow suggested that Weismuller might see better without his dark glasses. Who smacked whom first was disputed, but some smacking incontestably occurred. On nights like that, Billingsley felt, he might as well put out a sign inviting the police in.

Now, a year later, the raid alarm finally did go off.

This time there were too many bottles out, including the large wine basket, to dispose of them hastily, and the raiders were too fast. Billingsley didn't seem to recognize any of the agents. What was more, they had U.S. attorneys with them. That was something new.

Where was Bolan? Why hadn't the inspector tipped him off?

Billingsley stood by glumly while they inventoried the alcohol and rounded up nine waiters, three bartenders, two concessionaires, and more than a dozen kitchen workers, some of them doubly prosecutable as illegal aliens. Then, to his shock, the raiders began stripping the club, tearing out plumbing and gas lines and hauling out stoves, refrigerators, rugs, mirrors, even the piano. That had never happened before. A raid was a raid. But to destroy his club!

In a panic, he called his lawyer, M. Michael Edelstein, who had bad news. A recent Supreme Court decision had upheld the seizure of not just a speakeasy's liquor but its furnishings, as well. That case took place in Butte, Montana, but it could apply across the country. Clearly, it was a new government tactic.

Frantic, Billingsley sent Edelstein downtown for a restraining order to halt the demolition.

In federal court Edelstein argued that the Montana decision didn't apply. There, he said, the defense admitted that the seized goods had been used in violation of the Volstead Act. "We make no such admission," he declared.

But the club stayed closed, guarded by federal agents, while the court case wound on. Then Billingsley heard from his racketeer partners. Dwyer had a great idea: they could bribe a federal judge. All it would take, he assured Billingsley, would be $15,000.

Billingsley could hardly have been shocked. In their bootlegging days, he and his brothers had paid off sheriffs, mayors, and agents around the country. But this looked especially dubious. He'd hand over the money and hear that the bagmen had lost it. Or something. He told Dwyer no thanks.

In late January 1932 the ruling came in: the United States indeed had the right to seize all furnishings and equipment used in any room where

NEW DINING ROOM • STORK RESTAURANT • 51½ EAST 51ˢᵀ • NEW YORK CITY

A PERIOD POSTCARD OF THE FIFTY-FIRST STREET
STORK CLUB'S DINING ROOM

liquor was being sold, although agents could not destroy it without a court order. With that, five lesser Stork Club employees pleaded guilty to Prohibition violations and paid small fines. Charges against twenty-three others were dropped. Then, a day shy of a month after the raid, Billingsley had to stand by as federal agents dismantled his Stork Club on West Fifty-eighth Street. A raucous crowd of onlookers stood by, heckling.

He immediately began scouting midtown for a new location. Meanwhile, he decided, he had to break free of his troublesome partners and all their crazy friends and enemies, whatever it took.

He tried to reason with Frenchy. He had advanced their clubs thousands of dollars. They could keep that. They could keep all the other clubs, too — hell, they were theirs, anyway. But the Stork Club was his.

Frenchy frowned. He was not happy.

Billingsley had, meanwhile, found a new location, an elegant five-story town house at 53 East Fifty-first Street, off Park Avenue. It was built as a home, not a restaurant, but could accommodate two hundred patrons at a time, a good number of them around an impressive twenty-foot-square bar of Circassian walnut that he had picked up for the new club's centerpiece.

He rented the third floor of the adjoining town house at number fifty-one as an apartment for himself and Hazel and their daughter, Jacqueline, now nearly six. Then, finding the address of the club confusing, he deviously changed it to 51½ East Fifty-first Street. Now, if the agents got a padlock order, they'd find themselves dealing with the poor jerk next door.

He was still working on getting the place fixed up in February 1932 when Mad Dog Coll, accompanied by a bodyguard, made a late-night stop in the London Chemists' Shop, across from his rooms in the Cornish Arms on West Twenty-third Street. While his bodyguard settled himself at the soda fountain, Coll, in a dark suit with $101 in his pocket, headed for a telephone booth in the back.

Outside, a black sedan with three men rolled to the curb. One stayed in the car, one planted himself outside the drugstore, and one went in, unlimbering a machine gun from under his dark coat.

As if by prearrangement, Coll's bodyguard at the counter melted away.

The man with the tommy gun halted outside the phone booth where Coll was engrossed in his call. Then he announced, "All right, everybody keep cool, and no one will be harmed." He kept his promise with one exception, stitching the booth with gunfire.

Coll crashed down, riddled with fifteen bullets, two through the forehead. The shooter backed his way out, stepped into the waiting car, and sped off.

Uncannily, Winchell had flagged the rubout hours earlier in his "On Broadway" column in the *Mirror*. "Five planes brought dozens of machinegats from Chicago Friday to combat the Town's Capone. . . . Local banditti have made one hotel a virtual arsenal and several hot-spots are ditto because Master Coll is giving them the headache."

Unfortunately for Coll, he hadn't read the papers. Winchell was soon grilled by a grand jury on his source of information — it may have been Texas Guinan — but remained mum.

There were too many people who wanted Coll dead to easily narrow the list of suspects. But one name kept coming up.

Schultz.

Now Billingsley *really* wanted out. He offered Frenchy, Madden, and Dwyer three times what they had paid — $30,000. He just needed time to raise it.

Frenchy seemed hurt. And after all they had done for him . . .

Billingsley made finding the money look as hard as possible — he didn't want them to think they could squeeze him for more — so he went around borrowing small sums from a lot of people who would surely talk. Then he handed it over to Frenchy, and was once again free.

Or so he hoped.

SIXTEEN

WITH COLL ELIMINATED, Schultz reigned unchallenged. In fact, Billingsley had barely gotten his new Stork Club on East Fifty-first Street running when the dead-eyed mob boss came calling. Billingsley knew Schultz owned the dining room union as a way of pressuring saloons and restaurants into buying his beer. He had figured it was only a matter of time until they got around to him.

After all he'd been through, Billingsley had little stomach for a fight. He signed with Schultz's men for the dining room, assured that that was the end of it. But soon afterward, in the middle of a dinner hour with two hundred customers in the house, organizers came to the door demanding recognition of the kitchen workers union on threat of a walkout.

Furious, Billingsley stormed back into the kitchen. Certain they had some of the kitchen help primed to support them, he jumped up on an icebox, called the several dozen of them together, and warned them that they had better not walk out until all customers had been served. He stood there menacingly, ready to enforce his order. No one dared leave.

When the night was over, he summoned the kitchen and dining room workers together again. This time he fired them all.

Keeping Gregory Pavlides and loyal captains and waiters, he quickly recruited a new crew. He also called up his high-level police connection, the icy Jim Bolan, who arranged for two retired detectives, well paid by Billingsley, to shadow little Jacqueline to school and the playground. At the same time he built a third-floor catwalk in the hidden rear of the building to connect the club with his apartment. That way he could go back and forth without showing his face on the street. That summer, when Jacqueline went off to camp, he had Hazel's sister, Aunt Marion, take her in one car while he followed behind, at a crucial moment stalling his car in the middle of the road, blocking traffic to thwart any pursuers.

He didn't hear from Schultz for a while. Then the checkroom union started clamoring for recognition, dispatching four fat women to march outside the club, haranguing customers and workers. This was too much. Couldn't they at least send pretty pickets?

But another crisis was brewing. A customer who felt cheated by the quarter slot machines Billingsley kept alongside the bar had complained to the police.

For several nights Detectives Ray Stilley and Robert Jones had reconnoitered the Stork Club, passing freely though the entranceway with the cautionary sign NEVER RECOMMEND AN ACQUAINTANCE OF ONE DAY. On an evening in late August 1932, they played the slots and snaked their way to the dance floor, where the ten-piece orchestra was pumping out "Happy Days Are Here Again," the pro-wet anthem appropriated by the Democrats and their presidential candidate, New York governor Franklin Delano Roosevelt.

Before the number finished, they signaled for quiet, and Jones took over the microphone, which carried the music to upstairs party rooms, the lobby, and staff quarters. "This place is in the hands of the police for violation of the prohibition law, but we wish to cause no one inconvenience. Please finish your meals at your leisure, pay your checks, and go home."

Pandemonium erupted, patrons jamming the dining room to share what many were convinced was part of the scripted entertainment. They then returned laughing to their tables.

Detective Stilley stepped to the front door and waved.

Seven plainclothesmen from the chief inspector's office surged into the club, taking up positions to control the entrances and exits. They waited for guests to weary of the thrill of eating and drinking under the eye of the law and then commenced the business of raiding, arresting five employees. Unlike the old Stork Club, where the alcohol had been cleverly hidden behind trapdoors and false panels, the bottles here — one hundred at the bar and more than four hundred more in the fifth-floor wine "cellar" — brazenly stood out in the open.

Outside on the street, the limousines and taxis of fleeing patrons snarled themselves with those of unsuspecting arrivals in a colossal traffic jam that recalled opening night at the opera. Reporters who rushed to the scene monopolized the telephones in the Stock Club lobby to call in their bulletins, enraging Billingsley. They suddenly found that the receivers in their hands had all gone dead.

All in all, said a woman who swept out of the club with her escort, "It was the nicest raid I have ever seen."

With repeal seemingly around the corner, Billingsley reopened almost immediately. Cautiously, however, he now listed himself as "managing director."

"We Buy the Best to Serve the Best," he boasted in menu leaflets that listed his suppliers. He bought groceries from Francis H. Liggett & Company (Premier Brands) and Seeman Brothers (White Rose brand), bread and rolls from the Marseillaise French Baking Company, nut bread from R. H. Macy & Company, milk and cream from Sheffield Farms, ice cream from Louis Sherry, and soda and ginger ale from Schweppes. He was proud enough of his fare, in fact, to offer patrons authentic-looking Stork Club refund checks for a hundred dollars . . . "if" — and this was in small print — "you can find anything in the line of food or beverages at the Stork Club that's not the best that money can buy." The lavish offerings made for a stark contrast with the privations around the country, where 13 million were now unemployed and the newspapers carried a story about fifty people fighting over the contents of a garbage can.

SEVENTEEN

THIRTEEN YEARS, ten months, eighteen days, and a few hours after it ushered in the most lawless era in American history, Prohibition expired on December 5, 1933, at 5:32 P.M., Eastern Standard Time. Utah became the decisive thirty-sixth state to approve the Twenty-first Amendment, which repealed the Eighteenth. Few mourned the demise of a statute that had bred universal contempt for authority and established organized crime as a fixture on the American scene. A day after repeal even such an intractable foe of liquor as Henry Ford astounded luncheon guests at the Dearborn Inn by serving beer.

World reaction was positive, if smug: we told you so. In newly Nazi Germany, the wine-country newspaper *Rheinisch-Westfällische Zeitung* called Prohibition "one of the most gruesome farces any civilized nation ever undertook in order to stay civilized."

Prohibition's toll was grim. One hundred seventy-eight civilians and ninety-two federal agents killed. More than half a million people convicted of alcohol violations and fined more than $80 million — worth more than $1 billion today. More than 200,000 jailed. And more than $200 million worth of property seized.

Repeal meant more than just the return of the "immemorial beverages of civilized man," said H. L. Mencken, it signaled "a restoration of one of the common liberties of the people."

The victory, spearheaded by a prim socialite army called the Women's Organization for National Prohibition Reform, was in large part credited to an unlikely warrior, Pauline Morton Sabin, the nation's leading woman Republican and daughter of Paul Morton, Theodore Roosevelt's secretary of the navy. Sabin had worked tirelessly to elect Herbert Hoover over the Catholic Democrat Al Smith, but days after Hoover's victory, she resigned as a Republican committeewoman in disgust over his refusal to confront the scourge of Prohibition.

Before the month was out, twenty-four like-minded women from twelve states had met at the Drake Hotel in Chicago and picked Sabin as their leader. By April 1930 the growing movement, now 100,000 strong, met in Cleveland, going on record, unanimously, for repeal. That November the group held a "Victory Luncheon" at the Astor Hotel in Times Square, declaring: "The evils of Prohibition touch every cause close to the hearts of women."

It wasn't just women who agitated for repeal. The United Repeal Council, an umbrella group of anti-Prohibitionists, supported wet candidates, furnished speakers for public meetings and radio broadcasts, and placed newspaper articles and ads advocating repeal. Skewering the hypocrisy of the day, the organization's Crusaders distributed a "speakeasy map" of Washington with 934 black dots marking the places where raiders had discovered liquor in 1930. The biggest concentration was within blocks of the Capitol.

As the first night of legal liquor loomed, a panic seized the East. By thoughtlessly voting so late in the day, Utah made it impossible for many establishments to obtain their supplies from the few licensed warehouses before closing time. Thus, many citizens determined to hoist a glass to repeal had to do so with bootleg booze.

In a rush to down the first legal drink in thirteen years, comedian Joe Weber stationed himself at the Astor Hotel, where thirty seconds into the new wet era, he tossed back a glass of champagne. At the Park Lane, an exuberant guest lofted a golden daiquiri and intoned, "To those of us who love the thing that we call freedom, all hail!" At the St. Moritz on Central Park South, a large crowd filed out at midnight to drown an effigy of Prohibition in the Central Park Lake. A figure of Old Man Prohibition was gaily lynched from a lamppost at Broadway and Fifty-first Street, and throughout Times Square peddlers hawked gag whiskey bottles and miniature drink sets. Reid's bannered a novel sensation: champagne ice cream, "a new and exciting repeal flavor of fine old vintage."

On the first day of repeal, as it waited for newly legal liquor to be delivered from besieged warehouses, "21" (known in its speakeasy days as Jack and Charlie's) pressed patrons into service as a kind of bucket brigade to haul in liquor from suppliers too overburdened to make deliveries. Billingsley and other speakeasy owners celebrated by giving away their Prohibition alcohol.

At the very least, repeal immediately spelled savings. The price of a drink dropped by half, to about thirty cents for cocktails, to sixty cents for scotch. A bottle of wine sank to $2.50, champagne to eight dollars. But as former Police Commissioner Edward P. Mulrooney, now the chairman of the State Liquor Authority, noted, "The rush for liquor will be somewhat dampened because the public is short of money."

One initial casualty of repeal was the bar. It was still illegal to serve drinks except at dining tables. Inventive proprietors, however, got around that proscription by slapping together rolling carts to wheel drinks tableside.

As New Yorkers took to legal liquor with expected gusto, Commissioner Bolan stepped up his attacks on the now-reviled speakeasies, "smoke joints," and "shock houses" where rotgut was still being dispensed at five cents a shot. But if old habits were hard to break, new ones were also raising eyebrows. Where wine and beer had once been the beverages of choice for many pre-Prohibition drinkers, the public now clamored for highballs, cocktails, and straight drinks. Even ladies called for martinis.

With an eye to the strange new serving regulations, Billingsley removed the large, square bar where customers had been able to drink and look at one another, and built a new bar the length of the building on the third floor with space for musicians to play behind the bartenders. Then he raised the tables so that they would be on the same level as the bar. The bar was still there but, at least technically, the drinks were being served at the tables.

THE STORK'S FINAL LOCATION ON FIFTY-THIRD STREET

CHRYSLER AIR COOLING SYSTEM WILL KEEP THE STORK CLUB, 3 E. 53RD ST. COOL DURING THE SUMMER MONTHS

Now, all he lacked was a liquor license. Thousands of applications were piled up in the control board offices, and with their superior connections hotels were getting priority attention. But with the help of his friend Bronx boss Ed Flynn, Billingsley not only managed to get his license on the first day of issuance but also may have snagged the first one granted to a restaurant. The Stork's license, dated December 7, 1934, listed Hazel and her sister Marion as stockholders. Billingsley's name did not appear, though two years later he would be emboldened enough to list himself once again as managing director.

While the Stork Club's business was now booming, so was the competition's. Billingsley needed more space for dancing and musicians. By late 1934 he found a new location, the ground floor of a limestone doctors building at 3 East Fifty-third Street, around the corner from Fifth Avenue.

To design his new club, Billingsley hired the renowned architect Arthur Loomis Harmon, whose credits included the Italianate chain of moderately priced hotels called the Allerton houses, the Shelton Hotel on Lexington Avenue, and the deco masterpiece of 740 Park Avenue, one of the city's premier apartment palaces. In 1929, moreover, Harmon had joined the architectural firm of Shreve & Lamb, which was designing the Empire State Building.

Harmon, a small man, arrived at the Stork Club wearing a brown suit, salmon-colored shirt, green tie, tan hat, and tan shoes. The color scheme of the finished club precisely matched his wardrobe's that day. The bathrooms were also small, just like him, Billingsley marked with distaste. He immediately set about having the place redone.

Then one afternoon, three specters from the past came strolling in — Frenchy, Madden, and . . . Schultz.

EIGHTEEN

WHAT WITH ONE THING AND ANOTHER, the gangster threesome had been keeping themselves busy. In March 1932, after Colonel Charles A. Lindbergh's baby son was kidnapped, Madden and other underworld leaders had shrewdly offered their assistance. Al Capone, who was awaiting transfer from the Cook County jail to the federal penitentiary in Atlanta, came forth to speculate that "some mob did it" and offered a $10,000 reward for information leading to the return of the child and arrest of the kidnappers. If he could only get out of jail, he said, he could *really* help.

Madden's involvement took on a semi-official cast after the *Daily Mirror* prodded a prominent lawyer, Dudley Field Malone, to act as an intermediary with the as-yet-unannounced kidnappers. Malone was quickly deluged with tips from gangsters looking to cash in. He turned over the job of vetting the offers to Morris Rosner, a shadowy gangland figure who in turn engaged Madden as a consultant and go-between.

For a week Madden camped out in Malone's apartment, sleeping on a couch in the library. Whenever an informant proffered information, Malone asked him, "Do you know Owney Madden?" When the answer was yes, Madden himself materialized, usually sending the tipster fleeing. Madden was even said to have spent three nights at the Lindbergh home, strategizing with the colonel. But the efforts all came to naught when the baby was found dead.

By summer Madden was back in Sing Sing to finish out the last three years of his 1915 manslaughter conviction. (Although nine years had passed since his parole in 1923, the authorities decided that he had violated the conditions of his early release and ordered him returned to prison.) Madden and Dwyer deemed it an auspicious moment to shut down their huge brewery. The plant, protected by city police officers, had been sacked by Prohibition agents two years before, but on appeal the government had been ordered to return the seized property, because the search warrant had been improperly issued.

Within a year Madden was paroled again after his friends were alleged to have offered a million dollars for his release. A member of the state parole board, when questioned, acknowledged that "tentative" offers had been made on Madden's behalf but insisted no actual bribe had been tendered or received. At the same time, Sing Sing warden Lewis E. Lawes denied that he had used his own automobile to ferry delicacies to Madden in his cell block.

As for Frenchy, in October 1932, while Madden languished in Sing Sing, he was in their Park Avenue Club, formerly Belle Livingston's deluxe Country Club on East Fifty-eighth Street, when Prohibition agents raided. While they inventoried the furnishings and put the cash register's $486 into a canvas bag, they kept Frenchy and twenty-four employees locked up in the mirror-paneled dining room. But somehow Frenchy found his way out and disappeared through a service door. When the agents' money bag was opened at the Fifty-first Street station house, it was empty.

Now, two years later, Billingsley found himself facing a trio of problems he believed he was long rid of. But here they were again, the reptillian Frenchy, the reparoled Madden, dapper as ever, and the fearsome, blank-eyed Schultz. Had he actually taken over from Dwyer?

After Madden said a casual hello and then wandered off, Frenchy and Schultz began to eye the club with interest. Frenchy appraised the room and said they wanted to buy in.

Billingsley attempted a laugh, but it came out weak. "Prohibition is over," he said. "This place will be run like a bank."

Frenchy wasn't about to be put off. "We have to have some things going for us, and you better have some of us boys in with you."

"Why?"

Frenchy looked at him in disbelief "Do you need a brick building to fall on you?"

"What do you mean by that?"

Now Schultz spoke up with a blank gaze. Billingsley could see why he terrified people. "If you don't have us in with you, you will have plenty of trouble with the unions."

Billingsley knew Schultz still controlled the kitchen workers but tried to feign unconcern. "I'd rather have union trouble than partners."

Schultz gave him a last dead look. "You can have other troubles, too."

NINETEEN

OGAN, WHO HAD MIGRATED EAST after his Seattle jailbreak, was meanwhile building a lucrative real estate empire in the Bronx. His prominent emergence in New York after so many years amazed Seattleites who were somehow led to believe he had been lost aboard a yacht that vanished off Cuba in 1920.

He had made his mark on the Grand Boulevard and Concourse, New York's answer to the Champs-Elysées, where he put up what was billed as the world's largest apartment hotel, the Theodore Roosevelt, fourteen stucco towers covering an entire square block between 171st and 172nd Streets, which cost more than $2.5 million. Its three hundred suites comprised twelve hundred rooms, and its dining hall and restaurant delivered meals to residents by dumbwaiters. An Italian sculptor was commissioned to create a courtyard statue, the Fountain of Strength, with two-and-a-half-year-old Logan Jr. as the model, and picture postcards went out promoting the complex as "a remarkable advance toward perfection."

Next Logan led a syndicate in investing $2 million to buy up thirty-two plots along East Fordham Road, the main travel artery to and from New England, where, perhaps not coincidentally, the New York Central was about to build a bigger new train station and plaza. He and his Bronx investors also bought 17,000 acres on the west coast of Florida, a huge tract with twelve miles of frontage on the Gulf of Mexico and Suwannee River, where the Florida West Coast Railroad was building a new line.

His personal life, meanwhile, was a shambles. After almost seven years of marriage, he and Hattie Mae split up in 1926 (two years after Sherman's visit with Dee Dee), Logan accusing her of adulteries with various military officers. He sought custody of Logan Jr., but the boy, frail and sickly, was to die young.

In early 1928, seeking an influential new power base, Logan took over the faltering Bronx Chamber of Commerce. Within a year he had built it

LOGAN BILLINGSLEY WITH A BEVY OF FLAPPERS

into the third-largest business panel in the nation and the most active civic association in the city. With his newfound connections, Logan sought a city franchise to build a $400 million subway and vehicular tunnel connecting the northeast Bronx, through Manhattan, to Brooklyn. The grandiose plan came to naught, but by 1936 the city's master builder, Robert Moses, was to succeed with an aerial version called the Triborough Bridge. Logan also tried to drum up interest in a World's Fair in New York to commemorate the two hundredth anniversary of George Washington's birth in 1932, but Chicago, which was planning a similar exposition for 1933 to celebrate its centennial, raised such a protest that the New York plan was shelved, to be resurrected in 1939.

The stock market crash devastated the building industry. But ever optimistic and anticipating the New Deal still three years off, Logan urged Americans to spend their way back to prosperity. "One building plan filed is worth a ton of statements," he declared. "Let the government start erecting post offices and other public buildings. . . . And let the railroads start hiring additional carpenters, plasterers, masons and bricklayers, instead of press agents."

Calculatingly, Logan also organized an offshoot of the Bronx chamber, called the Manhattan Board of Commerce, listing among its members U.S. Attorney Charles H. Tuttle, New York Yankees owner Jacob Ruppert, and other leading lawmen, merchants, and politicians.

The step proved to be a serious miscalculation. In April 1930 the Better Business Bureau, curious about the new entity, queried its members about their affiliation, and drew puzzled responses. Some said they had never heard of it. The bureau dug further and unearthed Logan's unsavory past as a bootlegger, his arrest in the killing of the two Seattle policemen, and his prison record. It ultimately branded the Manhattan Board of Commerce a "racket."

Drawing on the bureau's discoveries, the *New York Enquirer,* a Sunday afternoon newspaper, then carried a damaging story on Logan's sordid past. For one of the city's most prominent civic leaders to be unmasked as a felon and con man was a sensation. Denouncing the Better Business Bureau as an unlicensed detective agency, and the *Enquirer* as its handmaiden, Logan filed suit. "They are making a mountain out of molehill," he maintained. "The most important charge seems to be that I shipped liquor in pre-Prohibition days from a wet state into a dry state and got into jail for it. If I did, what of it? It was my liquor and, incidentally, it was good liquor."

But challenging the Better Business Bureau in court was another big mistake. Logan was ordered to submit to pretrial questioning under oath. Hammered by the bureau's lawyer, he acknowledged having been arrested in the Seattle police killings and "perhaps a hundred times" for liquor violations. He also admitted to having served time in a federal penitentiary while claiming that he couldn't remember for what or for how long. Outside court, he told newsmen that his arrests were a matter of principle — a deliberate strategy to stand up for freedom as president of the "National Personal Liberty League." But when he refused to produce records of his Manhattan organization, he was found guilty of contempt and sentenced to fifteen days in jail and a $250 fine.

By January 1931 Logan withdrew his defamation lawsuit, but the contempt sentence stood. He compounded his problems by dropping out of sight and turning up in Atlantic City a few days before he was ordered to surrender. To make matters worse, he sent the Bronx sheriff a mocking postcard: *Reserve one outside room for me, American plan, your Hotel, after Monday.* This insult infuriated the judge. Logan appeared in court to beg forgiveness. "Your Honor, if I said anything during my examination before trial that was construed by the court to be disrespectful, I am awfully sorry and I want to apologize. I didn't intentionally say anything that would embarrass or be disrespectful to the court. I was sick at the time of the examination — under a nervous breakdown, ready to snap at any minute; it was a very embarrassing matter."

The jail term was dropped, he paid his fine, and the episode was over. And over the years, somehow, the Better Business Bureau file on Logan disappeared.

Across the country, meanwhile, brother Fred was making his own news. In September 1932, going under the alias Fred Erwing, he was being treated for pneumonia in a Los Angeles hospital when he grew delirious, seized a pistol secreted under the mattress, and mortally wounded his physician. The district attorney theorized that Fred had been overcome by "a haunting fear that enemies he may have made in his early life were threatening to kill him" but filed homicide charges nevertheless.

Logan flew to his bedside, saying he had no idea why his *half brother* — as he called him — was using the pseudonym. A coroner's jury found that Fred had indeed been hallucinating, and murder charges were dropped.

TWENTY

I N HIS NEW — AND FINALLY LEGAL — STORK CLUB, erased of
all traces of Harmon's effete salmon, tan, and green decor, Billingsley
staged a string of opening-night extravaganzas. Winchell, Runyon,
George M. Cohan, Mark Hellinger — they all came. Every reporter in the
city with a byline was presented with guest card number 353 as a clever reminder of the address.

"*Alors le deluge,* as we linguists say," wrote Archer Winsten in his *Post*
column as the parties wound down after New Year's 1935.

Lucius Beebe, the wry and literate *Herald Tribune* columnist, dropped
in from his regular perch at Bleeck's saloon to marvel at the fresh stone crabs
and other seafood that Billingsley was managing to fly in from Florida. If
Billingsley had a motto, Beebe speculated, it had to be "Come and get it!"

The Stork Club also attracted the sparrowlike Leonard Lyons of the
New York Post, one of the best-liked of his ilk. Born Leonard Sucher, he
had grown up poor on the Lower East Side and put himself through law
school. On the advice of a sweetheart, Sylvia Schonberger, who admired
his chatty letters and whom he later married, he contributed a weekly column of witticisms and advice to the English-language section of the *Jewish
Daily Forward.* It was the section's editor, Nathanial Zalowitz, who gave
him the nom de plume of "Lyons." Hired by the *Post* in 1934, just as the
Stork Club was being reborn on Fifty-third Street, Lyons became a stead-
fast chronicler of the night, making Billingsley the subject of his first column. Lyons didn't believe in writing about romances and divorces. Nor, it
was said, did he ever violate a confidence. He rarely drank, accepting at
most an occasional glass of wine. He corresponded with world leaders and
literary giants, and on the few occasions when he was away and unable to
write, Lyons turned his column over to the likes of Ferenc Molnár, Sinclair
Lewis, and James Michener, among other "real" writers, and once, Billingsley himself.

Winsten was another ardent admirer. "He looked like the man voted 'handsomest' in the class of '20, with his charming smile, fresh color, thinning hair and regular profile," he wrote of Billingsley, and then went on to quote him at length on the secrets of his success, a formula that started with the Stork's food and drink. He asked Billingsley about his labor troubles and printed his reply verbatim: "This gahdam Union gets my goat."

By now the cabbies were also testing him, particularly a tough clique that liked to monopolize hack lines outside the city's fanciest clubs. They chased away honest drivers and parked outside, meters already ticking, to victimize the unaware, the timid, and the drunk. Were they Schultz's doing, too?

Some drivers even invaded the club, planting themselves at the bar and tables, staring ominously at Billingsley. When he started receiving threatening letters and phone calls, he hired six beefy guards; gave them bottles of whiskey, cigarettes, and playing cards; and stationed them in a room next to where the help dressed.

Within an hour he got another phone call. "We know you have the FBI agents or coppers here, but we'll fix you in another way."

At least, Billingsley figured, he could rely on his inner circle, Steve Hannagan, Morton Downey, Gregory Pavlides, Albino Garlasco, and, of course, Yetta Golove. He had also put relatives on the payroll, figuring they would be less likely to steal from him. Hazel's sisters, Dodie and Marion, worked the register and the bar. His own sister Pearl baked pies and monitored the kitchen, while her husband, Andy Gray, procured provisions and supervised personnel. Billingsley also gave an assistant manager's job to Logan's son Glenn, the child he had had with Chloe Wheatley and the little boy Logan had perched on top of the little red wagon when he had dispatched Sherman to sell beer to the Indians in Anadarko. Family or not, however, they still had to open their bags for the obligatory security search at closing.

To spread the word about the Stork Club, Billingsley ran ads in college papers, with coupons for free food and drink, figuring their families would also be sure to come in to see what kind of place their kids were frequenting. He obtained the names and addresses of movie stars from a Western Union clerk in Hollywood and sent them circulars from the Stork Club, and did the same with Broadway stars. Runyon brought the sports people in. John Powers sent his models.

Two competitors were already well established: "21" (which the Kriendler brothers and their cousin Charlie Berns had started as Jack and Charlie's) at 21 West Fifty-second Street in 1930, and El Morocco (Elmo's, to the cognescenti), opened in 1931 on East Fifty-Fourth Street by John Perona, who had left his native Italy to train in the haute cuisine restaurants of London. To Billingsley's dismay, Elmo's distinctive blue-and-white zebra stripes showed up spectacularly well in photographs.

To keep tabs on his rivals, Billingsley hired private detectives to make the rounds of the clubs. One night he was sending a detective over to El Morocco when the gumshoe said, "No use of me going there. I know all about that place." As he explained, he did the same kind of work for Perona.

With all his promotional schemes, Billingsley was still struggling. On one slow night, with not a customer in the house, he went out for a walk and returned to find a party in full swing. His delight quickly turned to consternation. The *staff* was partying. Sportsman Dan Topping had stopped by, found the place dead, and called the employees together for a bash. Still, it paid the bills for a while.

When the disgraced Mayor Walker and his second wife, showgirl Betty Compton, returned to New York in October 1935 after three years in European exile waiting for corruption charges to blow over, Billingsley threw him an all-night welcome-home party at the club. He was sure the gala would make page one in every paper in the city. But the next day, to his dismay, he couldn't find a line about it. It just went to show, he said, "When the king is dead, everything about him is dead."

One of the first entertainers he hired was a sultry brunette, a twenty-ish singer from New Orleans born Mary Leta Dorothy Slaton but who had given herself the name Dorothy Lamour, a felicitous adaptation of her stepfather's name, Lambour. A few years earlier she had won the Miss New Orleans beauty contest but ended up operating an elevator at Marshall Field's in Chicago. Then a friend persuaded her to try out as a singer with band leader Herbie Kay's radio show *The Yeast Foamers*, sponsored by Fleischmann's yeast. A marriage to Kay didn't last, and she came to New York, where she found her way to the Stork Club at fifty dollars a week. But after little more than a month Billingsley yanked her as talentless. Her agent begged; she'd perform for free, just for the exposure. He'd split his earnings with Billingsley, all he made from her, all he would ever make. Billingsley was unswayed. It was perhaps a lucky break for her. She soon met Louis B. Mayer and ended up in a sarong opposite Bob Hope and Bing Crosby, earning nearly half a million dollars a picture.

While Billingsley struggled to publicize the Stork, Schultz continued to test him with pickets and union agitation. Figuring that the Dutchman had infiltrated his own men into the Stork, Billingsley rented a room across the street from the offices of Schultz's restaurant union on Eighth Avenue at Forty-third Street, down the block from the *New York Times,* and put three of his most trustworthy employees on surveillance duty with binoculars. They spotted half a dozen likely stooges. One of Billingsley's spies even sneaked into Schultz's hangout and filched lists showing which of Billingsley's employees were in league with the mob boss.

Then came a fateful break. In January 1933 Tom Dewey, the brash federal prosecutor then just thirty years old, had brought evidence to a grand jury that Schultz was evading income taxes from his beer racket. The panel voted an indictment, but Schultz dropped out of sight. Two years later he was finally flushed out to stand trial in the neutral venue of Syracuse. The government put on a strong case, but the jury was hung. In the summer of 1935 Schultz was retried in the small border town of Malone, New York. This time he was acquitted.

He came back to New York vowing vengeance against Dewey, since named a special state prosecutor. The vendetta didn't worry Dewey as much as it worried Schultz's mob rivals, who did not relish the heat that Dewey's murder would surely bring.

On the night of October 23, 1935, as Schultz dined in the Palace Chop House in Newark with two bodyguards and his accountant, gunmen riddled all three with bullets. Schultz alone survived, clinging to life in the hospital for twenty-two hours, during which he raved most poetically. Then, at age thirty-four, he died, leaving, or so it was rumored, a fortune of $7 million in a steel box somewhere upstate. It was never found.

TWENTY-ONE

FTER JACQUELINE'S BIRTH IN 1926 doctors had cautioned Hazel against a second pregnancy, fearing she might not survive the strain. But five years later she had gone to term with another child. If it turned out to be a boy, they planned to call him Fred, after Sherman's brother. Then, as the obstetricians had suspected, Hazel's labor became life-threatening, and Billingsley was asked to consider choosing between saving his wife or son, for it was a boy, after all. Billingsley was speechless, and the baby eventually died in delivery. The doctor asked Billingsley if he wanted to hold his son one last time. Billingsley shook his head and went in to comfort Hazel.

Now, five years later, Hazel was about to give birth again.

Billingsley, who could no longer bear to be inside a hospital, sat in the Stork Club's front room at table 1 with a telephone before him, dialing the floor nurse every few minutes for bulletins. This time there was good news. Their second daughter, Barbara, was born in April 1936 without complications.

That summer Billingsley took ten-year-old Jacqueline to visit Oklahoma. It was his first trip back in eighteen years and his first break from the Stork Club in a year and a half. The Dust Bowl years of the Depression had turned the land into a cloudscape of choking red dust and suffocating heat. Before cutting the arduous trip short, Billingsley visited some of the old-timers who swore they remembered him. He stopped in at Billy Gregg's roadhouse, where it cost a dime to dance, unless you ordered a chicken dinner, in which case it was free. The taxi ride from the train station to the hotel cost fifteen cents. He tipped a waitress a dollar, and she looked at him suspiciously, taking his generosity as an indecent overture. As always he admired the girls, "really beautiful, nice comfy cornfeds, healthy and swell complexions."

*   *   *

Billingsley's tireless promotion of the Stork Club finally seemed to be paying off, for at a time when many restaurants and cabarets were still going bankrupt, the Stork was emerging as one of New York's premier nightspots. On New Year's Eve 1936 the celebrants included Hoover and Tolson, caught in a gag photo showing the FBI boss in a funny hat raising his hands in mock surrender to a fashion model, Luisa Stuart, wielding a toy gun.

The club was doing a million dollars a year in business, an extraordinary sum in the Depression, and Billingsley was becoming a rich man. To be sure, he was working seven days a week from noon to 4:00 A.M. and rarely took a day off. He was also spending freely to ensure that the Stork had the best amenities. Seven thousand dollars a year for flowers. Twelve thousand dollars a year for lights. Fifteeen hundred dollars a week for his two orchestras. His two hundred employees earned more than union wages, which was the only way he could keep the unions at bay. And each year he got stuck with about $15,000 in bad checks.

Maybe the Stork Club was just a glorified café, but it was a *society* café. Encouraged by the media-savvy Hannagan, Billingsley worked that angle. He engaged the band of Haywood Powers, who was in the *Social Register,* and socialite-singer Gay Adams. It sure wasn't for her voice, Billingsley said, but she did draw her blueblood friends. He also consid-

THE STORK CLUB'S MOST FAMOUS ICON

ETHEL MERMAN AND IRVING BERLIN

ered Powers's music undanceable, but Powers, too, attracted a tony crowd. To further promote his beau monde image, he hired socialite Marion Cooley of Philadelphia, whose grandfather had developed the silk thread paper for American banknotes. She helped decide who was to be seated where, according to social standing.

Billingsley continued to court the columnists and soon had a powerful new friend in Dorothy Kilgallen, the hard-driving newswoman who had taken over the *Journal-American*'s "Voice of Broadway" column, thus becoming the first female rival to Winchell.

Among the stars discovering the Stork Club was Ethel Merman, who had opened on Broadway in 1936 with Bob Hope in the Cole Porter musical *Red, Hot and Blue!*, which introduced the hit "It's De-Lovely." After the show she often showed up with the cast for a late-night champagne dinner.

With her inimitable swagger and brassy bellow — she sounded like a band going by, said Cole Porter — Merman, born Ethel Zimmerman in Astoria, Queens, had transformed the musical stage. In 1930 she had burst onto Broadway in *Girl Crazy*, which introduced audiences to such Gershwin brothers' classics as "Bidin' My Time," "Embraceable You," "But Not for Me," and, most memorably, "I Got Rhythm," which invariably stopped the show.

The following year she returned with Rudy Vallee and Ray Bolger in *George White's Scandals* and then in 1934 — the year her romance with publishing scion Walter Annenberg broke up — starred in *Anything Goes,* popularizing a cornucopia of Cole Porter's greatest hits, including "I Get a Kick Out of You," "You're the Top," "Anything Goes," and "Blow, Gabriel, Blow."

And then she met Billingsley.

It was a glamorous and passionate pairing — the queen of Broadway and the king of clubs. "Billingsley liked me from our first meeting," she later recalled. "I liked him and the Stork Club. Why wouldn't I? I was treated like royalty." He was, she said, "spectacularly generous" with her. A chilled bottle of champagne from the Stork Club was always waiting in her dressing room after the show.

Hoover and Tolson were immediate fans of Merman and showed up for the premiere of her *Red, Hot and Blue!* Hoover enthusiastically plugged the show to a *New York Post* critic — which may have guaranteed its miserable reception.

Despite his affair with Merman, Billingsley remained intensely possessive of Hazel, herself still a head-turner, and he grew furious if he caught other men stealing glances at her. He doted on Jacqueline, too, who was beginning to develop her mother's lovely looks. She had come home from school one day in tears, saying a classmate had called her father a bootlegger. He comforted her. "Ask your friend," he said, "'What side of the bar was *your* father on?'"

A BALLOON PARTY AT THE STORK

Billingsley's shrewd promotionalism was imbuing the Stork Club with an aura of high society and glamour. Little perhaps was so mesmerizing to a glamour-starved nation as the sight of pampered debs at their banquettes using their personal gold swizzle sticks to stir the bubbles out of their expensive champagne.

The public also chuckled over Billingsley's giveaway nights, when balloons containing prizes were suddenly let loose from the main-room ceiling to be popped by frenzied patrons (and sometimes hatpin-wielding staff members as well) in frenetic competition for hundred-dollar bills and other treasures.

One spring night in 1938 sixteen-year-old Brenda Diana Duff Frazier, a society heiress with a doll-like wide-eyed gaze, blue-black hair, pale skin, and a thin-lipped mouth slashed with shocking red lipstick, arrived at the Stork in black silk and pearls on the arm of a Yale undergraduate. Pictures of Brenda taken by Stork photographer Chic Farmer soon began popping up in New York's fourteen daily newspapers and the Brenda Frazier–Stork Club link was established, although few could say exactly what made her unique.

She was at the club on a balloon night in 1940 when Tallulah Bankhead captured one of the coveted C-notes. Cattily, Tallulah offered it to Brenda, saying, "Here, I thought you might need this."

Brenda coolly accepted the gift, in the process vengefully catching the eye of Tallulah's date, John "Shipwreck" Kelly, a ruggedly handsome former football star and café society bon vivant whose nickname had begun as "Wrecker" in his gridiron days and had been modified after he worked one summer on a steamship. It wasn't long before Shipwreck asked Brenda out. Their date blossomed into a courtship during which they appeared at the Stork Club for twenty-three consecutive nights. In June 1941 they married.

Shipwreck was Billingsley's kind of man — dashing, sporty, and social. Since Kelly didn't have a lot of money, Billingsley was ready to stake him so he could woo Brenda properly, fully aware that their romance would create a publicity bonanza for the Stork Club. And when the couple had a daughter, Billingsley sent pearls — for the baby.

Though Tallulah lost a beau, she had plenty of others, and she and Billingsley remained friends. From her room at the Gotham Hotel a few blocks away across Fifth Avenue, she phoned the Stork one night for an order of sandwiches. Billingsley mischievously decided to deliver them himself and took along Shipwreck and writer Irving Hoffman.

They found Tallulah in bed, nude. She gazed at them coolly and said, "I've been figuring out which one of you I want to stay here with me, and Sherman, it's *you!*" Billingsley broke for the door and made it into the elevator before realizing he was alone. But Yetta, for one, didn't buy the story. "He wouldn't run from sex with a three-legged porker," she insisted.

But Billingsley had a puritanical side. He was sickened by mothers who all but thrust their daughters into the arms of wealthy and prominent men, married or not. He had seen girls marry their sisters' boyfriends. He had seen mothers steal their daughters' boyfriends. He knew a married man who had gotten a girl pregnant and paid another man to marry her. He knew a man who had seduced and married his brother's wife, and he knew a man who had slept with his daughter-in-law. And these, he reflected, were all *high-society folks.*

One night Billingsley discovered the madam Polly Adler sitting with a man in the Stork Club. Repulsed, he ordered them to leave, but they refused. Never one for subtlety, he had waiters remove the table in front of them, leaving them sitting exposed in the middle of the room until they fled.

His scruples notwithstanding, Billingsley sometimes let himself be drawn into sordid domestic dramas. A mother begged him for help in snuffing out her daughter's affair with a girlfriend who the mother was sure was only after their riches. He talked with both girls, urging them to end their romance, but they cried and proclaimed their mutual love. What could he do? He told the mother that he would never get in the middle of anything like that again.

He had an even closer encounter with a husky detective who came in one night a little high. The dick came over to Billingsley's table and bent over to whisper something but instead bit Billingsley on the ear. Stunned, Billingsley burst out laughing, sending the humiliated detective fleeing.

A few days later he came in again and sat down at Billingsley's table with a confession. "Here I am, out putting people in jail every day, and I am more queer than any of them." For once, Billingsley was speechless. He never saw the man again.

One night a doddering old man appeared at the Stork Club door. He looked a little intoxicated, and the doorman barred the way. "I'm Sherman's friend," the old man announced. "We went to school together down in Oklahoma." The doorman laughed; the old guy had to be ninety. Still, he was insistent, and Billingsley was summoned.

The old man stuck out a bony hand. "Howdy," he said, "I'm Emmett Dalton." Sherman stared, dumbfounded. Shortly before the Billingsley clan arrived in Oklahoma, a Santa Fe passenger train steaming south through the Cherokee Strip had been halted by a swinging red lantern. As the engineer brought the train to a stop, two bandits leapt aboard, sending

the engine and cash-carrying express car down the track to cronies, including the three notorious Dalton boys, Bob, Grat, and Emmett. Four months
later the gang was all but wiped out in a botched two-bank robbery in Cof-
feyville, Kansas. Of the Daltons, Emmett alone survived, though so badly
wounded he was easily captured. Now, here he was at the Stork Club.

TWENTY-TWO

IN THE SUMMER OF 1937 Billingsley was once again on a collision course with his staff. Rumors flew through the Stork Club that Billingsley had hired a new crew from out of town and would soon be cleaning house. Thirteen waiters rushed to join the New York City Hotel Employees and Restaurant Employees International Union, affiliated with the American Federation of Labor. That September Billingsley fired them, claiming later that they were "incompetent, insolent, unruly and dishonest"; drank with customers and stole drinks; confused checks; cleaned their nails in the dining room; and had "garlic breath."

Billingsley hadn't built his bootleg booze empire and battled Prohibition agents and Black Hand gangs to be told how to conduct business in his own club. He had also never forgotten the threats of Schultz and his goons. Now Schultz was dead and Jimmy Hines was in jail, but their reign of terror over the food and drink industry continued.

Schultz and one of his beer collectors, Big Julie Martin, had organized the corrupt waiters union, Local 16, and the Metropolitan Restaurant and Cafeteria Association, nothing more than a multimillion-dollar shakedown racket, despite its grandiose name. You either joined it and put up its sticker in the window, or faced stink bombs, labor trouble, vandalism, or worse.

Legitimate union organizers didn't stand a chance. Benny Gottesman, the frail and bespectacled secretary of Local 1 of the waiters union, had been trying to organize the Elkwood Restaurant on Broadway and Eighty-first Street when Big Julie appeared. Julie was "protecting" the Elkwood and demanded that Gottesman call off his pickets. Gottesman refused, explaining that he was the official representative of two thousand members.

"Schultz will send his machine guns down," Big Julie threatened, "and you'll see what they can do."

At that, Gottesman buckled, but Big Julie promised, "I'll do for your union the same as I'm doing for Local Sixteen. You'll get protection, and I'll take care of everything." In fact, he elaborated, "If you have twenty-five or fifty members who are squawkers, I'll take care of them. I won't kill them, but I have a way."

Max Gottfried, the president of Local 1, had also heard from Big Julie with demands to withdraw the pickets from the Elkwood.

"Who are you?" Gottfried asked.

"Never mind," Big Julie told him. The place, he said, belonged to Local 16.

Gottfried was unswayed. "What business is it of yours?"

Big Julie was incredulous. "You don't know who you are talking to?" He threw Jimmy Hines's card on the table. "Call him up and see." When Gottfried hesitated, he added: "The Dutchman is behind us."

When Gottfried still didn't seem suitably impressed, Julie stuck a gun in his ribs. "Either you take off the picket line, or off you are."

Gottfried got the point.

Leo Lindemann, owner of the famous Lindy's that Runyon had called "Mindy's" in his Broadway fables, had also come under the gun in 1933. He and other restaurateurs had been discussing ways to defeat Schultz's goons when a stink bomb went off in his establishment. That was persuasive.

Lindemann then visited the union offices at Eighth Avenue and Forty-sixth Street, where he asked Paul N. Coulcher, secretary and strong-arm man of Local 16, for help in running Lindy's. How, he asked innocently, could he get rid of waiters who were no good?

Coulcher said he would leave the amount up to Lindemann.

Lindemann suggested $150 a month, which Coulcher said sounded fine, and Lindemann had his protection. Then, when another Broadway restaurateur, Louis I. Brooks of Jack Dempsey's, went after Lindemann for an unpaid debt, Brooks got a visit from Big Julie. "You leave Lindy alone."

Spiros C. Pappas, who owned a bar and grill on East Twenty-third Street, balked at signing with the cafeteria workers union. When he fired a union bartender he caught stealing, he was ordered to take him back.

Pappas refused.

Two days later his kitchen caught fire.

Pappas closed his restaurant.

Billingsley read with interest but little surprise these revelations from the state supreme court in the 1936 extortion trial of seven men and the Metropolitan Restaurant and Cafeteria Association. Dewey, still being hailed for his prostitution conviction of Lucky Luciano and his war on loan-sharking gangs, was spearheading the attack on the Schultz gang. (Schultz himself, executed in the Newark chop house, had already been definitively convicted by a higher court of no appeal.)

Earlier, Dewey's grand jury had indicted thirteen union leaders and the restaurant association on charges of running a two-million-dollar-a-year extortion racket. One of the union defendants, Max Pincus, who had pressured bar owner Pappas, was also accused of embezzling union funds. With the trial about to start, a porter in Pincus's building in the Bronx walked into the courtyard and saw Pincus hanging by his fingertips from a windowsill between the fifth and sixth floors. He called out, but at that moment Pincus dropped, plunging to his death.

Violent death had also claimed Schultz and Big Julie Martin, along with two more of the thirteen defendants. And the day the trial opened in January 1937, another of them pleaded guilty, agreeing to testify against his cronies. That left seven.

The jury took only three and a half hours — including two hours for a meal — to convict all seven. Dewey praised the verdict. "For the first time a complete industrial racket has been presented to a jury and the verdict has established that racketeering can be crushed. This conviction should free two large labor unions, which have a great opportunity for service to the workers, from the grasp of racketeering officials." Dewey was hailed as a giant-killer. Since targeting the city's major racketeers, he had brought fifty-eight to trial and convicted all fifty-eight.

Judgment on April 7 was swift and harsh, with sentences of up to twenty years.

Emboldened by the outcome, Billingsley soon fired the waiters, who appealed to the New York State Labor Relations Board, claiming retaliation for union organizing.

The panel held hearings for nearly six months, until March 1938, and then took until November to hand down its decision: Billingsley had illegally dismissed the staff. He owned the nine back pay minus whatever any of them may have earned in replacement jobs. He was to cease interfering with their right to organize, disband his company union, maintain no worker blacklist, and post the board's order for all to see.

Billingsley appealed, but a judge upheld the labor relations board. Billingsley owed the workers about $20,000. Outraged, he appealed to a higher court. In May 1939 the appellate division reversed the lower court: Billingsley was within his rights to have fired the workers.

Now the union appealed.

In desperation Billingsley's lawyer, George Vanderveer, who had defended him in Seattle, contacted Dave Beck of the Teamsters Union. Beck of was no help, however, for he himself was destined for prison.

In March 1940 the state's court of appeals, in its first decision reviewing the deliberations of the labor relations board, reversed the appellate division, ruling that the board had reasonable grounds for its decision against the Stork Club and therefore must be upheld. Billingsley had to take the nine back. By now their back pay had risen to more than $57,000. Tired of fighting, both sides settled on a quiet compromise: Billingsley would take some of the waiters back, but he could discreetly weed them out in time.

While Billingsley had been enmeshed in court in September 1939, one of his unbeloved ex-partners, Frenchy De Mange, succumbed quietly to a heart attack in his room at Manhattan's Warwick Hotel. The fifty-five-year-old former Hudson Duster, master safecracker, kidnap victim, and nightclub angel had been living quietly on a sizable estate in Florida and in Hot Springs, Arkansas (where his partner Madden had also found peace) in between occasional trips to his old Broadway haunts.

The funeral was announced for four days afterward, but for secrecy's sake his friends gathered a day earlier at the John Simons Funeral Home on West Thirty-fourth Street, not far from Madden's old Phoenix brewery on Tenth Avenue. Madden was there, in black, as were a weeping woman and children pointed out as Frenchy's widow and offspring, although Billingsley was surprised to find he had a family. The large metal casket was mahogany-colored, and the hearse was followed by six automobiles with floral offerings, one, more extravagant than the rest, tied with a ribbon and bearing the legend: "You helped everybody; God will help you." The donor cards were faced in, concealing the names. Behind the flowers, twenty-five cars escorted Frenchy to his final resting place in Woodlawn Cemetery in the Bronx.

TWENTY-THREE

THERE WAS NO UNION PROBLEM between Billingsley and Merman. They rendezvoused regularly, carrying on their passionate version of "I Get a Kick Out of You." Yetta noticed that they sometimes both came back with bruises. Once, Merman came into the club rubbing her rump and glowering. As the story circulated among the Stork's staff with titters and guffaws, the lovers had been in Billingsley's car when one of them dropped a lit cigarette onto the seat. Merman, not seeing it, had sat on it with her bare butt.

Merman became a vampish presence at the Stork. Sometimes upon passing Albino, the doorman, she would flip up her skirt, revealing nothing on underneath. Albino found the gesture crude. He would have preferred a tip of more tangible currency. "I can't put food on the table with *that*," he scoffed.

Hoover and Tolson also remained fervent Merman fans. On one of her opening nights they sent her a telegram: "Sincere good wishes to you and your new show. We're sorry we can't be in the front row to hiss — no kiss you. Tenderest regards. John Edgar Hoover. Clyde Tolson." That had to have been from Clyde, Merman decided; he was the one with the sense of humor. John was quiet and withdrawn.

Shortly after the opening of the 1939–40 World's Fair in New York, Billingsley took Merman, Hoover, and Tolson to dinner at the Italian Pavilion. Afterward they walked the fairgrounds of Flushing Meadow Park. At an arcade shooting gallery, Hoover and Tolson hoisted rifles and expertly picked off the rabbits and ducks.

Somehow Merman had gotten the idea that Billingsley and Hazel were estranged. Moss Hart's former flame Paula Lawrence, who inspired Kurt Weill's *One Touch of Venus* and who played opposite Merman in *Something for the Boys,* broke the truth to Merman one night at the Stork Club. Hazel was not away in the Midwest somewhere but in New York and was actually the owner of record of the club.

"I wish you hadn't told me that sitting here," Merman said. "You mean I'm eating *her* food?"

Billingsley spent lavishly on Merman. Among the staff it was whispered that Billingsley had bought Merman a yacht, which they berthed at the Seventy-ninth Street boat basin on the Hudson River and used for their assignations. Gregory was shanghaied into service as their cook. It was distasteful duty for the straitlaced family man, mortified to be an accessory to another's tawdry infidelities, but Gregory served uncomplainingly. During the Boston tryouts of her 1939 show *Stars in Your Eyes* with Jimmy Durante, Sherman sent a catered supper to the entire cast. He also gave Merman a dazzling diamond-and-ruby bracelet spelling out FROM SHERM TO MERM.

Winchell heard about the extravagant present and waspishly dropped a reference into his column linking his pal to "a prominent musical comedy star." Billingsley was furious, but there was little he could do. He and Winchell had their ups and downs but were bound together. "Sherman and I know too much about each other," Winchell said, by which he clearly meant women and perhaps a speakeasy Winchell owned in Harlem.

If Hazel was aware of the relationship, she didn't let on, certainly not to her daughters. But Barbara noticed. Once Merman gave her a stuffed toy, which she excitedly took home. When she told her mother where it came from, Hazel burst into tears. Visiting her father one night at the club, she noticed Merman's hand brazenly on his knee. Barbara kissed her father good night while reaching down and removing the offending hand, digging her fingernails deep into Merman's knuckles for emphasis.

In fact, the stormy romance was entering its terminal phase. At the club one day Merman pitched a vase through the glass of Billingsley's upstairs suite. By the end of 1940 she had thrown herself into the first of a string of marriages, beginning with a Hollywood actor's agent named Bill Smith. She informed Billingsley of her nuptials cursorily, in a telephone message left with Yetta.

Sherm and Merm, as Winchell might say, were *pppfffttt*. Years later Merman discreetly acknowledged the romance, adding sourly: "I'll only note it was one of those times when I'd have been better off if I had listened to my mother when she said, 'Ethel, are you sure you know what you are doing?'"

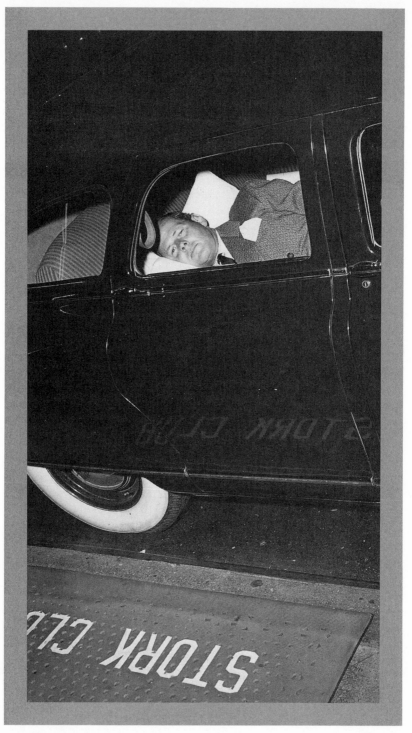

THE STORK CLUB'S PROPRIETOR CATCHES UP ON HIS REST.

STORK
CLUB
TWILIGHT

TWENTY-FOUR

FADING DIVA MARGO CHANNING commandeered a Cub Room table graced with a gift box of Sortilege and looked around. Millions gazed around with her. By staging a dramatic scene in his 1950 masterpiece *All About Eve* at the Stork Club, movie director Joseph Mankiewicz paid tribute to the iconic hold Billingsley's midnight oasis had on America's sophisticates. But in the biting script and the mocking delivery by a sardonic Bette Davis, there lurked an ambiguous message: "Isn't this a lovely room? What a clever name. Where the elite meet."

The Stork Club may have reached its pinnacle, but if so, there was only one way it could go.

In the summer of 1950 Billingsley got his own *Stork Club* show on the embryonic medium of television. Just weeks before, he had been discussing television with Winchell in the club. Winchell was intrigued by its possibilities, but Billingsley persuaded him to stick to his column and radio. Adding a television show, he argued, might be spreading himself too thin. Had Billingsley known more about the curious new medium, he might have said that Winchell was hot while television demanded cool. Winchell delayed his debut, but Billingsley would have done well to take his own advice and stick to what he knew best. What seemed at first like an extraordinary stroke of good fortune soon underscored how the Stork Club and America were on divergent paths.

Early television had few established formulas to fall back on, but even so, Billingsley, though affable enough, proved to be an awkward on-air host. He could barely smile without a cue card. As his upstate neighbor and longtime Stork habitué Tallulah Bankhead was to write later, "*The Stork Club Show* developed out of the Stork Club itself as naturally as indigestion out of Brussels sprouts."

The idea of a Stork-based television show was borrowed from the 1949 *Dinner at Sardi's* on WOR-TV Channel 9 in New York. That program, in turn, was an expansion of a Sardi's celebrity interview radio show, produced in the forties by a onetime CBS radio prodigy named Gary Stevens. Hired at fifteen as a prolific celebrity profiler, Stevens was taken on his first visit to the Stork Club. Later he advanced his career by contributing items to Winchell, like one about "the producer who offered a starlet a scotch and sofa — she reclined."

In the Cub Room one night Billingsley pitched some CBS executives the concept of a Stork Club show, which would give people around the country a privileged glimpse of the celebrity life. He had commissioned some market research, he explained, that found the Stork Club to be New York's best-known nightclub. The runner up, "21," was mentioned by only half as many respondents as knew of the Stork, and more than twice as many people interviewed said they would like to visit the Stork Club. But entertainment was named the most popular reason for visiting nightclubs — seeing celebrities ranked low. As for watching a nightclub program on television, the results were also not encouraging: a substantial majority was simply not interested. Those who were, again preferred seeing entertainment; the idea of interviews with celebrity guests left them indifferent. Still, Billingsley pressed his case. Arthur Godfrey, Billingsley's partner in the perfume business with Morton Downey as well as a CBS star, also lobbied CBS president William Paley for a Stork Club show. Sardi's was piker stuff, Billingsley argued. The Stork Club was big-time.

Stevens was surprised one day when CBS producer Irving Mansfield, the husband of not-yet-bestselling novelist Jacqueline Susann, dropped in at Sardi's to look around. Mansfield, the quintessential man about town, was said to spend a thousand dollars a year just to check his hat. Mansfield obviously thought the format was worth copying. The next thing Stevens knew, the Stork Club show was on the air, premiering as a fifteen-minute feature Monday, Wednesday, and Friday nights at 7:45. Stevens was later brought in to help, and at $600 a week, how could he turn it down? To assist with scripts, CBS hired comedian Abe Burrows, who had just written the book for Broadway's *Guys and Dolls* and whose talent for devising comic sequences came in more than handy for the show's programming.

CBS spent $100,000 to build a mock Cub Room on the fourth floor of the Stork Club, planting microphones in the wine baskets and flower bowls — this bugging, at least, was done openly — and covering the tables with chartreuse tablecloths, which televised white. The network also gave Billingsley several thousand a week in licensing fees. It was an astonishingly good deal for Sherman, who essentially got paid for allowing CBS to air the world's longest commercial for his club.

*　　*　　*

The Stork Club show opened to the tinkly piano strains of "Autumn in New York" and a shot of three champagne glasses poised on a tablecloth stenciled with the Stork logo. An orchid was then placed between the glasses, champagne was poured (and occasionally spilled — it was all live), and a pack of Fatima cigarettes was set down, as a lady's bejeweled hand selected a cigarette. A voice intoned: "Fatima, best of all king-size cigarettes, takes you to the world's most famous nightclub, the Stork Club. Anyone you ever heard about, read about, or dreamed about at some time or other comes to the Stork Club." Then, as a second camera panned the room, there was Billingsley, introduced as "the world's most fabulous host," chatting stiffly with one or another of his guests. If he appeared more hirsute than usual, it was thanks to a toupee that Gregory was entrusted with carefully combing. Billingsley also liked to have doorman Albino Garlasco hovering somewhere in the background, for his booming laugh. But after fifteen years of blasting his whistle and scuffling with interlopers, Albino was about to retire, taking as a treasured souvenir from a soon-to-be remodeled canopy the glass marbles spelling out the words S*T*O*R*K C*L*U*B.

Nobody, it seemed, knew quite how to act yet in the strange and intimidating glare of the cameras, which Billingsley insisted be operated by technicians formally attired in dinner jackets. Guests froze. Billingsley froze. Sometimes he forgot the names of people he was talking to. He had a long conversation on camera with an uncomfortable and anonymous actress who plainly wished Billingsley would introduce her to his audience.

During one Fatima commercial, he took a drag and choked. The camera stayed on him mercilessly as he grabbed for a glass of water.

One night his guest was Prince Ali Khan, who mentioned that he had a daughter named Fatima. Billingsley took that as a cue to pull out a carton of Fatimas and offer it to the prince, along with a promotional ashtray marked, even more tastelessly, "For Fatima Ashes Only."

"Well, now," Billingsley said, "you certainly will enjoy these Fatimas."

"Oh, no, I won't," Khan rejoined. "I happen to prefer Camels."

On another occasion Billingsley was interviewing a guest when he noticed a cigarette burning a hole in a nearby banquette. He jumped up, smothered the fire, and returned to his seat, not noticing that a diligent waiter had removed the empty chair. He fell down with a crash, injuring his back.

Celeste Holm, who costarred in *All About Eve,* had opened that fall at the Royale Theatre in the Broadway comedy *Affairs of State.* Gushing over her during one program, Billingsley said, "You light up the room, Celeste. I want tickets to opening night."

"Well, actually, Sherman . . ."

SHERMAN PREPARES FOR THE *STORK CLUB*
TELEVISION PROGRAM.

"No, no, Celeste," he insisted. "I want to be there opening night."

"We're doing very well . . . the critics . . ."

"I want tickets for opening night," Billingsley stubbornly repeated.

"Well," Holm finally said, realizing the situation was hopeless, "if you insist, I will go down on my hands and knees under the seats and try to find you tickets from opening night. We opened eleven days ago."

His gaffes could be painful. "By the way, Admiral," he asked Admiral Bull Halsey, "what year did you graduate from West Point?"

Flailing around for a topic, he stunned an English actress by blurting, "How old are you?"

"Uh, twenty-fivish," she managed to mumble.

Billingsley couldn't help snorting in derision. "Twenty-fivish? You'll never see thirty again."

One night he sat down at the table of Winston Churchill's daughter Sarah as she nibbled a stalk of celery.

"What are you doing?" he asked.

"Eating celery."

Billingsley pondered that. "And what else do you do for a living?"

The critics snickered, but he was undeterred. He had newspaperman Bill Slocum prompt him with large cue cards or notes concealed in the table flowers and coffee cups.

One night an incredulous Gloria Swanson turned to Billingsley and asked, "Sherman, why are you doing this show? You are such a great club host. But you're so awful at this."

Stricken, he tried to shrug off the remark. "Oh, Gloria, you're always kidding."

"No, Sherman," she said intently, "I'm *not* kidding."

Disaster had a way of finding him. One night the script had alotted three minutes for an interview with Bette Davis. He opened by asking her, "Bette, what is the difference between television, radio, and stage?"

She stared at him with her large, unblinking eyes. "There's absolutely no comparison."

That left two minutes and forty-five seconds to kill.

Sometimes guest entertainers tried a shortcut by lip-synching songs to records, a practice that lasted until Les Paul and Mary Ford appeared to sing "Tiger Rag." In the middle of their performance the record began to skip, and they suddenly found themselves miming to "Hold that tiger . . . Hold that tiger!" while off camera the music boomed, "Here, kitty, kitty, kitty . . ."

Humiliations abounded. When a hero of both world wars, General Clarence R. Huebner, visited with his wife, Florence, Billingsley sent over a tin of caviar, champagne, a bottle of Sortilege, and red Stork Club suspenders.

Mrs. Huebner was all atwitter. "Oh, Mr. Billingsley . . ."

"You don't have to call me Mr. Billingsley," the gracious Sherman assured her.

"Oh, then," she said sweetly, "may I call you . . . Herman?"

In the control room, Gary Stevens buried his head in his hands.

Winchell wouldn't let the gaffe drop, and for days thereafter his column harped on a certain "herman," lowercased, as if the S had been accidentally dropped.

Upon signing on as a sponsor, a Chesterfield executive called the FBI to voice concern "that Billingsley will in due time let undesirable characters get on the TV show." A Hoover deputy, Louis Nichols, assured him that the bureau would not hold Liggett & Myers, the company that owned the brand, or executive vice president Ben Few responsible for anything Billingsley might do on the air.

Milton Berle on his TV show offered up a savage parody of Billingsley as host, after which Berle, once again, was banned.

Billingsley bravely plowed on. "It's wonderful," he later told *Daily News* columnist Ben Gross. "Everywhere I go now, people recognize me. But get this clear, Ben, I've never pretended to be one of those slick professional emcees."

*   *   *

CBS had assigned a tall and slim twenty-one-year-old redhead from Texas, Sally Dawson, to the production team of *The Stork Club show*. By an odd coincidence, her cleaning lady, Nellie Cliff, had been Winchell's first dance partner and lover in vaudeville in 1914. By the show's second season in 1951, Sally left the network to join Billingsley as his technical adviser.

To add some needed professionalism, CBS also hired actor Yul Brynner as the show's director. Brynner was adept at jumping in to ad-lib when Billingsley's guests became tongue-tied. But one night he announced, "Wish me luck, kids, I'm going to audition for *The King and I*" — and he was gone.

As on-air talent Billingsley employed the musical comedy team of Peter Lind Hayes and his vivacious wife, Mary Healy, who had long been treasured patrons of the Stork Club. The boyishly crew-cut Peter, who had meanwhile been instrumental in launching the career of a tenor named Mario Lanza, was as facile and limber as Billingsley was leaden and self-conscious. He liked to call Billingsley "cowpoke," a term that unaccountably baffled the Oklahoman until he looked it up and decided he liked the description.

SHERMAN, MARY HEALY, AND PETER LIND
HAYES RELAX AFTER A TELEVISION TAPING.

JACKIE, BARBARA, AND SHERMANE BILLINGSLEY

SHERMANE ENTERTAINS JACK WEBB

Other Billingsleys were getting into the act, too. Jacqueline, by now an aspiring actress, made appearances on the show when she had time. Her younger sister Barbara, however, shied away from the camera after a girlfriend told her it added pounds to her figure, and Hazel had no interest at all in taking part in the show. Shermane, by now a chubby-cheeked tot in corkscrew curls, cavorted easily before the camera, as she was young enough to take the new medium for granted. She was clever, too. When Johnny Weismuller was supposed to present her with a rabbit but suddenly went blank, Shermane had the presence to feed herself her own line, sending the audience into convulsions: "You know, my father once gave me two rabbits, and in a short time I had two hundred!"

Shermane also gave away puppies on the air. She presented one to a child who wanted a dog and had written in to say, "My mommy says that with five kids around the house, all we need is a dog and I want to make her happy."

Priceless unscripted moments like these endeared *The Stork Club* to its audience, whatever the carping critics wrote. But the fifties were witnessing new social pressures that took Billingsley and the rest of America by surprise.

TWENTY-FIVE

THE STORK DISCRIMINATES AGAINST EVERYBODY," Winchell once said. "White, black, and pink. It's a snob joint. The Stork bars all kinds of people for all kinds of reasons. But if your skin is green and you're rich and famous or you're syndicated, you'll be welcomed at the club."

That assessment was not entirely accurate. Billingsley did favor a homogeneous look and type, his client of choice being young and good-looking, famous, influential, successful, rich, well born, and preferably WASP. Plenty of Jews frequented the club, to be sure: Winchell, of course, Leonard Lyons, Billingsley's lawyer Monroe Goldwater, Al Jolson, Bert Lahr (né Lahrheim), and many of Hollywood's leading moguls. Irving Berlin was a regular in the Cub Room and it was there one night in the summer of 1951 that President Truman called to thank him for his graciousness to First Daughter Margaret, who had just sung a recital of Berlin's songs at Carnegie Hall.

Black and dark-skinned Latin celebrities were admitted to the Stork Club, too, but hardly as hospitably as whites. Other black customers might gain entry if they were accompanied by a club favorite, like artist and Hollywood columnist Irving Hoffman, who sometimes brought in black friends. Duke Ellington and singers Lena Horne and Thelma Carpenter got in, although a rumor circulated widely that Horne and George Jessel had been rebuffed one day at the door. As the story went, the pair had been asked frostily who had made their reservation, and Jessel had responded, with impeccable timing, "Abraham Lincoln." (Years later Horne confirmed that the incident had occurred — but not at the Stork Club. It happened at "21.")

But there was no question that blacks, if alone or obscure, were often turned away or shuttled into the large and empty Blessed Events Room, usually reserved for private parties.

The Stork Club was hardly unique in its discrimination. Although New York was certainly the most progressive, liberal, and heterogeneous metropolis in America, the entire society remained color- and caste-divided.

Around the country, top hotels, country clubs, restaurants, private schools and colleges, sports teams, and better jobs were still reserved for white Gentiles. The military had been racially segregated all through the war, and Jim Crow still ruled the South.

One notable exception to the restrictive policies, however, was Café Society. Opened in 1938 in basement quarters on Greenwich Village's Sheridan Square, with an uptown annex appearing two years later on Fifty-eighth Street near Park Avenue, the cabaret gained renown as a kind of *un*–Stork Club, a sendup that twitted the pretensions and prejudices of its more self-important prototype.

The creation of Barney Josephson, a former shoe salesman committed to racial and social equality, Café Society clad its waiters in tails while guests came in wearing attire as casual as rumpled sweaters. Having admired the shockingly exuberant cabarets of prewar Europe, Josephson sought to re-create the phenomenon in Manhattan, complete with political satire and jazz. He made a point of welcoming the unions, signing a pioneering entertainment contract with the American Guild of Variety Artists (an agreement that did not spare him from being picketed by the stagehands when he refused to hire an electrician to change a lightbulb). With its cheery slogan — "The Wrong Place for the Right People" — and its ingenious name, the club soon attracted bohemians and intellectuals, New Dealers, WPA-ers, and artists. It also made a point of courting black patronage and engaged black musicians, including Billie Holiday, who stirred patrons with her piercing anti-lynching lament "Strange Fruit."

Unsurprisingly, Café Society attracted the watchful eye of the FBI. Indeed, the money to start the club may have come from the Communist Party. Josephson's brother, roommate, and business partner Leon was a leading American Communist in the twenties and thirties, and Barney himself acknowledged membership for a brief time in 1937. Hoover, who regarded the brothers as a security threat, placed them and their club under surveillance, and by 1949 Josephson was hounded out of business. But if nothing else, Café Society demonstrated that a powerful social revolution was beginning to take form.

If the stirrings of the organized civil rights movement were still several years off, times clearly were changing. It was Billingsley's unhappy fate to trigger an explosive racial case that not only would roil the city but would forever taint the Stork Club, hastening its demise.

Exactly what happened that night was never clear. But the aftermath was unforgettable.

On Tuesday evening, October 16, 1951, Broadway star Roger Rico and his wife, Solange, arranged a late after-show dinner at the Stork Club.

THE BAR AREA

JOSEPHINE BAKER

Rico, a bass at the Paris Opéra, had replaced the Metropolitan Opera star Ezio Pinza in the long-running *South Pacific*. Rico had been well cast as the French planter; he himself was the son of wealthy plantation owners from Algeria and had spent the war fighting the Germans.

As their guest, the Ricos had invited Josephine Baker, the sleek and sensuous dancer, singer, and ecdysiast extraordinaire, then forty-five, who had become an early black sex symbol of the mass entertainment era. Rico had known Baker since her days on the Paris stage and had served with her during the war in Algeria, where she had played a fittingly dramatic role, undertaking spy missions for the resistance.

Baker was born in St. Louis in 1906, overcoming a bitter slum childhood to become the toast of Paris and the Continent, then America and the world. Tempestuous and whimsical, the incandescent entertainer with the mocha skin and penchant for exuberant nudity had accumulated countless lovers of both sexes while indulging her extravagant tastes, which included letting white mice scamper over her body under her robe, and lining the interior of her automobile in snakeskin.

Baker's companion that night at the Stork was Bessie Allison Buchanan, a light-skinned black performer with a notable stage career of her own. At sixteen, she had performed at Owney Madden's Cotton Club, going on to appear in the legendary Jazz Age Negro musical *Shuffle Along* on Broadway in 1921 and in *Show Boat* in 1927. She and Baker had become lovers, a common practice among lonely and often male-abused chorines. Bessie, who sometimes passed for white, was dancing at the famed Savoy Ballroom in Harlem when she caught the eye of its West Indian owner, Charles Buchanan, and in 1929 quit the stage to marry him. (Buchanan would later finance his wife's political ambitions, bankrolling her 1954 election to the New York Assembly as the first black woman in the state legislature.)

Rico, who had often visited the Stork Club, clearly had some forebodings about bringing Baker there, and asked several people at the theater if they thought it would be all right. They all ridiculed the question. This was 1951; she was a world-renowned star, currently headlining at the Roxy. Of course he could take her to the Stork Club.

But Bessie Buchanan may have had a deeper agenda for their visit, and as her husband, Charles, acknowledged later, "Bessie plotted everything." Singer Thelma Carpenter also said she had warned Baker in her dressing room at the Roxy that Bessie was out to provoke an incident at the Stork Club. Carpenter had been invited to come along but, fearing trouble, begged off.

Maude Russell, another dancer in *Shuffle Along,* also later viewed Buchanan as the instigator who told Baker, "You're a big French star. Go on in the Stork Club and break the barrier."

Josephine, radiant in a blue satin Dior gown with her hair trailing in an elegant ponytail, arrived at the Stork Club with Bessie and the Ricos about midnight. Gregory was on the door, recognized Baker, confirmed Rico's reservation, and led them to the Cub Room.

They passed Winchell and *Journal-American* columnist Jack O'Brian and his wife, Yvonne, sitting at table 50, and were seated at a banquette at the far end of the room. Winchell complimented her on her ponytail.

Winchell not only knew Baker but had also been an ardent fan of hers since 1939, when he wrote: "Josephine Baker is really *fabulous* . . . the word was made for her." Championing her in a column after France capitulated to the Nazis, he said, "Josephine Baker, the stemmers hear, is destitute on the French Riviera and isn't permitted to work because she's married to a non-Aryan."

In 1949 he had hailed her return to the Folies-Bergère, and gratefully acknowledged her help in raising $20,000 for the Damon Runyon Cancer Fund that he and Billingsley had created.

As recently as January 1951, nine months before their fateful encounter in the Stork Club, Winchell, bearing roses, had caught her act nightly at the Copa City in Miami Beach, owned by Baker's progressive Jewish manager, Ned Schuyler, who was determined to break down the color barrier. With Schuyler's encouragement, Baker stayed grandly and daringly in his white-occupied Arlington Hotel and insisted that blacks be admitted freely to her shows along with whites, a major breakthrough in segregated Florida. Afterward, Baker cabled Winchell: THANK YOU FOR YOUR WONDERFUL WORDS OF PRAISE *AU REVOIR* FOR A LITTLE WHILE GOOD HEALTH TO YOU AND YOURS.

At the Stork Club, the Ricos, Baker, and Buchanan were served a round of drinks and were given menus. Baker ordered a steak and a bottle of vintage red wine. Her years at the best tables in France had made her an oenophile.

George Amodio, the club's deliveryman who was working as a waiter in the Cub Room that night, later recalled standing by his station and seeing Billingsley walk past the room, look in, and do a double take, demanding, "Who the fuck let her in?" The captains soon passed the word, Amodio said — no service for the Baker table.

Billingsley later denied any snub, maintaining that a waiter had just gone on break, leaving the table unattended. Adding to the delay in service, he explained, was the fact that Baker had ordered a filet mignon, which was not on the menu. The wine she had selected was also hard to locate. Then, too, the club was crowded that night, and many diners had to wait for service.

Still after waiting nearly an hour, the Rico table's order had not yet arrived.

Rico tried to signal waiters, to no avail. Finally taking it as a snub, he began to protest.

Incensed, Baker and Rico headed for the phone booth to call her lawyer, Walter White, executive secretary of the National Association for the Advancement of Colored People, whose number Baker seemed to have handy.

As they passed Winchell's table, Winchell, misinterpreting the scene, turned to O'Brian and said, "That's nice. They are going dancing."

When Baker and Rico returned to the table, menus were hastily offered again. Baker changed her order to sirloin, and the food and wine soon arrived. But by then Baker refused it.

Rico was told that there would be no charge, but he threw money down, and the group stormed out. Winchell and the O'Brians had already departed for a late-night screening of *The Desert Fox* at the Rivoli.

After fleeing the Stork Club, Baker spent the wee hours in frantic activity, speeding to the home of Walter White to complain about her treatment and discuss legal action.

White sent her to WMCA radio host Barry Gray. He was just winding up his show at Chandler's Restaurant near Grand Central a few minutes before 3:00 A.M. when Baker swept in with her account of the night's events. It was too late to go on the air, Gray said, but she could come back.

Although it was near dawn, Baker roused Ned Schuyler's lawyer, Shirley Woolf, at the Park Sheraton Hotel, where they were both staying. Woolf had just returned from Judy Garland's comeback concert at the Palace. When Baker knocked on her door denouncing Winchell, Woolf thought her anger oddly misplaced. Had Winchell even been aware of any snub? Woolf cautioned Baker about picking a fight with the influential columnist. Woolf said she wouldn't patronize a place where her people weren't wanted.

Baker cuttingly responded: "No darling, *your* people would buy the store."

Baker next gathered at the Roxy with her press agent, Curt Weinberg, Buchanan, Schuyler, Woolf, and a second lawyer dispatched by a friend at the French consulate. (Baker was, after all, a French citizen, and any mistreatment of her had the potential of setting off an international incident.) Joining them was Henry Lee Moon, public relations director of the NAACP, and Ted Poston of the *New York Post,* the first black reporter on a major New York daily. He sensed a big story.

Baker announced that she wanted to picket the Stork Club but was worried that she could be sued by Billingsley. Moon called Thurgood Marshall, the NAACP's counsel, who confirmed that she could be sued, but he encouraged her to picket anyway.

Weinberg argued that Winchell had done a lot for Baker and asked why they were directing their fury at him if he didn't even witness the incident.

Moon was unmollified. "It's about time we got after Winchell anyhow, to show him up."

The story broke in the *Post* the following day, October 18, Poston quoting Baker as saying: "I do not intend to take such treatment quietly. If it is necessary to for me to picket the Stork Club to call attention to such racial practices, then I will picket it. I have no intention of suffering deliberate humiliation without striking back."

Billingsley, Poston wrote, could not be reached for comment.

Later in the day, Moon called a surprise press conference in Baker's dressing room at the Roxy to announce that middleweight boxing champ Sugar Ray Robinson would resign from the board of the Damon Runyon Cancer Fund in protest.

Weinberg, who had not been consulted about the conference, warned Baker again about involving Winchell, not to mention the Runyon fund and Sugar Ray. She had to control Moon and the NAACP, Weinberg demanded.

WALTER WINCHELL (AT HEAD OF TABLE) CELEBRATING HIS
FORTY-SIXTH BIRTHDAY, IN 1943

Baker replied that it was none of her affair and insisted she didn't
know Winchell. The only reason she was even aware that Winchell had
been in the club was that the Ricos had told her, she said, adding that she
wouldn't have recognized him. Her argument was ludicrous: Winchell was
not only the most identifiable journalist in America, but he had also spoken
to her many times and paid court to her outside her dressing room at the
Copa City earlier that very year.

Infuriated, Weinberg quit as her press agent.

Baker dropped plans to picket the Stork Club. But stoked by the
Post, the affair was growing into a firestorm.

The next day the NAACP sent a telegram to J. Edgar Hoover asking
him, as head of the FBI and a patron of the Stork Club, to express his disapproval and take action against Billingsley.

Hoover ignored the plea, scribbling under the message, "No answer
required. I don't consider this any of my business." Walter White of the
NAACP, meanwhile, offered Winchell an olive branch, praising his
progressive record on race relations and calling on him to repudiate
Billingsley.

Instead, Winchell explained on his ABC radio program that he had left the Stork Club by the time of the "alleged discourtesy." He did not de-nounce Billingsley. He did, however, quote some of White's flattering statements about himself.

Furious, White cabled ABC's president, Robert E. Kintner, demand-ing airtime for a rebuttal. Baker, too, protested. The incident was bigger than her, she told Poston. "It is a matter that concerns America itself."

Kintner, whose loyalty was to Winchell, immediately sent the colum-nist a copy of White's telegram, assuring him that ABC would not give White airtime. Kintner even showed Winchell a draft of his reply, which Winchell approved.

Winchell was clearly in a bind, but he was not about to capitulate to Baker's tactics. "After 20 years on the air and almost 30 in the newspapers, I thought my record was crystal-clear when minorities are getting kicked around," he wrote. "I am appalled at the agony and embarrassment caused Josephine Baker and her friends at the Stork Club. But I am equally ap-palled at their efforts to involve me in an incident in which I had no part."

Sugar Ray Robinson, meanwhile, had retreated, denying that he had given any thought to quitting the Runyon fund. He was very sorry for what-ever happened to Baker but believed that she was being unfair to Winchell. With that, Robinson discovered a sudden need to leave town for business in Washington.

As tensions rose, someone called in a bomb threat against the Stork Club. Detectives searched the building for an hour and found nothing.

On the evening of October 22, six nights after the incident, the picket-ing of the Stork Club began — sans Baker, who was performing at the Roxy. (Winchell ducked out of the club shortly before the protesters arrived.) Back and forth with signs like FAMOUS NITE SPOT JUST A WHITE SPOT marched Walter White, Bessie Buchanan, Thelma Carpenter, and writer Laura Z. Hobson, who had exposed postwar American anti-Semitism with her novel *Gentleman's Agreement,* made into an Oscar-winning movie with Gregory Peck.

Mayor Vincent Impellitteri, a Stork Club regular, had been on vaca-tion when the affair began. Now, reported Poston, the crisis was about to be dumped into his lap.

Next, Baker took her complaints to President Truman, prompting Poston to report: "The battle over bias at the Stork Club today stretched from E. 53d Street to the White House." A nervous Mayor Impellitteri an-nounced that he was boycotting the Stork Club and would conduct "a vig-orous investigation." The state liquor authority indicated that it was reviewing the Stork Club's liquor license. Not to be outdone, the city council vowed its own sweeping bias inquiry.

The NAACP called on sponsors of the *Stork Club* television show to withdraw their support, and the picket line swelled. The second night's protesters included Duke Ellington's sister, Ruth James, and cast members from *South Pacific* and *Guys and Dolls*.

And in a particularly bad omen for Billingsley, a business agent from the Hotel Employees and Restaurant Employees International Union visited the picketers.

Some patrons, embarrassed to be seen crossing the picket line, stopped their cabs a few doors east and tried to slip into the club quietly. But Billingsley assured his television audience, "We're so crowded that we had to turn away people at lunch."

From his winter quarters at the Roney Plaza in Miami Beach, Winchell began a venomous counterattack, unearthing an Associated Press item from 1935 reporting that Baker had backed Mussolini in his war to conquer Ethiopa, pledging: "I am willing to recruit a Negro army to help Italy. I am willing to travel around the world to convince my brothers Mussolini is their friend."

Daily News crime reporter Curley Harris, meanwhile, let his old friend Winchell know that he was trying to dig up material on Baker's rumored associations with Axis groups in South America and her "violently anti-colored record." But Harris also revealed that the only people he could find who seemed to sympathize with Billingsley were other saloonkeepers, including Toots Shor.

Others rallied to Winchell, including ex-Communist Howard Rush-

WINCHELL AND SHERMAN

more of the *Journal-American,* who had been a writer for the *Daily Worker* until he was fired in 1939 for refusing party orders to pan the movie *Gone With the Wind,* and George S. Schuyler, an independent-minded archconservative black columnist for the black newspaper the *Pittsburgh Courier,* who told Winchell that Baker "has been successfully hornswoggling the colored brethren into accepting her as a group heroine and champion."

Winchell next reported that before the Stork Club affair, Baker had made similar complaints about the service and food at Sardi's.

That column brought a stinging denial from Vincent Sardi, who cabled Winchell that it was untrue and demanded a retraction.

Winchell refused, saying Baker had made the statement to one of his informants.

And then the war spread to the airwaves.

Radio host Barry Gray, like Baker's agent Ned Schuyler, had helped break the color line by inviting black performers onto his show at the Copa Lounge in Miami Beach. The lounge then mysteriously burned to the ground, later to be resurrected as the Copa City, where Winchell paid court to Baker. The gangling Gray, who had broken into radio after World War II as a gofer at the Mutual flagship station WOR, had then made his way back north and convinced WMCA to let him anchor a late-night celebrity talk show from Chandler's Restaurant on East Forty-sixth Street off Lexington, starting in May 1950.

Anticipation was running high when Gray, opening his show at Chandler's before several hundred late diners just after midnight on October 25, 1951, announced "a lengthy discussion and probably the true story" of the Josephine Baker affair, as told by the NAACP's Walter White.

As for the other side of the story, Gray said that Billingsley had also been invited but had not responded.

White began aggressively. As someone who hated communism and fascism, he said, "I am frightened for my country, because an incident like this in a phony place like the Stork Club does a thing of this sort, where a man who has prejudices which he brought up from Oklahoma smears and lowers the prestige of America all over the face of the world, because of his stupid little policy here in New York."

Gray played devil's advocate. If the Stork Club was anti-black, why had Baker been admitted at all and her table served drinks?

White couldn't explain it.

White painted Billingsley as anti-Jewish as well, but here Gray interjected that "many people that I know who are obviously of the Semitic races have attended the Stork Club."

A few days later White received a typed letter, replete with errors, on Stork Club stationery. It was dated October 24, the day before Gray's show.

> May I take this opportunity to express my feelings concerning the exagerrated "incident" which took place recently on these premises.
>
> Because of the exclusive nature of our clientele, we find it necessary to exclude certain types of persons whom we know would be regarded as obnoxious by the majority of our patrons.
>
> I am greatly displeased with the action your organization has taken, particularly the involvment of Walter Winchell in this matter, since he was in no way concerned and should never have been drawn in.
>
> Be advised that despite pickets and other agitation, the policy of this establishment as regards the exclusion of obnoxious persons will not be altered.

It was signed, "Sherman Billingsley."

White, livid, demanded an apology.

Billingsley, who didn't type, branded the letter a forgery and demanded an investigation. District Attorney Frank S. Hogan promised to pursue the matter.

The dispute soon claimed its first, unlikely, victim. Shortly after the story broke, the producers of *South Pacific* asked Roger Rico to quit his contract. Rico, who had already performed for eighteen months and had six to go on his contract, indignantly refused. But complaining that they were receiving bomb threats, the producers insisted on buying him out, stipulating, perhaps to minimize bad publicity, that he not leave the country until the contract expired.

And so, with six paid months on their hands, he and Solange got a trailer and saw America, driving from Niagara Falls to El Paso, Texas.

TWENTY-SIX

THROUGHOUT THE AFFAIR BILLINGSLEY KEPT A LOW PROFILE, leaving Poston to write no-news leads like "Sherman Billingsley continued today his defiant silence . . ." Behind the scenes, however, he collected anti-Baker items that he funneled to Winchell. Among them were Baker's memoirs, published in 1949. Saying that Baker "out-Goebbels Hitler," Winchell stepped up his offensive, quoting her own words:

> In Harlem the Jews subject the Negroes to slavery. In Harlem all the bosses are Jews. They burden all the Negroes. All the movies, the one-price stores, belong to the Jews. The salesmen are Negroes and they are robbed like nowhere else. Negroes cannot work without Jews. They cannot go to work on Broadway without the help of the Jews. They depend completely upon the Jews. They are in their hands, completely subjected to their harsh demands.

Stung, she directed her lawyer, the eminent Arthur Garfield Hays, to issue a statement on her behalf backhandedly making a key concession: "Miss Baker accepts Walter Winchell's statement that he was not present at the time of any discourtesy, but this is beside the point."

Baker defended her war record and said that Winchell "took out of its context a statement in my book." In fact, she said, the book as a whole showed her "happy and affectionate relations with Jewish people (and incidentally, I married a Jew)." As for supporting Mussolini's invasion of Ethiopia, "It is so obviously ridiculous that it does not requite comment. It is not so, period."

Winchell was incensed; after all, he had the Associated Press clipping with her statement from the October 1, 1935, *New York Post*. He had been ready to drop the matter, he acknowledged, "but they keep tell-ing lies."

Billingsley, meanwhile, sent the Anti-Defamation League and the Mayor's Committee on Unity his first official version of the incident with a declaration of his guest policy.

> *Miss Baker made a reservation one afternoon. That night, with three other people she came into the Club. She was seated at an excellent table in the crowded Cub Room — where world celebrities gather. For an hour or more she and friends were served drinks of their choice and seemed to be enjoying themselves. Because of an unusual food order for that time of night — it was after the theater — there was an un-usual service delay. Unfortunately this sometimes hap-pens — even to our best customers. It is the policy of the Stork Club — as it always has been — to cater to a clientele made up of the peoples of the world, natu-rally giving preference to those who have been our constant patrons through the years. This seems broad enough — and understandable enough — to explain our joy at serving ladies and gentlemen from the four corners of the earth without discrimination — as we have for twenty years, and always will.*

The mayor's panel found the statement "insufficiently forthright" and requested clarification. Billingsley then repeated his assertion that the club catered to "the peoples of the world," this time adding: "For the life of me I can't understand what group is omitted in our policy statement."

The committee still had some quibbles but issued its report on De-cember 20. The document ran less than two pages and concluded, "We find nothing to substantiate a charge of racial discrimination."

The case was closed.

But it refused to stay closed. Two nights later Barry Gray, calling it "*the* celebrated case of 1951," announced the start of a three-night radio marathon reexamining the whole affair — "a radio trial, if you will." And, Gray asked, who better to serve as "her own moderator, investigator, ques-tioner" but Baker herself?

She began by turning her fire not on Billingsley and the Stork Club, but on Winchell. How dare he report that Immigration authorities were in-vestigating her? She had Walter White step forward to read telegrams from the Department of Justice and State Department denying the charge. Then she moved on to her war record, introducing a former French intelli-

ED SULLIVAN AND NEW YORK CITY MAYOR
VINCENT R. IMPELLITTERI

gence officer and resistance fighter, Jacques Abtey, who had been her fellow combatant (and lover, though she didn't reveal that) in Algeria. (What
she also didn't disclose was that she had written Abtey two letters laying
out her version of the Stork Club affair and instructing him to mobilize the
North African press on her behalf and come to America to support her.)

Baker next addressed the charge of anti-Semitism. Yes, she admitted,
she had written about "the discrimination and exploitation practiced against
my people in Harlem and elsewhere," but she announced that she had just
celebrated Hanukkah with the American Jewish Congress in Chicago.

Gray then hushed the crowd to take an important call. The audience
heard him say, "Ed Sullivan?" When he hung up, he said it had indeed been
the *Daily News* columnist and host of the *Toast of the Town* television show.

S ullivan and Winchell had despised each other since
1927, when they both worked on Bernarr Macfadden's
quirky prototype tabloid, the *Graphic*. Later, when Sullivan was on the
News, he wrote an open column to Woolworth heiress Barbara Hutton asking for a contribution to ease the plight of suffering children during 1934's
Depression Christmas. Winchell ridiculed him as a blackmailer, and the
feud was on.

Sullivan, too, was a media pioneer two times over. A former radio host
during that medium's first decade, he had also helped usher in television in

1948 with his Sunday revue show that was to be called *You're the Top*. With his somber, leaden mien, he became the target of scathing reviews and widespread jokes. ("While he doesn't sing, dance, or tell jokes," said Bing Crosby, "he does them equally well.") But his stoic coolness suited the new medium, and his program became one of television's legendary successes.

Two nights after his call to Gray, Sullivan joined him at the microphone before a capacity crowd of three hundred packed into Chandler's. Gray was breathless with superlatives, glossing over Sullivan's questionable motives and praising his initiative as "probably the most courageous and wonderful phone call that ever occurred on any program of this kind or any kind."

Sullivan, in turn, called Gray a fine American and praised his "impertinence," another way of saying that he hadn't forgotten the times that Gray had bloodied him. He unexpectedly began his discussion of the Baker affair by announcing, "I as an American despise communism." He loved "old-fashioned Americanism, where you get a great thrill in your heart when the Star-Spangled Banner goes by in a parade and you take off your hat." He hated, he told the audience, anything un-American. "But of all things that are un-American, to me the gravest affront is character assassination. So I despise Walter Winchell for what he has done to Josephine Baker."

The room rang to applause.

"I despise him," Sullivan repeated.

Senator Joseph McCarthy was a character assassin, Sullivan said. "But I call your attention to the fact that long before Senator McCarthy came into this character-assassination racket, there was a guy by the name of Walter Winchell. Walter Winchell was one of the originators of character assassination."

All he had had to do was say he was sorry about what had happened at the Stork Club, Sullivan continued. But no, he had to drag in Mussolini.

And why was Winchell such an apologist for the Stork Club, anyway? What was he, the owner? Why didn't he ever mention "21" or El Morocco or Le Pavillon or the Colony? What was wrong with the Colony, which Sullivan plugged as "one of the great operations of New York"?

Dismissing Winchell as "an empty trumpet that's sounding off," Sullivan told Gray that "a lot of us are in your corner — a lot of us. A lot of us who have demonstrated that we can take care of him."

The restaurant thundered with clapping and cheers.

Gray tried to make himself heard, telling Sullivan that what he admired most was "that innate something called class that goes hand in hand with personal courage," but he was all but drowned out by the ovation. Gray had never heard anything like it.

TWENTY-SEVEN

THE MAIL brought Billingsley new grief.

He had so often been the target of threats that his name frequently appeared in FBI files with the designation VIKEX, Bureau shorthand for "victim of extortion." In one case Billingsley had received a letter postmarked Crosby, Minnesota, from a woman who claimed that he was the father of her daughter and wanted $4,500 for an unspecified operation for the child. The FBI had no trouble identifying the sender, because she had thoughtfully included her name and mailing address. She proved to be a demented soul whose closest contact with Billingsley was reading an article about him in *Life* magazine.

The end of 1951 now brought a new series of threats. A penny postcard postmarked Miami warned: "We've decided to send our men to dynamite your place on Xmas's [sic] Eve or New Year's Eve. If we fail to do this your life will be in danger at any time."

The FBI determined that the message was typed on either a pre-1947 Remington Noiseless typewriter or an Underwood Noiseless made between September 1929 and September 1935. But there the trail ended cold.

A few days later Billingsley received an anonymous typed letter postmarked Woodmere, Long Island:

> Mr. Billengsley:
> This is to warn you that you better close the joint
> up or we will blow it up. Take HEED of this warning
> we mean Bussiness.
> P.S. You better close up by THURSDAY.

The FBI opened a new investigation. It, too, went nowhere.

The first mail after New Year's 1952 brought yet another anonymous note, the vilest to date. This one, handwritten, came to the Park Avenue apartment of Sally Dawson, Billingsley's svelte redheaded television assistant.

In obscene terms, the writer demanded explicit sexual favors from Dawson on threat of revealing ugly secrets. It was signed, "a captain."

Reluctantly, Billingsley turned this letter, too, over to the FBI, asking that it not be shared with postal authorities. This was one matter on which he didn't want any publicity.

A second handwritten note quickly followed:

> To A know Good Son-of-Bitch:
> Just because you are getting a little business you are letting it Go to your fucking Jewish head — you know the shit you are doing is wrong, I have spoke to some of your help, boys + Girls And they All say you are a baster – I myself would like to put my foot in your ass — And dont be surprise if you dont get it. — you forgot you were a working man once, so dont be so God dam smart are I will fuck you up myself —. My sister work At your place and she has told me some Awful shit about you — yes, you are all for yourself — you have treated people like they were dog's — my sister told me how you treated the Colored boy you fired about 4 weeks ago — boy if I was him I would wait for your ass And let you have it — in your fucking big nose, you know Good cock sucker — To show you how I feel aboiut you, I hope your wife drop dead with A Cobb uP her Ass —
> And you had better treat my sister right Are I will beat your Ass up — I Am from Rome

The FBI started running that letter, too, through its laboratory.

Although he would hardly admit it publicly, Billingsley was clearly worried about the Baker affair. He had sent Morris Ernst, the prominent civil rights attorney and lawyer for the Runyon Cancer Fund, with a peace offering to Walter White, suggesting they "shake hands and forget the incident" and an invitation for White and Baker to come back as his guests for an evening at the Stork Club.

White informed Ernst that he couldn't settle with Billingsley without a guarantee that the club would end discriminatory policies.

The *Post* was also unwilling to abandon the Baker affair, and began to run a multipart series that promised to go on for weeks. With no pretense to objectivity, the pieces, prepared by the editors and seven reporters, were an obvious journalistic contract hit.

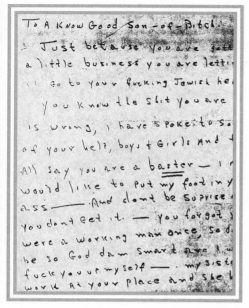

To A KNow Good Son-of-Bitch
Just because you are so
a little business you are letting
Go to your fucking Jewish he
you know the shit you are
is wrong, I have spoke to so
of your help, boys, & Girls And
All say you are a bastard — I
would like to put my foot in y
ass ———— And don't be surprise
you don't Get it. — you forgot
were a working man once so d
be so God dam smart. Are I w
fuck you or myself ——. my sist
work At your place and she

ONE OF THE THREATENING LETTERS
SENT TO SHERMAN

Two of the articles dealt exclusively with Winchell and Billingsley. The *Post* had dug deep, sending a team to Miami Beach to rummage for dirt on the columnist. A reporter had also called the FBI to check on a tip that Billingsley had been investigated as an alleged "pusher" of stolen bonds in 1943. A Bureau spokesman told the *Post* that the information was "absolutely not correct."

But Hoover, notified of the *Post's* inquiry, wanted to be sure, and queried subordinates, "Was Billingsley involved in any way?" The files were checked again, this time more thoroughly. There *had* been a stolen-bonds prosecution in 1943, as it happened, but Hoover could rest easy: "Billingsley was not in any way involved."

The first *Post* article, on January 21, set the tone for the series, starting off: "John Sherman Billingsley's Stork Club symbolizes Walter Winchell's success in life and the double standard by which he has lived." It called the Stork Winchell's "dream world," which "he rules with an alternately ruthless and benevolent hand."

The article drew on many blind sources, a technique for which Winchell himself was notorious, and resorted to amateurishly unsourced pejorative quotes that rang as fabrications. "In the words of many who have witnessed the story of the Stork since birth: 'Billingsley is Winchell's valet.'" It recounted Billingsley's notorious antipathy toward unions, ignoring the history of labor corruption that seemed to explain at least some of his antagonism, and disclosed apparently for the first time to New Yorkers Billingsley's bootlegging conviction in Michigan and imprisonment in Leavenworth.

The *Post* also tracked down Logan in his Westchester development office. His brother berated Sherman for flaunting his bootlegging history and childhood poverty when their father was "one of the oldest and wealthiest settlers," although here it seemed that Logan was the revisionist.

In its second article on Winchell and Billingsley, which ran the

CLYDE TOLSON, J. EDGAR HOOVER, AND LUISA STUART,
NEW YEAR'S EVE 1936

following day, the *Post* reexamined the entire Josephine Baker affair, hammering Winchell as two-faced. "He had maintained his palship with Sherman Billingsley, the lord of snobdom, even while appointing himself custodian of the grave of Franklin Roosevelt." It again quoted Logan, this time to more incendiary effect. "'Far as I know,' he said, 'Sherman's only got it in for one race — that's the drunken, brawling Irishman. But as to Niggers, well, you know he caters only to the finest people and it wouldn't do him any good to let all the Niggers in there. But I remember Sherman was real nice to a Nigger boy named Nappy who my father took in when he was only three. When Sherman opened the club he took Nappy with him.'"

Winchell went on the attack against Barry Gray. After his last Baker program, he and his wife had left for a European vacation cruise. He returned three weeks later to find himself savaged constantly in Winchell's column as "Borey Pink," "Borey Red," and "Borey Yellow."

Pressured by Winchell, guests fled Gray's program, along with sponsors. Averted eyes and silence greeted his entrance in restaurants. Exiting Longchamps on Madison Avenue at Fifty-ninth Street one night, he was about to get into a friend's car when he was belted from behind and pummeled into unconsciousness. The investigation went nowhere, and as *Post* columnist Earl Wilson wrote, "The suspect list has narrowed to 1,000."

Gray had been back on his feet for only a few months when, entering the Du Mont Television Studios one night, he was smashed in the head with a hard metal object. After his recuperation he moved to Westchester and hired a bodyguard.

Winchell, who kept a newspaper photo of the battered Gray over his bed, continued his vilification, publishing Gray's home address as an invitation to hate-mailers.

Remembering Ed Sullivan's vows of support, Gray left numerous messages for the TV host, to no avail. There was no word from Josephine Baker, either. He soon lost his show at Chandler's and drifted from studio to studio, struggling to pull his life together.

Baker's career, too, had suffered, with stages and nightclubs boycotting her in deference to Winchell. From Havana cabaret owner Louis Coto cabled Winchell: MONTMARTRE CLUB HAS CANCELLED JOSEPHINE BAKER HOPE YOU APPROVE.

Baker was doing herself little good, turning up soon in the Nazi haven of Juan Perón's Argentina, where she blasted America as a "barbarous land living a false-Nazi-style democracy." Her diatribes alienated, among others, Representative Adam Clayton Powell Jr., the fiery black congressman and minister from Harlem who had led some of New York's earliest and most effective protests against discrimination and who with his wife, Hazel Scott, had helped escort Baker to appearances in New York the year before. The truth, Powell declared, "is that the United States has been very kind to Miss Josephine Baker," whom he branded a "manufactured Joan of Arc."

No less an icon than Louis Armstrong also chimed in, albeit privately. Sitting around with friends after a concert in Portland, Oregon, while his ever-present tape recorder rolled, Satchmo said he was fed up with watching Baker "malign the U.S. and praise France for its handling of race problems. . . . She is not trying to represent nothing but herself, grab all that loot and cut out and go back to France." He went on: "When you have ability you don't have to go through a lot of who struck John. See, if she had talent she wouldn't raise no hell at all. She wouldn't have to open her mouth; her ability would speak for itself." He wrote her off: "I don't dig her."

By March 1952, meanwhile, the Baker case had cooled off enough for Mayor Impellitteri and members of the Board of Estimate to venture into the Stork for the first time since the previous October, when the mayor had declared: "I will not go to the Stork Club or any other club that practices discrimination."

The *Post* of course caught them.

One of the mayor's party explained lamely, "We had been at City Hall all day and were hungry."

Impellitteri wearily confirmed his visit. "The Stork Club incident," he declared, "is closed."

But the flow of hate mail continued. There was another anonymous letter.

DEAR BUM,
I AM WRITTING YOU THIS LETTER TO
LET YOU KNOW WE ARE GOING TO BRING
THE UNION INTO THE STORK CLUB, BE-
CAUSE YOU ARE GETTING TO COCK SUCK-
ING SMART FOR YOUR GOD DAM PANTS.
WE WORK THE BEST YEARS OF OUR
LIFE FOR YOU AND YOUR STINKING FUCK
WIFE AND YOU. . . .
JUST WATCH OUT FOR OUR POWER . . .
FROM THE WAITERS WHO HATE YOUR
GUTS
P.S. THE POST NEWSPAPER IS WITH US.

With a certain weary routine, the FBI once again compared the letter with earlier notes. But this time agents found some startling stylistic resemblances to the "I am from Rome" letter.

Billingsley had been poring over staff lists to come up with suspects in the latest letters to him and Sally Dawson. He remembered an employee he had fired two years before, after which he had received some filthy letters he then foolishly threw out. But Billingsley did recall his name. The FBI tracked the man down and took handwriting samples from him, but he was quickly ruled out.

On June 4 agents returned to the club to give handwriting tests to an elevator operator and eight bar workers. One of them, James Henry Carman, was a thirty-one-year-old black bartender with two years on the job who had just been told he was being let go in a staff cutback. He seemed excessively nervous.

As an agent recited words and phrases from the threatening letters that Carman was instructed to print and write, the suspect labored slowly and deliberately, as if trying to disguise his hand.

But a few details jumped out. For the word *writing* he had printed *WRITTING,* and he had also dotted his *i*'s with little circles — just as they had appeared in the obscene letter to Dawson.

In an URGENT Bureau cable to his agent in charge in New York, Hoover seized on the matches and asked for additional samples to be

INTERNATIONAL HOSTESS ELSA MAXWELL WITH GUESTS

taken. As the FBI lab continued its analyses, agents felt confident enough to leave a note in Carman's home mailbox asking him to call the FBI.

Instead, he fled, boarding, as the FBI quickly established, an evening Northwest Airlines flight to Los Angeles.

In Los Angeles, "stops" were placed with all airlines, bartender unions, employment agencies, and bars where he was thought likely to turn up.

Then, on June 23, agents in Carman's hometown of Louisville intercepted a letter from him sent from Los Angeles giving his return address at the YMCA on South Hope Street. As Carman walked in the next evening, he was surrounded.

He readily admitted writing the "I am from Rome" letter to Billingsley and the obscene letter to Dawson — out of rage, he insisted, at poor working conditions and the Baker affair. Within days the racist "DEAR BUM" letter had also been conclusively attributed to him.

What Carman did *not* write, tests showed, was the insulting letter to Walter White over Billingsley's signature.

In Washington Hoover waited impatiently for word of Carman's sentencing September 2. ADVISE IMMEDIATELY RESULTS COURT ACTION TODAY, he cabled his L.A. office.

The answer came quickly: $150 fine and three years' probation.

DANCING THE NIGHT AWAY AT THE STORK

It was hard to say which was more ludicrous, the outcome, or the effort that had been expended on the case. Billingsley had long taken a dim view of the legal system, but this left him seething.

The FBI was left to agonize over how the triumph was to be reported publicly.

Often when it broke a dramatic case, the Bureau issued what it called an "Interesting Identification" write-up. But how could it trumpet its success here without subjecting Dawson to embarrassing public scrutiny? The Bureau then came up with a dubious solution. Change the names.

> Hanover Studley,* owner of a night club in
> New York, has, like many other well-known persons,
> received his share of anonymous and "crank" letters.
> However none of these letters was more vicious and
> disgusting than one he received in March of 1952. . . .

The asterisked footnote acknowledged the name as fictitious. The FBI account cited the obscene letter to Dawson, but only after also changing her name — and sex.

She became "George Fork."

TWENTY-EIGHT

WITH THE BAKER AFFAIR FINALLY BEHIND HIM, Billingsley was free to concentrate on issues closer to home. His eldest daughter, Jacqueline, twenty-six (but already sensitive about her age and calling herself twenty-five) had declared her intention to marry, the seigneur's opposition notwithstanding.

He had bought his family a castle of sorts, a five-story Italianate mansion at 33 East Sixty-ninth Street, between Park and Madison Avenues, that had cost, in 1950, $125,000, but today might be worth a hundred times that amount. It boasted some two dozen rooms, including a double-height, glass-domed marble foyer with towering columns. The ground floor also featured a library, bar, and garden. Above was a living room, dining room, and largely superfluous kitchen — Billingsley liked to have meals delivered from the Stork Club. He and Hazel had picked out twin connecting apartments on the third floor. Barbara and Shermane did the same on the fourth floor, and the fifth floor, with a terrace, was reserved for Jacqueline. What would become two years' worth of renovations were making the place habitable.

He had sent his daughters to Spence, for the best education and the schooling in social graces that he had been denied. He paid for dance instruction at the Colony Club, golf lessons at the Wingfoot, swimming lessons at the Atlantic Beach Club, tennis lessons at the Lake Placid Club. And although all three girls were badly myopic and needed glasses, he was forever urging them to go without so that admirers could see their beautiful eyes, even if it meant at times that the girls couldn't quite see what they were eating or who was waving to them from across the room.

Jackie was blond and strikingly pretty in a coiffed and glamorous, movie-starlet kind of way. After Spence she had attended the proper Finch College for two years — a compromise, for she had long since set her heart on an acting career. She majored in drama and afterward entered radio

THE BILLINGSLEY FAMILY: HAZEL, SHERMAN, BARBARA,
SHERMANE, AND JACKIE

school, studying acting, commercials, and scriptwriting. Then she began training with her own drama coach, specializing in languages and dialects. She broke in on a show called *Blind Date* and on radio's *Perry Mason Show* and within a year had been on seven soap operas and commercials, winning a minor spot as Edna Pierce, the nurse, on NBC's *Young Widder Brown,* then in its eleventh hit year of what would become an eighteen-year run.

There was nothing seemingly objectionable about Jackie's prospective fiancé, a tall and lean, heartstoppingly handsome twenty-six-year-old former FBI clerk and university graduate named Alexander I. Rorke Jr., whom she had known for four years. The son of a prominent attorney, Rorke was president of his own vending machine business and had served with distinction as a paratrooper and intelligence specialist in Europe during World War II.

What was wrong with him was that Billingsley hadn't selected him. Worse, this young man had a mind of his own and didn't shy away from voicing his opinions, even if they differed from those of his possibly future father-in-law. Billingsley, in return, called him shiftless and argumentative. Whether he might have found anyone worthy of his daughters was questionable.

Billingsley wrung from Jackie a promise to keep an open mind and date other men, but he saw conspiracies everywhere. He accused the couple of concealing their romance behind phony escorts who picked up Jackie and then delivered her to Alex.

The couple finally decided to marry with or without Billingsley's approval. Jackie sent a girlfriend to the Stork Club with a note asking for his blessing and inviting him to the wedding the next day at the Rorke family's place of worship, the Roman Catholic Church of the Holy Trinity on West Eighty-second Street.

But before the note could be delivered, news of the nuptials leaked to reporters at City Hall. They called Billingsley, catching him by surprise.

"I know nothing about it," he declared coldly. He boycotted the wedding and the reception for three hundred. *Daily News* society editor Julia McCarthy sided with the lovebirds, complaining to Yetta, "The nerve of this Okie!"

Billingsley blamed Hazel. "I'm knocking myself out twenty-four hours a day for you and the kids so I can give you everything. I'm killing myself with the goddamn TV show, the club, the perfume business. Nobody helps me. Nobody does like I tell them. Shit! You let her screw up her life running off with some know-it-all who'll never amount to a damn."

Behind his hostility, Jackie suspected, was his terror of growing old. What was his child's marriage but another nail in his coffin? And if she had kids, what would they call him? *Grandpa?*

Barbara was struggling with her own identity crises. An intense and dark-haired version of her glamorous older sister, she was ten years younger than Jackie and eight years older than baby Shermane, a position in which she felt she had to assert herself.

Barbara also felt a special bond with her father. She loved it when the two of them walked down the street, far ahead of her lagging mother and sisters, harmonizing a spirited rendition of "Oklahoma!" with a special emphasis on the "okay!" On those occasions, Hazel huffed that it was beneath her dignity to be seen in their company, and that suited Barbara just fine. Her father would sometimes pull her into a doorway to wait for her mother to catch up, and then spring out with a loud wolf whistle. Her mother would blush and keep walking, too embarrassed to admit she was flattered by the tribute.

Barbara had always felt especially proprietary toward her father in the Stork Club, where she was appalled by the attention he got from other women. Without knowing the details, she sensed the threats to the sanctity of their home and instinctively invented childish stratagems to ward off the danger. Barbara contrived to have a conversation in the ladies' room with a girlfriend that a woman she deemed overfriendly to Sherman would be sure to overhear. "I'm glad my dad isn't like those dumb celebrities who don't care about their families and who get divorced. You know, just this morning I heard Dad tell Mom that he had no respect for some friends of theirs who had gotten a divorce. Dad says that he thinks divorce is a disgrace when there are children involved."

Years later Billingsley confirmed Barbara's fears, confiding: "Ethel offered half a million just for me to leave Mom. I was the one. I couldn't leave."

Barbara had suffered other burdens as a Billingsley. At Lake Placid, where they summered while Sherman remained in New York, one of her girlfriends told Barbara that she could forget about invitations to the top parties because the Billingsleys were nouveau riche, and her father was just a glorified head captain. Important people had money for at least three generations. Sobbing, Barbara called her father. Wounded himself, he urged her just to ignore it.

But the girl, as it turned out, was wrong. Back in the city Hazel and Barbara were inundated with invitations to mother-daughter teas, the first step in the pre-debutante whirl of dances culminating in the proper coming-out party. Whether or not her popularity was just a matter of socialites currying favor with Billingsley for a good table in the Cub Room, Barbara was much sought after. Now, if anyone questioned her social bona-fides, she had a smart answer ready: she would rather have a crisp new hundred-dollar bill than an old single.

A number of the functions required Barbara to bring an escort or two and to pay the boys' way, which Barbara decided was beneath her dignity. Sometimes she even ripped up the invitations, horrifying Hazel. One escort she did favor was Mort Downey's son Sean, a childhood friend who was to gain fame later as the Morton Downey Jr. of tabloid TV. When they grew up, they decided, Barbara would write plays and Sean would score them. But the social arbiters deemed Sean unacceptable, the Downeys being Irish Catholics and too, well, *café-ish,* and Barbara and Sean happily boycotted the society parties.

At Spence, Barbara was known for her gravity and seriousness, which passed in a 1950s teenager for profundity. She discussed the injustices of life with her best friend, Wiki Cheatham, who grew up in River House, one of the East Side's most palatial towers, but as Barbara had rarely been east of Park Avenue, she thought Wiki must inhabit some poorhouse. Barbara invited Wiki to Pound Ridge for a weekend, cautioning her father not to flash large bills for fear of shaming the girl.

Jackie's unsanctioned marriage had made Billingsley more protective than ever of Barbara. Whenever she left the house, he demanded to know where she was going and with whom. He was terrified she would get into a boy's car and be crippled in an accident. "You're my beautiful Babsy," he lectured. "For God's sake, just listen to me. Honey, young girls have no judgment when it comes to men. Some grubby guy comes along and sees a beautiful young girl like you with money in her family, and these guys figure they'll never have to work." Treating her like the little girl she no longer was, he swept her out of the club to catch the Good Humor wagon. They would sit on a bench licking burnt-almond ice-cream pops, and he would tell her again how poor he had been as a child. "Who ever cared about me? So that's why I'm telling you what a lousy, cruel world it is, and why your mother and I want to protect you."

On one of these afternoons Barbara told him that she wanted to study journalism at Northwestern University in Chicago. He wouldn't hear of it. "God knows who you'd meet halfway across the country." No, she would go to Vassar in Poughkeepsie, an all-girls college less than two hours' drive up the Hudson. "Besides," he said, "it isn't what you know — it's who you know, and I know everyone: Hearst, Berlin, Winchell, Kilgallen, Sobol, O'Brian. I did that just for you."

At times like that, she thought she hated him, that he was crushing her. But inevitably she melted. He was the one who seemed lost. She sometimes felt that she was the grown-up, comforting a lonely little boy.

When he continued to insist on Vassar, she showed him by slacking off her studies at Spence. They finally compromised on the fashionable Bennett School in Millbrook, New York, near Vassar. She could go there and transfer later to Vassar.

Upon graduation, Spence girls were sent off with a prophecy. Barbara's future, the school decided, was to write a novel. Its title: *Life Is Real; Life Is Earnest.*

TWENTY-NINE

I N EARLY FEBRUARY 1953 Steve Hannagan flew to Nairobi for Coca-Cola, then controlling nearly 70 percent of the American soft drink market and eager to expand abroad. He was in his hotel room in the Kenyan capital when a sudden, massive heart attack killed him. He was just fifty-three. The news shattered Billingsley, who couldn't imagine the club without the bluff, bearish figure he had come to rely on for sage advice and friendship since the Stork's earliest days. It also occurred to Billingsley that he had recently lent Hannagan $100,000, cash he could now never recover.

At the packed funeral mass at St. Patrick's Cathedral, Billingsley sobbed openly, seeing in Hannagan's death his own likely ignominious end. He joined Winchell, Morton Downey, Gene Tunney, Jock Whitney, Lowell Thomas, Charlie Berns of "21," and nemesis Toots Shor as honorary pallbearers. Also prominent among the mourners was Ann Sheridan, Hannagan's longtime love through his strained second marriage to model Suzanne Brewster.

For Billingsley, Hannagan's death was the latest in a series of setbacks that seemed to be coming with increasing frequency. Soon afterward, a bass player at the Stork Club, Christopher Emanuel Balestrero, was arrested and charged with two holdups in Queens after victims picked him out of lineups. Protesting his innocence, Balestrero was indicted and put on trial. By the time an aggressive defense lawyer and state senator, Frank D. O'Connor, rounded up twenty-three witnesses to support Balestrero's alibi and the police caught the real robber — who looked astonishingly like Balestrero — his wife had suffered a nervous collapse and spent nine weeks in a sanitarium. Three years later Alfred Hitchcock was to film the dark story as *The Wrong Man* with Henry Fonda as Balestrero, and Billingsley playing himself in a cameo.

DESI ARNAZ AND LUCILLE BALL

On the surface, business at the Stork Club seemed strong. Movie stars, political titans, captains of industry, and awestruck tourists continued to line up at the gold chain. The Kennedys often filled the Cub Room, and Gregory sometimes had to spirit Jack's companion, Marilyn Monroe, out through the kitchen when wife Jackie unexpectedly showed up. Careers were still made there. A willowy, green-eyed brunette not yet twenty, Giovanna Scoglio, who had come to America from Rome at fourteen, was given a job selling cigarettes. Billingsley didn't care for her looks and moved her to the checkroom. But one night the cigarette girl was ill, and Giovanna was sent back out on the floor, where the male customers went wild over her. Two weeks later she had a modeling contract, and several months after that Hollywood discovered her as Gia Scala. She went on to roles in *The Guns of Navarone* and several other films before dying, at thirty-eight, of an overdose of drugs and alcohol.

Mindful of the damage done by the Baker case, Billingsley tried to woo black stars into visiting the club. He sent Eartha Kitt takeout dinners, hoping that might lure her in. But still angry over the Baker affair, she petulantly refused, and in a clever song, "Monotonous," by Arthur Siegel and June Carroll in the Broadway revue *New Faces of 1952*, Kitt twitted him in her best feline purr:

> T. S. Eliot writes books for me,
> King Farouk's on tenterhooks for me,

THE DUKE AND DUCHESS OF WINDSOR (LEFT AND SECOND FROM
RIGHT) WITH GUESTS AT TABLE 50 IN THE CUB ROOM

Sherman Billingsley even cooks for me,
Monotonous.

Something was wrong; Billingsley couldn't deny that the climate had
changed. As society doyenne Elsa Maxwell complained, "Today, New York
is without a face. It is just a blur. New York isn't a place to live in. It is a
great big ice-cream freezer." Was it, as the *Post* speculated, that the war
had sounded the death knell for the world of privilege, leisure, extravagance, and escapism that reached its apotheosis in the soigné precincts of
the nightclub? Was it a somewhat lesser catastrophe — the marriage of
Brenda Frazier? Or was it a growing distaste for the self-indulgence of a
spoiled class that seemed suddenly out of place in the serious rebuilding
that was reclaiming a bomb-ravaged world?

Inside the club there was unrest, too. Manager Ed Wynne, a former
baseball umpire who had been with Billingsley since 1944, seethed when
he learned of Billingsley's cancellation of a reservation Wynne had made
for a special Sunday morning breakfast for prelates attending a conclave at
St. Patrick's. Whether Billingsley had anything against Catholics or just
didn't feel like opening the club earlier than usual on a Sunday, Wynne
took it as a personal affront. And once again labor trouble was simmering.

Vito Marcantonio, the dark and wiry leftist political leader of East
Harlem who had served fourteen years in Congress in the thirties and forties,

ALFRED HITCHCOCK WITH SHERMAN AND HENRY FONDA
DURING THE FILMING OF *THE WRONG MAN*

had begun organizing the kitchen workers. He picketed the Stork Club, but Billingsley, sensing that Marcantonio might want to run for the House again in 1954, had some of his political pals call him off. Marcantonio and Billingsley got to talking civilly and met several times in the dark back rooms of restaurants around the city. They made an odd couple, the WASPy Billingsley and the Latin Marcantonio, who had long allied himself with Communist positions while always denying being a Communist. But Billingsley, who had been fully prepared to hate his union tormenter, found himself unexpectedly charmed by the fervent little man. But whatever prospects existed for a reconciliation would die with Marcantonio after he collapsed with a heart seizure on a rainy City Hall sidewalk in 1954.

Yetta, Billingsley's gal Friday since 1940, had also grown increasingly disenchanted with his crude and dictatorial ways. He had started to turn on her, haunted by a fear or premonition that she would quit. "Don't ever even talk to another restaurant owner," he warned her repeatedly. When after one blowup or another, she did storm out, he usually knew where to find her — sitting in Hanson's drugstore near the Taft Hotel on Seventh Avenue. Billingsley would stand on the sidewalk looking in the window. She would pretend not to see him and look away, and he would beckon her and cajole and always win her back. Sometimes Winchell drove Yetta home from Hanson's, but she didn't care for his detours to crime scenes.

But in the summer of 1953 the day finally came. Wynne and another manager at the Stork, Frank Harris, had quit to open their own club, which they called, combining their names, the Harwyn. The start-up money had been supplied by seventeen disaffected Stork Club patrons, each of whom contributed $3,000. Wynne and Harris located the Harwyn at 112 East Fifty-second Street, about three blocks from the Stork, and chose a decor of pink and black, with flattering pink lights that drew quick approval from the ladies.

Wynne and Harris were soon joined by other Stork Club defectors, including Yetta. To Billingsley it was a most treacherous betrayal; he saw it as desertion, pure and simple. "I began to become too big," he rationalized. "A group got together to try to take everything from me. They stole my mailing lists and lists of everyone I did business with, addresses of all the people that were good enough to help me through the years. All the recipes for special dishes from the kitchen . . . same procedure with the bar."

Yetta denied any theft, insisting that the Harwyn built up its own lists by subscribing to *Celebrity Service*. But Billingsley was unconvinced. He still had some good sources of information. And if he couldn't recognize his clientele, who could?

Phil Manos, too, joined the exodus. Manos had worked at the Stork from 1948 to 1951, when he went into the army. On his return in 1953, he became the champagne popper on the *Stork Club* TV show, readying the bottle that was poured into the three glasses in the opening shot. Once, he hit Winchell in the head with a flying cork. He was also written in for some of the awkwardly self-conscious byplay on the show. When Peter Lind Hayes was served a cup of coffee, Manos had to ask, "Sugar?" That gave Hayes the chance to respond, with a corny wink at Mary, "My sugar is next to me."

Manos had also once delivered tea to Billingsley in his seventh-floor suite, finding him in bed with a girl. Manos was more embarrassed than Billingsley.

Another defector was Frank Carro, Billingsley's onetime shadow and prompter on the TV show. Knowing that Billingsley got tongue-tied, he had worked late into the night writing notes on the tablecloth and Billingsley's shirtcuffs. But he was incensed by the mere fifteen dollars his father Carlo had been handed as a retirement bonus after working at the Stork Club since the speakeasy days. Frank signed a union card, as did Billingsley's driver, George Amodio. Both were fired, and both took jobs at the Harwyn.

The Harwyn attracted its own share of celebrities. Mickey Mantle, Phil Rizzuto, Yogi Berra, and other Yankees made it a favorite gathering place, as did lesser-knowns who found Wynne's folksy welcome a refreshing contrast to the frosty once-over at the door of the Stork. But for some reason, the press never gave the upstart much ink. Billingsley hadn't had to spell it out for his newspaper friends: the Harwyn was anathema.

That, however, didn't stop Billingsley from staking out the Harwyn to see for himself who had the nerve to patronize it. When he encountered

Amodio in the street one day, Billingsley fell into step with him. "I'm going to shoot you bastards," he said. "You guinea bastard, you deserted me."

Amodio was indignant. "What do you want? You fired me."

"Well," Billingsley reasoned, "you joined the union. You wouldn't have had these problems."

In long stream-of-consciousness memos stitched together with elipses like a Winchell column, Billingsley claimed to his lawyers that he was the victim. *The last thing I get is a threat that I'm going to get knocked off . . . it's supposed to be this Harwyn Bunch . . . then I get another call in a woman's voice saying they want to take over all my business . . .* Billingsley blamed his troubles on Frank Costello's onetime bodyguard, Matty Brown, who he suspected was a silent owner of the Harwyn. Billingsley called Ed Wynne merely a front and complained that his brother was a police inspector who had it in for the Stork Club, and besides the whole thing was cooked up by the secretary of the waiters union . . . and Toots Shor "is a part of the whole thing."

When it came to the Harwyn, Billingsley made no allowances for even loyal customers. When one longtime Stork patron made the mistake one night of lighting up a cigarette with a box of matches from the Harwyn, Billingsley spotted it from across the room. "Get your ass out of here!" he yelled, banishing the mortified host and his guests. Tom Corbally, whose days at the Stork went back to the thirties when he was fifteen and one of the preppie jelly beans so prized by Billingsley, tried one night to get away with mischievously declaring something a "hard win." Billingsley promptly threw him out. Corbally's exile lasted seven weeks and ended as abruptly as it began when someone called from the Stork Club and said, "Sherman wants you to have a bite." Corbally was glad to return. Some of his most magical memories were bound up with the club. Throughout his life, in fact, he would carry around in his head the telephone number of the Stork, PLaza 3–1940, which was unforgettable in a way that no home number he ever had was. He recalled a night when an infatuated young man presented a deb with an expensive ring. "Oh, thank you," she said, dropping it into her bag and walking away. Clearly, he thought, a Stork Club girl. The way Corbally divided the world, there were girls you slept with and took to the Copa, and there were girls you bought a black dress for and took to the Stork Club.

THIRTY

ILLINGSLEY WAS BELEAGUERED AT HOME, too, although blessedly, perhaps, he had little idea of what was going on with Barbara. She started at Bennett but, predictably, found much to despise in her father's choice. Initially, she liked the attention she got from the other girls, who asked endlessly about the Stork Club, and enjoyed sharing the foie gras and other delicacies her father regularly sent her. But

THE STORK CLUB EMPORIUM AT ROGERS PEET

soon everything got on Barbara's nerves. The girls were loud, their language foul. All they talked about was sex. They drank too much. They stayed up too late laughing and screaming, and the bathrooms were so filthy that Barbara wouldn't take a shower without putting a towel underfoot in the tub. The pâté and crackers left crumbs all over the room, and the stacks of dirty dishes went unwashed.

The one thing she did like was Bennett's policy on freshman home visits: they weren't allowed. If it were up to her father, she'd come home every weekend. He didn't like the thought of her up there dating strange boys, and to keep tabs on her, he called her room every night. If she happened to be out, he phoned every twenty minutes until he reached her. The dorm bulletin board was papered with messages from him. If she didn't get back to him by 10:00 P.M., when the switchboard closed, his calls were routed to the main office, where she was embarrassingly summoned. To further curb her wanderings, he and Hazel routinely ignored the "car permission" slips Barbara kept sending home for them to sign. Without one, she couldn't even take a taxi off-campus, much less accept a ride from a teacher, classmate, or date.

Finally, on a visit home the exasperated Barbara searched out the combination to their house safe in a secret passageway between her parents' separate bedrooms and cracked the vault to retrieve the signature stamp her mother used to sign the Stork Club's payroll checks. She used it to approve the car-permission slip herself and at last had mobility.

Her debut threatened. She tried to steel herself, but each prospective escort was worse than the next. One young aristocrat studying for the ministry was driving her on a date when he was cut off by a black driver, and burst out with a stream of racist profanity. "You're some man of God, aren't you?" said Barbara. "I may vomit." She fled to the Stork Club, where she told her father that she couldn't go through with her coming-out.

He tried to calm her. What if they called it a Christmas dance instead? He'd close the club, and she could fill the place with her friends.

Barbara was adamant: No debut. No Christmas dance. No anything.

Somehow her refusal was reported in the newspapers. Billingsley was furious. Had his own taping system picked it up?

The following summer of 1954 Barbara, then eighteen and feeling very grown-up, announced that she would spend her college vacation working in an office job in the city. With Hazel and nine-year-old Shermane shuttling between Pound Ridge Farm and Lake Placid, and Jackie away and married, Billingsley agreed to keep the Sixty-ninth Street mansion open at a cost of a thousand dollars a month so that Barbara would have a place to live while she proudly earned her thirty-five dollars a week.

Just before school started, Barbara threw a Labor Day party. One of the guests, John Rogers, a twenty-eight-year-old self-employed ship photographer, wooed Barbara, and they began a romance that continued when she returned to Bennett.

Billingsley got word of it and was enraged when he heard mistakenly that Rogers was forty-eight. He snatched up the phone and confronted Barbara. In vain she tried to correct his error, but Billingsley wouldn't listen.

During Thanksgiving vacation Barbara again broke into her parents' safe, this time to take her birth certificate. Then she and Rogers eloped to Folkston, Georgia, where the age of consent was eighteen, and a county judge married them.

Shermane, dressed for school the next morning, was surprised to find her father's bedroom door open so early. She went in and found him on the phone, frantically dialing Barbara's friends to find out why she had not come home that night. One of them finally told him.

Billingsley had already called Hoover at the FBI to demand a kidnapping investigation. Eventually, an agent telephoned with word that Barbara would soon be calling home.

Billingsley might have been relieved, but instead he was indignant, calling Hoover back to complain. "Now, how the hell can he tell me that and you say you don't know where she is!" If the FBI knew so much, couldn't it have kept the two of them from spending the night together? He slammed the phone down on Hoover.

It was an ill-judged outburst, poisoning their almost twenty-year friendship.

Two weeks later, in mid-December, the newlyweds returned, landing at Newark Airport to a warm welcome from Rogers's parents, who brought champagne and roses and put the couple up at their apartment on Park Avenue until Barbara could decide when and how to approach her father.

The press relished the story. LOVE CONQUERS SNOB APPEAL, crowed the *Daily News,* snickering that Billingsley had more control over his Stork Club guest list than he did his own flesh and blood. And this, the papers noted, was already the second daughter to abscond. At least the third one, Shermane, was still only nine.

THIRTY-ONE

THE *STORK CLUB* TELEVISION SHOW had not only survived the Josephine Baker debacle but prospered, winning a devoted audience despite (or perhaps because of) Billingsley's gaffes. In the summer of 1952 — with the number of TV sets in use in the country having more than tripled to 17 million since Billingsley's debut two years before — it doubled its airtime to fill a half-hour slot on CBS starting at 7:00 P.M. Saturdays, hours before clubgoers would be climbing into their dinner jackets and gowns for the real thing.

Critics continued to snipe away. Jack Gould of the *New York Times* said the show turned the Stork Club into a persuasive argument for home cooking. The new format introduced a discussion period. One week's intriguing topic was "What makes glamour?" But the panelists were more concerned about a debutante whose coming-out party had been photographed by *Look* magazine — which then never did use the pictures! — and a woman who had a bikini made for her poodle.

One night in the Cub Room actor Broderick Crawford offered Billingsley some gratuitous advice: "Stick to saloonkeeping. You're not a very good actor."

Billingsley picked up a bottle, waving it at his large antagonist. "Get out of my club, you son of a bitch." Broderick joined the banned.

One viewer sent Billingsley a signed telegram from Washington: YOUR SHOW STINKS. Billingsley — who had not yet broken with Hoover — turned it over to the FBI for investigation. Agents ran the sender's name through their files, finding no federal record. They traced the telephone that the telegram was called in on, made a pretext call to that number, and identified the sender as a man who lived in the rural northern Virginia town of Hague. They considered taking the inquiry further but, given the difficulty of conducting it discreetly in such a small community, decided to drop it.

Little Shermane, meanwhile, remained a feature of the weekly proceedings, drawing her own fan mail. From Chicago, Sadie Edwards wrote to her at "Stork Club/New York City."

> *Dear Shermane,*
> *I see you every Saturday night at 6 o'clock and*
> *you do so much good for the little girls and boys I just*
> *love to look at you with your daddy he sure does love*
> *you lots. I love dogs too. I wish I had one. Here is a*
> *penny you may like to save as it is 100+ years old.*

But the show remained disaster-prone. The night that society singer Adelaide Moffett was booked for her television debut, the preparations began with a routine rehearsal of her banter and songs. The crew took an hour's break, and the show went on. Billingsley walked to Moffett's table and asked the scripted question.

She didn't answer.

He repeated it.

No reaction.

He tried to answer the question for her.

She sat frozen.

Billingsley was desperate to be away from there and onto someone else, but the cameraman and director seemed caught by surprise as well.

Finally, after what seemed like an eternity of ghastly silence, the glowing red eye swung over to a more forthcoming guest — Yul Brynner, who had once helped emcee the program before moving to Broadway. Facile as ever, he filibustered, discoursing about his stage makeup, and went about ordering a meal. A headwaiter identified as Society Joe recommended the lobster or boned squab. Brynner pondered his advice and ordered scrambled eggs, caviar, and a raw hamburger. In the *Times,* columnist Jack Gould scratched his head. "Let's get together, boys."

Tough-guy columnist Westbrook Pegler nervously made it through a show and in departing shook Billingsley's hand. "Never before," he said. "Never again."

Winchell hadn't even wanted to try making an appearance, although he did finally join Billingsley and Senator John Sparkman of Alabama one night as they talked on camera. Winchell asked the pair a few questions, thus making his low-key television debut.

With the 1954–55 fall television season, the fifth for the Stork Club, the show moved again, this time to a 10:00 P.M.Saturday half-hour slot on ABC. Trouble quickly followed. A switching problem in Denver left viewers of *The George Gobel Show* on NBC suddenly watching *The Stork Club.*

SHERMAN RECAPTURES HIS YOUTH
AT POUND RIDGE FARM

There was never any telling what the show would bring, wrote *Times* critic Val Adams. One night Billingsley walked over to a couple's table and lofted the chocolate chiffon pie they had ordered. He eyed it critically, then set it back down and walked away. Not a word weas exchanged.

Entertainment columnist Marie Torre of the *World-Telegram and Sun* said that she treasured the moment when an announcer intoned, "And there sits Mrs. Gloria Vanderbilt in a honey-bear *peau de soie.*"

Billingsley was sitting with Bette Davis one night when a phone near him rang long and loud. He grimaced; the Stork operators knew not to put calls through during the show. He mumbled a garbled apology and snatched up the receiver.

"What the hell are you ringing the phone here for when we're broadcasting?"

"Mr. Billingsley," said the operator nervously, "I don't know what you're going to do, but I'm leaving right now. I just got a call. A man said a bomb was going off here in ten minutes and would blow the whole building up."

Telling himself it was just another phony threat, he replaced the receiver. Struggling to appear nonchalant and not bothering to share his information with his guests, he returned his attention to Davis. But he couldn't keep his eyes off the clock. The minutes crawled by — uneventfully.

One night as Billingsley was introducing the fashion show, a waiter in the corner of the screen seemed to lose his footing, tripped, and sent a tray of dishes crashing to the floor, in full view of the home audience. Hundreds of phone calls and letters poured in begging Billingsley not to fire the hapless fellow. In fact, as Billingsley later revealed, the mishap had been cleverly staged for publicity. From then on, he liked to say, he always kept a waiter in reserve with a tray of dishes, to be dropped on command. One night he staged another mishap. Someone bumped into him, knocking a fortune in diamonds out of his hands.

Next, the show moved to Sunday nights from 9:15 to 10:00, before finally bowing out with a final embarrassment.

The program on May 8, 1955 — the tenth anniversary of VE-Day — began familiarly with Billingsley's earnest introduction: "Hi there and happy Mother's Day. Let's give all the mothers in the room orchids. And now let's watch Bert Lahr coming through the Morton Downey Room."

As a camera panned the studio, an announcer ran through some of the celebrity guests of the evening: Danish singing idol Carl Brisson — Rosalind Russell's father-in-law and "the only entertainer ever to have been knighted by two kings" — Tito Guízar, who began his career in Billingsley's speakeasy more than twenty-five years before, and *Wonderful Town* star Edith Adams — not yet known as Edie — who was married to comedian Ernie Kovacs.

Ella Logan came on to sing a medely of "It Happened in Monterey," "In a Little Spanish Town,"and "The Darktown Strutters Ball" — perhaps not the best choice in view of the Josephine Baker episode.

Billingsley leafed through photographs of Lahr as the Cowardly Lion in *The Wizard of Oz* and in other film and stage roles and then said, "Let's see what some of our guests have ordered for dinner."

A couple dined on "smothered pheasant which has been browned in a hot oven for ten minutes placed in a casserole and moistened with two cups of stock and let slowly simmer for about twenty minutes." Denmark's deputy consul general and his wife were waiting for the baked Alaska. The Lahrs were waiting for watermelon. To fill the time, the announcer told a story about society entertainer Frances Maddox, who as a supposed gag had borrowed $500 from Billingsley for a fur stole and more than ten years later had never paid the money back. "But that's the way things go sometimes," he concluded. Tito Guízar reprised the first number he had played for Billingsley in 1929, "La Cucaracha," and then it happened.

SHERMAN WITH BERT LAHR

THE PHOTO THAT IGNITED THE BILLINGSLEY–TOOTS SHOR FEUD. BILLINGSLEY IS AT FAR LEFT, SHOR AT RIGHT.

Billingsley pulled out a new batch of photographs he had clearly prepared in advance and said to Carl Brisson, "Let's see who's been here recently."

He turned over the first picture and said with ill-feigned surprise, "Well now how did this picture get in here? That's Toots Shor and a man I don't know." Viewers could clearly recognize the bulky figure of Billingsley's detested rival sitting alongside others at the bar of the Stork Club. "This proves that Toots and I were friends once."

Watching the broadcast at home on Sixty-ninth Street, Hazel guessed what was about to happen and whispered, "Oh, no, no, *no,* Sherman, don't!"

"Want to know something?" Billingsley said, reading from a cue card that the staff had prepared well in advance. "I wish I had as much money as he owes."

Brisson looked puzzled. "Owes to you or somebody else?"

"Everybody," Billingsley said. "Oh, a lot of people."

Hazel buried her head in her hands.

The music came up, Ella Logan swept into a closing rendition of "I've Got the World on a String," and Billingsley posed with his dog, Boy, for a final word. "It's about time to say good night," he said. "See you next Sunday with Polly Bergen." At last the show was over.

Shor immediately announced that he would sue for defamation and won a court order to examine a film of the show. He brought suit against

Billingsley, the Stork Club, ABC, and the production company for more than a million dollars, charging that Billingsley's statements falsely portrayed him as "insolvent and financially embarrassed, unable or unwilling to pay his just debts and obligations."

ABC soon pulled the plug on *The Stork Club,* bringing Billingsley's television career to an ignominious end.

The Billingsley-Winchell friendship was the next casualty. There were conflicting versions of their falling-out. By one widely circulated account, packs of Old Gold cigarettes were sighted one night in August 1956 on Winchell's Stork Club table. Billingsley was getting paid to promote Chesterfields. Suddenly, gossip columnists reported, Billingsley was taking down Winchell's picture from the wall of the Stork Club lobby.

Winchell wouldn't set foot in the Stork again for more than two years.

THIRTY-TWO

THE HARWYN CLUB WAS GOING STRONG, much to Billingsley's disgust. Yetta had finally hit on a clever new strategy to force the press to take note of the Stork Club's upstart rival. When a hot new movie or Broadway show premiered, she opened the Harwyn to its players, free, for their cast party. The film version of *Guys and Dolls* brought Brando, Jean Simmons, and Samuel Goldwyn to the Harwyn, and an avalanche of publicity followed, as well as parties with Bob Hope, Rock Hudson, Sinatra, and Sammy Davis Jr. One night affianced Prince Rainier and Grace Kelly dropped in, and the prince requested "Your Eyes Are the Eyes of a Woman in Love." The band didn't know the song, but Wynne rushed a busboy over to Colony Records for the sheet music, and half an hour later the royal couple was whirling around the dance floor to the tune. Readers of the columns the next day could well have assumed that the Harwyn was where the storybook romance had first unfolded, when in fact in fact it had taken place at the Stork.

Billingsley, who had showered his celebrity guests with gifts that amounted to millions over the years, unleashed a new wave of largesse. He sent cigars to President Eisenhower (perhaps not the wisest present for a heart attack victim) and a bottle of Eau de Bourrasque to Mamie, receiving notes of thanks from both. Bing Crosby got Sortilege and replied, "Very useful item of this rare essence, and I shall make good use of it." Cigars also went to Mayor Robert F. Wagner, who years later, as a widower, was to marry one of the last Stork Club girls, Barbara Jean Cavanaugh, the sister of his fire commissioner. Newlyweds Betty and Charles Ventura of the *World-Telegram and Sun* got a television and joked, "Even Milton Berle looks good on this wonderful set!" Augustine and William Randolph Hearst Jr. got Sortilege and vintage liquor, and Mrs. Hearst replied, "Nothing could have been more welcome than the rare and precious liquid 'gold' you gave Will and you know I'd rather have perfume than real gold!" Joan

Crawford sent thanks to Billingsley "for being so gracious to the children and to me." Cary Grant had supper at the Stork Club and by the time he got home to the Plaza, perfume and cologne were awaiting him. "You are an incredible man!" Grant wrote. An engraved thank-you note arrived from the Waldorf Towers with the message: "The Duchess and I and our friends are enjoying the fine contents of the two cases and appreciate your thought of us a great deal."

Billingsley received spectacular gifts in return: Irish jumper horses, automobiles, Patek Philippe wristwatches, prototype ballpoint pens, a vicuña overcoat (from Al Jolson), $500 suits, neckties by the thousand, a $2,500 massage chair, money clips, cuff links, tie clips, shirts with gold buttons, gold buckles and gold sock supporters, gold picture frames, liquor, bathrobes, slippers, hats, a pedigreed white pig, English cloth, wallets, luggage, cameras, television sets, rifles, autographed books (from

A THANK-YOU NOTE FROM THE FIRST LADY

THE WHITE HOUSE
WASHINGTON

Denver
October 27, 1955

Dear Mr. Billingsley,

You are always thoughtful, and have been especially so to think of us during this time of anxiety with such wonderful gifts. It pleases the President and me to be able to give presents to all of the people who have taken such excellent care of us during our stay in the hospital, and we delighted in seeing how much all of the nurses, doctors, and our other friends appreciated receiving bottles of the very fragrant Sortilege perfume and cologne. These beautifully wrapped bottles were welcomed by every one, and I do want to join with the others who have been fortunate enough to benefit from your generosity in expressing warmest thanks for your kindness, and every good wish always.

Mamie Doud Eisenhower

Mr. Sherman Billingsley
3 East 53rd Street
New York City, New York

SHERMAN WITH ERNEST HEMINGWAY (LEFT)
AND JOHN O'HARA (RIGHT)

Hemingway, John O'Hara, and Robert Ruark), and a foot-square solid gold Tiffany clock. One Christmas, in a touching gesture only a lawyer would think of, Ed Flynn marked Billingsley's bill of $20,000 "paid."

Billingsley hadn't thrown Yetta out of her apartment after she left for the Harwyn, but she could scarcely have remained his tenant for long. She found new quarters in the Coliseum Park Apartments on West Fifty-eighth Street, where one day soon after she moved in, her intercom buzzed. It was the FBI. Did Yetta know a certain Tony Ferruccio?

The question stunned her. Yetta had in fact found the love of her life, if a bit incongruously, in Ferruccio, an Italian bookmaker known on the street by the potent nickname Costello. (He was no relation to Frank, who was only an acquaintance.) Tony and Yetta had met in 1943 in Hanson's drugstore. For a man in a rough trade, he was consummately gentle, respectful of her, protective, and loving. She hadn't dared to breathe a word about Tony to her mother, who often warned that if Yetta ever married outside the faith, she'd sit *shiva* for her. Well, Yetta reasoned, they had never really considered marrying.

Yetta told the FBI agents to mind their own business.

Two weeks later two police detectives dropped in to see her at the Harwyn. Did she have a charge account at Saks?

No, she didn't.

Well, did she know someone named Fat Tony Salerno?

No, she said, she didn't know Salerno, then a rising power in the Genovese crime family.

Well, they asked, how come Salerno was paying for her charge account at Saks?

Yetta was aghast. Where did they get these stories? Suddenly she understood. "Listen," she said, "the only mobster I ever met was Billingsley. I know he sent you."

Yetta's mother started getting phone calls. Did she know that her daughter was a gangster's moll? Frightened and not understanding English well, she asked Yetta what it was all about. Yetta suspected that the calls came from the Stork Club but told her mother that it was just someone playing games. But now that her mother was being harrassed, Yetta became incensed.

Even Tony got a call one night from Costello — the real Costello. Could Tony get Yetta to cool it? She was making Billingsley crazy.

Tony respectfully disagreed. *She* was making *Billingsley* crazy? It was more like the other way around. Tony advised him of the calls to Yetta's mother, and the strange visits to Yetta.

Costello decided to leave it alone.

Yetta, still seething, told her story at the Harwyn one night to an enterprising young columnist for the Annenberg papers. She also told him about the hidden microphones at the Stork Club. And she called Manhattan district attorney Frank Hogan.

Hogan was already looking into the matter of electronic eavesdropping. In February 1955 detectives and phone company investigators raided an apartment at 360 East Fifty-fifth Street, uncovering a mysterious wiretapping center. The tenant, a film technician and electrical equipment supplier, and two telephone company workers had been busily tapping the phones of an eclectic group — the pharmaceuticals giant E. R. Squibb, burlesque dancer Ann Corio, the Knoedler art gallery, a Park Avenue art collector, and others. Strangely, no arrests were made, and the mysterious affair was hushed up. But a lawyer for a private civic group called the New York City Anti-Crime Committee finally gave the story to the papers. The three wiretappers were quickly arrested and charged, opening a window on what seemed an epidemic of illegal phone-tapping by police and private investigators, not only in New York but around the country. It was even revealed that as part of a Ford Foundation study of the jury system, court officials had approved bugging a federal jury's deliberations in Wichita, Kansas.

In the end, the arrested wiretappers implicated Steve Broady, who had escaped prosecution in the 1949 wiretapping scandal involving Mayor O'Dwyer. This time Broady, named as the mastermind, was convicted on sixteen counts of wiretapping conspiracy and was sentenced to two to four years in prison. But whatever he knew about the Stork Club, he never said.

After making her complaint, Yetta was assigned to D.A. Hogan's deputy, Al Scotti, to whom she confided her suspicions about Billingsley. "I just want him stopped from bothering my mother," she said. The calls tapered off but never quite stopped.

THIRTY-THREE

BECAUSE BILLINGSLEY WAS SO HARD on his staff, new help was always in demand. Tommy Wendelken had been working behind the soda fountain at Lamston's on Madison Avenue when Ray Brown, Aristotle Onassis's chauffeur who drove the tycoon to and from his Olympic Airlines offices upstairs, came in.

"How would you like a job in the Stork Club?" Ray asked Tommy, then twenty-one, an eager, bright-faced Irish kid, with the title of assistant fountain manager. "I can fix it up," said Ray. "The night manager is my brother Jim."

When Tommy arrived the next morning at ten, a man in a suit at the door stopped him. "I'm supposed to work here," Tommy announced.

"As a waiter?" the man asked.

"I hope so."

He was taken up to the second floor, where Gordon Swetland, the day manager, said, "Take him down to the cellar. Get him outfitted."

At lunch he kept getting asked for things he had never heard of, but he wrote them down confidently and then asked the other waiters what they were.

He was in the kitchen when he noticed other waiters shuffling around nervously. "Somebody has to take an order from Mr. B," one said. "Tommy, we've been taking care of you, you go."

Tommy shrugged and went up to the seventh floor.

The man sitting up in bed with an open shirt had a full, rugged face, squinty frosty-blue eyes, and thinning hair. It had to be the boss, Mr. Billingsley. Tommy was surprised to see that it was the same man who had stopped him at the door when he arrived.

Billingsley looked at him suspiciously. "I want a hamburger," he said. "No flowers. No water. No bread and butter. A fresh hamburger." He looked sharply at Tommy. "Do you understand?"

THE STORK CLUB MENU, WITH ALBERT DORNE'S
FAMOUS ILLUSTRATION

"Yes."

"You speak . . . English?" Billingsley seemed surprised.

"Yes."

"How the hell did you get in here?"

Tommy went back to the kitchen and delivered the order. He saw a cook select a filet mignon and put it through a meat grinder, carefully knead a patty, and drop it on the griddle. When it was ready, Tommy made sure there was nothing else on the plate and took it up to Mr. B, who seemed satisfied and tipped Tommy five dollars.

At the end of the shift, the pooled tips were distributed. He had never seen so much money.

One night Lana Turner came in. Billingsley called over the head-waiter. "Where is the American kid?" He put Tommy in charge of her table.

Then one day Billingsley said, "Get a tuxedo, you'll be my shadow."

GREER GARSON LOOKS ON WHILE SHERMAN TAKES A CALL.

Tommy went on nights, following the boss around as he table-hopped in the main room and Cub Room. "You're here to learn," Billingsley said, sipping cup after cup of diluted coffee — one-third water, one-third milk.

Tommy wondered why he never seemed to see anybody fat or ugly in the club. There were some black faces, but they belonged to the help. Everybody there looked the same, Tommy thought, remembering something Mr. B had said: "I'll let in who I want to." There were a lot of rules. No table-hopping (except by him) was one of them. "If you don't come in with them, you can't sit with them," Billingsley said. On the blackboard in the pantry where he posted staff messages was another: JESUS CRIST! IF YOU KNOW THEM, THEY DON'T BELONG IN THE STORK CLUB.

Some guests, Tommy saw, got extra-special treatment. When Greer Garson came in, Mr. B was alerted immediately. He scratched out a speedie for Tommy to rush to the bar. A bottle of Sortilege, an orchid, and champagne were waiting for her when she arrived at the table. Then, just as she was being seated, Billingsley strolled over and casually greeted her, "Hello, Greer."

Zsa Zsa Gabor came in with diamond pins so big that they threatened to pull down the front of her dress. *If only,* Tommy thought. Jim Arness was so tall, Tommy found himself staring into his large Western belt buckle. Brenda Frazier came in with a ghostly powdered face and scarlet lips and ordered a White Spider, a vodka concoction Tommy had never heard of.

Frank Costello ordered White Label scotch and had a gravelly way of talking. "I'm not a gangster," he growled. "I'm a gambler."

One night Tommy spotted a dapper, thin-faced man sitting opposite Costello in the Cub Room, and a shiver went down his back when someone whispered his name. Even Tommy had heard of Owney Madden. The last of the gangster trio who had taken over the Stork Club in the early days had been spending most of his time in Hot Springs, Arkansas, where he had married the postmaster's daughter. Tommy watched, transfixed, as Madden and Costello competed in a friendly rivalry over who could pledge more to Billingsley's doctor, T. Scudder Winslow, for a hospital charity.

One night Tommy worked a party that Gene Tunney threw for Jack Dempsey, and watched as Tunney stood to offer a toast: "To the greatest fighter who ever lived."

Dempsey's wife let out a shriek and said, "He was going to make the same toast to you!"

Not long after, Augustine and William Randolph Hearst Jr. threw a party for two hundred in a Stork Club room decorated with potted orange trees and stuffed birds. Afterward Mr. B said, "No check."

Tommy didn't think he heard right.

"No check," Billingsley repeated, and explained, "we'll never read anything bad about us in the Hearst papers."

Billingsley taught Tommy his eloquent vocabulary of hand signals. A

JACK AND JACKIE KENNEDY AT JFK'S THIRTY-NINTH
BIRTHDAY PARTY ON MAY 17, 1956

TEDDY, JACK, AND BOBBY KENNEDY AT JFK'S PARTY

finger to the nose meant, This guy stinks, don't take his check. A hand on his pocket square meant, Bring perfume. A stirring motion with an index finger, Free drinks for the table. A thumb up, Get these jerks out of here. A hand to the ear, Call me on the phone to get me the hell out of here.

Certain things you didn't joke about, Tommy found. When a woman came in and said, "Sherm, when did you get rid of the zebra stripes?" she was barred. You didn't joke in the Stork Club about El Morocco.

People were always getting barred. There were more of them, it sometimes seemed, than guests in good standing. Tennis player Frank Shields was barred for getting into fights, especially after a few drinks. Humphrey Bogart was so gentlemanly, it was hard to understand why he had been barred by "21" and El Morocco, until the night he came in drunk with author Quentin Reynolds and nearly assaulted Billingsley. People whose checks had bounced were barred. Harold Ross of *The New Yorker* had been barred for running a critical series on Winchell in 1940, although he was reinstated before he died. Elliot Roosevelt was *almost* barred after he falsely denied a Stork Club press release that he had gotten engaged to a society singer. But Billingsley soon relented. How could you bar a Roosevelt?

And sometimes entire groups and parties were banned. In the summer of 1956 a fashion group, the National Association of Fashion and Accessories Design, booked a banquet room for a Saturday night show featuring black models. The group sent out press releases, prompting a

MARILYN MONROE AND JOE DIMAGGIO

flurry of calls from the papers. Was this Billingsley's way of atoning for the Josephine Baker affair?

Billingsley took it as a provocation and called the fashion association in a rage. "You know, I was exonerated in the Josephine Baker case!"

Forty-eight hours before the event he canceled the show, telling reporters, "They can go to hell."

THIRTY-FOUR

IN 1956 THE STORK CLUB LOST $160,000, nearly a million today — or so Billingsley claimed on his tax returns. Whether he, like many other club owners, kept a second set of books that recorded a more favorable balance, it was clear that his palmiest days were behind him.

Before the end of the year the unions mounted a new organizing drive. Billingsley was in no mood to give in, for as he saw it, they were as crooked as ever, and the McClennan Committee's televised hearings into labor racketeering would only confirm his distrust. The one man who might have helped Billingsley avert a ruinous replay of his union troubles, Frank Costello, was in prison for tax evasion.

In the spring of 1956 Max Selinger, an organizer from Billingsley's old nemesis, Local 1 of the Dining Room Employees Union, offered labor peace at the Stork Club for $2,000. To show his good faith, he was willing to give Billingsley four signed checks of $500 each, made out to cash. If Billingsley had any union trouble, all he had to do was cash the checks and recoup his payment. Selinger left the checks with Billingsley and said he'd be back for his two thousand the next day.

Billingsley, no fool, photocopied the four checks and handed the originals back when Selinger returned for his money. Then Billingsley presented his tangible proof of union perfidy, and professing shock, the local fired Selinger.

By January 1957, claiming that patronage had dropped and he needed to cut staff, Billingsley ordered Chef Rene LeCrann to fire a butcher involved in union activities. LeCrann reluctantly complied. The next day Billingsley called a staff meeting. "It's going to rain, be cold, and snow," he said, "but I'm not going to let any union run my place. Any cocksucker who goes out that door is not coming back. No law can make me take them back." When LeCrann refused to pledge to cross a picket line, Billingsley fired him, too.

Four days later, charging that Billingsley was paying 25 percent less in wages than his competitors, twenty-seven of the club's thirty-eight kitchen employees, members of Local 89 of the Chefs, Cooks, Pastry Cooks and Assistants Union, walked out.

Billingsley protested that they hadn't taken into account the nightly rounds of free champagne and other drinks and the gift cartons of cigarettes he routinely distributed, but the strike was on. The next day the dining room workers joined the picket line, including sixty of the club's sixty-four captains, waiters, and busboys.

Billingsley stood on the sidewalk, taunting them. "See?" he said, taking off his hat. "I haven't got much hair. I'll sign up with your union right away if you can make hair grow on my head."

Frank Bottaccini, Local 1's business agent, regarded Billingsley's sparse crown with scorn. "Well," he said, "we can't do that — but we can march outside this place until the rest of your hair falls out."

Billingsley, however, had to have the last say. He climbed up to the Stork Club roof and bombed the pickets with bags of water.

Newsmen who flocked to the scene got a familiar earful from the irate Billingsley. "They've been trying to organize my place since Dutch Schultz walked in with Jimmy Hines, the Tammany district leader, and Jimmy said that the Dutchman could save me a lot of trouble, since he was running the unions. Well, that was twenty-five years ago, and I've had nothing but trouble with them since."

He rustled up replacement cooks and filled out the ranks of waiters with moonlighting Fordham University students eager to earn tuition money. Although they were inexperienced, Billingsley found that they learned fast and made a good impression on the guests. Some hot romances quickly flared with the cigarette and hatcheck girls.

Sensing that he was in for a long siege, Billingsley sold Pound Ridge Farm, with few regrets. It had become a headache to maintain, and Hazel had always seen it as the origin of all their troubles.

He sought a fresh start, too, with a new lawyer, someone who might strike fear into the unions, unlike predecessors whom he suspected of labor sympathies. Ed Flynn's son Pat suggested Roy M. Cohn, the pugnacious, narrow-faced counsel who became familiar to the nation whispering into the ear of Senator Joseph McCarthy at the end of his discredited crusade against Reds in the government. Cohn, then only thirty, had been coming to the Stork Club for more than a decade, introduced by Leonard Lyons, who found young Roy an avid gossipmonger. As his client list grew, Cohn began dropping juicy tidbits to both him and Winchell. Now he became Billingsley's top strategist.

A leader of the striking unions offered to meet Billingsley privately in his Forty-second Street office after hours to work out a compromise. When he got there, Billingsley was ushered into a conference room filled with three dozen union leaders and immediately stormed out. He returned to the club to discover union organizers everywhere, buttonholing the staff to sign up. He figured the meeting had all been a ruse to get him away for a few hours.

Next Billingsley picked a fight with Local 802 of the American Federation of Musicians — the only union he had ever allowed into the club. But, he figured, once you took on one union, you effectively took them all on, they were all so interconnected. The crime of musicians' leader Al Manuti was to have tried to mediate the conflict between Billingsley and the kitchen and dining room workers. Billingsley called it meddling and told his two bands that since they couldn't keep their union leader from "butting in," they, too, were fired.

Facing silent nights, Billingsley heard of a nonunion American band stranded in Ireland that was looking for a way to return home. He wired them money for tickets and tried them out. They stank. He hired two Dixieland jazz bands, also nonunion, in New Orleans and paid their way up. They also stank. He tried two more bands from the Mexican border; they were even worse. Then he found a nonunion band in New Jersey. They were perfect. After a few days, however, they suddenly quit, fed up with the nightly gauntlet and the need for bodyguards.

Morosely, Billingsley wandered into the staff locker room. "Any of you boys know where I can get a band for tonight?" he asked.

A cook looked up. "I can play the piano." A bartender said he played the drums, a doorman played sax, and a waiter, bass fiddle. Others shouted out their instruments. As it happened, they were all musicians in Manuti's union who hadn't been getting work and sought restaurant jobs in the interim. Billingsley was doubly thrilled: he had found another way to get back at the union. Best of all, they weren't bad.

The musicians union retaliated in newspaper ads. "Wake up, Mr. Billingsley! You and your Stork Club are in trouble." They had news for him. They didn't want his champagne and cigarettes — just an end to his "medieval" style of labor relations. "We suggest that you catch up with the rest of the 20th century."

Billingsley took out his own ads. "Come to the Stork Club. We have pickets at the Stork . . . but the food and service are better than ever. Besides, you see all your friends here."

Then he came up with the gimmick of hiring eye-catching models to march around, counterpicketing with signs like WE THINK THE STORK IS CUTE! and LOVE THE STORK AND THE STORK LOVES US. That ended when the unions won a court order barring counterpicketing. Billingsley, in turn, won an injunction against the unions' picketing, which was quickly overturned by the appellate division. While he was back on the familiar

SHERMAN WATCHES AS PICKETERS MARCH IN FRONT OF
THE STORK DURING A PROLONGED STRIKE.

seesaw of the courts, he was mollified when the striking workers were ordered not to block the sidewalk or interfere with Stork Club patrons.

In fact, many of Billingsley's longtime patrons thought nothing of crossing the picket line. Some, in fact, made a flamboyant point of it, turning
Easter 1957 into one of the Stork Club's more successful holiday celebra-
tions. But others boycotted the club, earning Billingsley's withering contempt. He felt particularly betrayed by his young debs and preppies. "Just to
get them in here, I let them have chopped sirloin, French fries, and salad for
a dollar-fifty, yet they'd rather go sit in some greasy hole in Greenwich Village,
with queers and dope addicts, and eat horsemeat at three times the price."

With the strike nearly two months old, Jackie Gleason, a longtime
patron, drove up with a blond companion. He circled the block several
times, yelling out, "What ho! Pickets? I can't go in!" But then he tried to
enter anyway.

Billingsley ordered him ejected, sending Sally Dawson, as a final ig-
nominy, to deliver the judgment.

At twenty-six, the redheaded Dawson was often at Billingsley's side.
She also patrolled the picket line, taking notes and preserving some of the
shouted slurs on a hidden tape recorder. When she and a marcher got into
an argument one day, she triumphantly whipped back her lapel, revealing a
tiny microphone. "You want to hear it played back?"

Billingsley also rigged up recorders in the club's doorway and along the facade, in hopes of capturing strikers' threats. Hidden cameras filmed the pickets, and roving Stork Club photographers were on hand to record any altercation. Audaciously, he and Dawson even set up recorders in Billingsley's mansion and invited Frank Costello — then briefly out of prison — over for a chat, in hopes of getting something on tape that they could use against the strikers. Maybe, too, Costello could help them get their garbage picked up. The carting union, headed by racketeer Longy Zwillman, had refused to cross the picket line, leaving Billingsley to humbly haul away his own mountains of trash. But Costello had too many problems of his own to take on Billingsley's. Convicted in 1954 of evading nearly $400,000 in taxes from 1941 to 1950, he had gone to prison in May 1956 on a five-year sentence but in less than a year won release pending further appeal. Two months later, while he was still free, a gunman, long presumed to be Vincent "the Chin" Gigante, later boss of the Genovese crime family, fired a shot that creased Costello's scalp. Miraculously, he survived to return to prison.

Then in early March, the mail threats started up again.

> Mr. B.
> *Every dog has his day, your time is up, regardless*
> *if you sign or not you are a dead duck. You have been a*
> *criminal all your life, now you are near the end.*

"PROTESTORS" HIRED BY SHERMAN TO COUNTER THE STRIKERS

Costello is in the can, he cannot be any help to
you. W. W. pitys you with joy at El Morocco.
   Toot Shore would pay any price to have the plea-
sure to spit in your your eyes. . . .

It was signed, *"X Boys."*

As before, Billingsley turned to the FBI. Once again agents searched the anonymous letter file, without results. But Hoover was no longer the confidant he had once been. The Bureau discussed the case with an assistant U.S. attorney, who shrugged off any suggestion of prosecution. Where was the extortion?

It was nearly 3:00 A.M.on March 27 when Billingsley dropped off Dawson by taxi at her brownstone apartment building on Park Avenue at Sixty-ninth Street, located handily just a block from his mansion. Walking the small Welsh terrier that she kept with her at the Stork Club, she stepped through the unlocked grillwork door and down four stairs to the tiled landing in front of a second locked door. She was fumbling for her keys when she heard the front door behind her open.

She barely had time to turn before two men rushed her. Dawson was six feet in her heels, but one of the men — light haired, in glasses and a topcoat and hat — was considerably taller than she. The other man, swarthy, was a head shorter. She felt something hard smash into her face. She took another blow from the other side and went down in a hail of kicks. The pair fled with a warning that she later recalled as "If you don't stop working for Billingsley and stay away from those cameras and shorthand and records, the next time we'll break every bone in your body." With a broken nose and other cuts and bruises, she made her way up the stairs and into her apartment to call the police.

Billingsley, meanwhile, had reached home, where a third-floor walk-in closet with a window afforded a convenient view of Dawson's apartment. He flashed his lights three times as a signal to her, and waited as usual for her answering flashes. When they didn't come, he grabbed his Luger and made for the door. At that moment his phone rang. It was Dawson, telling him what had happened.

He reached her apartment at the same time as the police, soon followed by reporters and photographers. With shiners blackening both eyes, Dawson begged them not to take any pictures, promising them that later that morning she would pose for them at the Stork Club.

A few days later, viewing a lineup at the police station, she picked out one of her assailants — the shorter one. He turned out to be Emanuel David, business agent of the waiters union, whom she recognized from the

SALLY DAWSON LEAVES FELONY COURT.

picket line. David's lawyer later suggested that she had falsely accused his client and that Billingsley, who often took Dawson home at night, had a motive to create a "connived situation" to defame the union. He even intimated that perhaps Billingsley had beaten her and was trying to pin it on the union. The judge angrily ruled the claims out of order, warning, "We're not trying Sherman Billingsley here, Counselor."

Before the case could be adjudicated, however, Dawson surprisingly withdrew her complaint, explaining that her father, fearing for her safety, had persuaded her to drop it.

Three weeks later a switchboard operator at the Stork Club, Rinette Pelletier, was in the apartment she shared with her landlady on East Sixty-second Street when her phone rang.

"Rinette?"

She quickly recognized the thick Irish brogue. "Mike Crowley. How are you?"

She was surprised that he was calling, although they had gone out a couple of times. He had been the club's paymaster and personnel manager until the start of the strike in January, when Billingsley fired him for threatening to beat up Gregory Pavlides. Crowley maintained that he was fired for refusing to pay off a worker beaten up by Billingsley's private Burns guards.

"Did you know that you were on your way out?" Crowley asked.

Pelletier was shocked. "What do you mean?"

"Billingsley is going to let you go."

"Where did you get your information?"

"Don't worry. I know everything that is going on in there." Then without warning he tore into her. "You son of a bitch. You're no good. How do you like sleeping with Mr. B and sucking his prick?"

She gasped. "What did I ever do to you to talk to me like that?"

"What I have against you is that you are still working for Sherman Billingsley, and if you don't get out you will get the same thing that Sally Dawson got."

Shocked speechless, Pelletier hung up. Hysterical, she called the Stork Club and got Billingsley, who in turn called Crowley. "Mike, why would you call this girl and make those threats and say those terrible things, and what is wrong with you, anyway?"

Crowley cursed and hung up.

Three minutes later a contrite Crowley called back and offered to meet Billingsley somewhere.

"So," Billingsley said, "come down and see me. What's stopping you?"

"I don't want to come to the Stork Club. I don't want any of the union officials to see me."

They agreed to rendezvous at Reuben's on East Fifty-eighth Street off Fifth Avenue. Billingsley immediately called the police to arrange for two plainclothes detectives to monitor the conversation.

Crowley, abject, blamed his behavior on drinking. He wasn't mad at Billingsley, but at some of the managers at the Stork Club. In fact, he said, he'd like to come back to work. "I'm sorry I made the threatening call," he said, as the detectives listened.

Billingsley watched the detectives get up and position themselves at the door. "I have to go," Billingsley said.

Then he did a double-take: sitting at the bar was Toots Shor, of all people. Without thinking, Billingsley marched up to him. The two glared at each other. Shor said, "You dirty prick!"

Facing charges of disorderly conduct in magistrate's court, Crowley denied everything. He denied having taken Pelletier out — he was, after all, married with a family in Ireland — or calling her or drinking or even apologizing to Billingsley. He insisted that he had called Billingsley only after receiving a mysterious threatening phone call and that Billingsley had entrapped him into the meeting at Reuben's.

Magistrate Jack L. Nicoll found that for disorderly conduct there had to be a breach of the peace and that the phone call to Pelletier — assuming it happened — did not meet that standard. He also harbored a reasonable doubt. Only a "moron," he suggested, would reveal his identity and then go on to threaten someone like that.

Accordingly, he dismissed the charge against Crowley.

Billingsley was dumbfounded. First Carman had gotten off with a slap on the wrist, and now Crowley was walking. There were so many more witnesses he could have called, he said. "There is very much more behind this."

"I'm sorry," the magistrate said.

Billingsley was enraged. "I'll tell you what I'll do. I'm going before the crime commission, and I will let it out."

"Please do," said the magistrate.

Billingsley exited fulminating, "I could mention a lot of other names."

THIRTY-FIVE

THE STRIKE GROUND ON with no sign of ending. After six months a union organizer told the papers, "Just when we think he's at the breaking point, he starts insulting the pickets again, and we know he's back in form."

One afternoon in June Billingsley stepped out of his house to find six strangers on his granite doorstep.

"Get the hell out of here," he demanded. He was expecting Shermane home from school any moment and knew she would be frightened.

One of the men answered back with a snide remark about Billingsley's daughter.

Furious, Billingsley pulled out his pistol, sending them fleeing, although he later insisted, "They all made a rush for me, coming inside of my home." The man he had argued with then walked the few blocks to the East Sixty-seventh Street station house to file a complaint that Billingsley had threatened him with a gun.

The men turned out to be housepainters who were working on the Austrian consulate next door and who had just sat down on Billingsley's stoop to eat their lunch. A detective lieutenant was dispatched to arrest Billingsley, who, when he saw the officer, was indignant. It was William Nevins, whom he recognized as a regular customer at the Stork Club. Billingsley remembered having given him wine, perfume, and even a pedigreed Welsh terrier.

Later that night, by prearrangement with Roy Cohn, Billingsley surrendered to face a charge of felonious assault.

He was booked and fingerprinted at the precinct, then taken downtown to headquarters for a mug shot before an appearance in night court. Cohn argued that Billingsley had been receiving death threats and that he had not actually pointed the gun at anyone. The judge agreed to release

Billingsley in Cohn's custody, provided he surrender his four registered handguns.

ARREST OWNER OF STORK CLUB

Under the bold black front-page headline, the *Daily News* splashed a large photo of Billingsley, grinning inappropriately and clasping an arm around Cohn's shoulders. The next day the charge was reduced to third-degree assault after Billingsley contended that he had only shifted his unloaded gun from one pocket to another.

Police Commissioner Stephen P. Kennedy, asked to explain why Billingsley was allowed to go around armed, vowed an investigation. But records showed that Billingsley had had a pistol license since at least 1949, when he declared he needed protection for "carrying cash receipts from business to home and return." On his application he had listed his bootlegging conviction and cited as his character references no lesser figures than

SHERMAN MAKES HEADLINES
IN JUNE OF 1957.

Hoover, Governor Dewey's secretary Paul Lockwood, and Associate U.S. Supreme Court Justice Frank Murphy.

The names were leaked to the press soon enough. Asked whether Hoover knew Billingsley and was aware that he was being used as a reference, an FBI spokesman had nothing to say. On an internal memo regarding the matter, however, Hoover handwrote: "I am 'no commenting' this matter. The facts are, however, I never knew Billingsley used my name on the application. The N.Y.P.D. did not contact me and I am acquainted with Billingsley."

The disclosure of his friendship with Billingsley and frequent patronage of the Stork Club embarrassed Hoover. A dismayed citizen wrote him from New York to inform him that "some years ago one of our local Supreme Court Judges stated to me that Frank Costello, the noted King of the Underworld, was the owner of the Stork Club." For the files, Hoover wrote, "Disregard," on the letter, and instead, the Bureau began an investigation of its author, finding that he may have sought to become an agent himself in 1926, and later popped up on a Bureau list of wartime Irish Republican Army informants and a mailing list maintained by the Bronx Communist Party. Or was it someone with the same name? The FBI couldn't be sure and dropped the inquiry.

At any rate, four months later, after the painter repeatedly failed to show up in court, his complaint was thrown out.

Billingsley had reason to be concerned for his youngest daughter. Thirteen-year-old Shermane had long chafed at the chauffeured rides to and from Spence, and she ultimately won her parents' reluctant permission to take the public bus. She was coming home one day, sitting in her usual seat comfortingly near the driver, when a man tripped — or pretended to trip — over her feet. He burst into a stream of curses while she reddened in fear and mortification. She looked away, too terrified to make eye contact. He took a facing seat, glaring at her, and then got up and kicked her painfully in the shin.

Instinctively, she turned to the driver for protection. To her even greater shock he was smiling, seemingly amused by the incident. When the bus stopped, she jumped off and ran home.

She burst in on her father, who was meeting with some men in the library, and breathlessly recounted what had happened. Enraged, he called the bus company. Who was the driver? A dispatcher said there were too many buses running to single out one.

Not long after, Shermane was called out of her eighth-grade class just before dismissal; middle-school supervisor Adelaide D. Parker needed to see her urgently.

She told Shermane to sit down; it was about her father. They didn't really know, it wasn't confirmed, a report merely, but they didn't want to take the chance she might hear it on the street after school.

"Hear what?" Shermane asked anxiously.

The headmistress's office had gotten a call. Sherman Billingsley had just died of a heart attack.

Shermane sobbed as school officials desperately tried to reach her family. The three o'clock bell sounded, and the halls echoed to the shouts of her classmates gleefully heading home.

Then the phone rang. The receiver was handed to Shermane.

"Are you all right, honey?" She was so shocked, she didn't recognize her father's voice for a moment. "What happened?" he asked.

"They told me . . . you were . . . dead." Tearfully, she told him about the call to the school.

He was fine, he insisted, but was *she* all right? Someone calling herself the school nurse had just phoned the Stork Club to say Shermane had fallen down the stairs and broken her neck.

He was getting spooked. In September 1957 Billingsley was being driven home early one morning by Stork Club doorman William O'Rourke when the man slumped unconscious. The car kept speeding down Park Avenue until at Fifty-ninth Street Billingsley managed to seize the wheel and steer them safely to the curb.

O'Rourke had suffered an ulcer attack. Billingsley blamed it on the unions, telling the papers, "He was ill because of the abuse he had to take from the pickets."

Two months later Billingsley was at a table in the bar one night about ten when *he* suddenly keeled over, toppling unconscious to the floor. He was carried to his seventh-floor Stork Club apartment, where a police emergency unit quickly arrived with oxygen. Then, with Dawson at his side, he was rushed by ambulance to Roosevelt Hospital. He quickly revived and by twelve-thirty was back in the Stork Club. God only knew, he worried, what had gone on in his absence.

THIRTY-SIX

I T WAS BARBARA'S LITTLE DAUGHTER, Pam, who spotted the picture in the newspaper first. "Look!" she said. "There mummy daddy in bed drinking coffee."

Barbara snatched up the *News* to see a front-page photo of her father in Roosevelt Hospital after his collapse at the Stork Club. Frantically, she called her mother and heard the story, packed up Pam, and drove to the city as fast as she could.

Barbara had been estranged from her father for several years, ever since her elopement at the end of 1954. Although Billingsley had initially shunned the newlyweds, he softened in time, but by then she had hardened and refused to see him. Shamed, he sent her lavish gifts — mink and sable coats, envelopes of hundred-dollar bills, even a car. She returned them all. When Pam was born, Billingsley offered a day nurse and a cleaning woman, but Barbara wasn't interested; she could run their little apartment in Riverdale in the Bronx by herself.

Billingsley's seizure in the Stork Club (he accused the union of slipping knockout powder into his tranquilizers) finally fostered a reconciliation between them. Barbara started bringing Pam to visit her grandfather, although she was careful to avoid the loaded term, telling Pam he was "Mommy's daddy."

Billingsley doted on the little girl, although he was astonished one day when he asked her to sing a song and she came up with "Diamonds Are a Girl's Best Friend." He was further alarmed to find Pam's scalp turning black, only to learn it was her dark roots growing in after Barbara had bleached her blond.

Jackie had also begun making visits home with her son, Alex III, and daughter, Hazel. But Billingsley still stubbornly refused to meet his sons-in-law, and Barbara and Jackie and the children were reduced to being dropped off and picked up by their husbands outside the Billingsley mansion.

In truth, Barbara's marriage wasn't going well. Her father's adamant refusal to accept Rogers was a factor, but she couldn't blame their troubles solely on that. Her husband seemed to be working all the time. His latest project was a resort upstate, for which he bought the land and immersed himself in the construction.

Grandiosely, Barbara began to think of herself as her father's natural successor at the Stork Club. (Jackie was preoccupied with her growing family, and Shimmy, as they called Shermane, was too young.) Barbara brought up the topic indelicately. "Listen, Dad," she said, "one of these days we'll be walking down the street, and everyone will wave . . . there goes Babs Billingsley and her dad . . . instead of the other way around."

"Thanks a hell of a lot," he said. His response was to exile her to the Stork's perfume office. He was giving out more Sortilege than ever. And his temper was getting shorter.

One night in October 1957 he showed up in front of the Harwyn bellowing for a captain he had fired to come out. When the man opened the door, Billingsley put his hand in his pocket as if reaching for a gun and cursed him, threatening to shoot. The captain slammed the door, and Billingsley stalked off.

Having been alerted to his erratic behavior, the *Herald Tribune* did some research and learned from a source in the police department of Billingsley's prison record. The paper then called the FBI to see if it would be proper to refer to him in an editorial as an "ex-convict."

The Bureau declined to offer an opinion but suggested checking whether the conviction had been reversed, a position endorsed by Hoover. "Right," he scrawled on the internal memo regarding the subject. "This is no business of ours."

The strike was growing nastier, and instances of sabotage in the club increased. Salt turned up in the sugar bowls, sugar in the salt shakers. The tap water came out of the faucets indigo blue. Telephone wires were cut, and the pay phone coin slots plugged with slugs. The toilets were stuffed with heavy rubbish, light switches were broken, fuses were removed. Refrigerators and freezers were disabled, spoiling food. Carpets were splashed with paint, mirrors were cracked, and chair and table legs weakened with saw cuts so they would suddenly collapse under patrons.

Billingsley assigned family members to round-the-clock shifts of guard duty. Barbara patrolled the club checking for booby-trapped furniture and straightening out the flatware that had been bent grotesquely out of shape. She threw out cracked water glasses and hunted for moldy bread that had been planted in the bread baskets. She made the rounds greeting customers and handing out lipstick, perfume, and cologne to the ladies, and shaving cream packaged in a Stork Club ashtray to the men. Billingsley himself took to sleeping in the club, and those nights when he did go home, he felt that he was tailed by mysterious drivers.

He had, thankfully, gotten his guns back. Entering his darkened house at night, he would go through the rooms and closets, pistol in hand. Finally satisfied there were no intruders, he would drop into bed and try to sleep through the eerie creaks and rattlings of the old mansion. Instead of sleeping late as he used to, he was up early to haul away his garbage and make the rounds of purveyors, picking up liquor and food supplies with an armed guard, sometimes a moonlighting cop.

Soon even the club itself proved no sanctuary. A thug came in one afternoon to pick a fight. He grabbed a water bottle off a table and started after Billingsley, who swung a chair and knocked him down. Cops monitoring the pickets outside rushed in for an arrest.

A few nights later three large strangers visited his seventh-floor offices. Their message was blunt: if he ever wanted his garbage picked up again, he had to pay them off. Labor peace would cost extra.

Billingsley snatched up the phone and told the switchboard operator to summon the police. Then he reached under the coffee table and pulled out a tape recorder. "Did you ever see one of these before? I have all your threats recorded."

The trio looked crestfallen and meekly accompanied the police out, never noticing that there was no tape in the machine.

On their next visit the racketeers came prepared. One picked up a spoon and started tapping on a Stork Club ashtray. Another cracked English walnuts. This time Billingsley had tape in his machine, but the din ruined the recording.

Still, he and Dawson had managed to collect eight reels of tapes of talks with union representatives and threats on the picket line, summaries of which they turned over to the district attorney, federal prosecutors, and Senate investigators. They then handed the tapes themselves over to the FBI, along with a Midgetape recorder and amplifier. Hoover was miffed. Since when did the Bureau get its information after everyone else?

FBI agents listened to the tapes and decided that if anything, the case was a local, not a federal, matter. The tapes and equipment were returned to a bitter Billingsley.

The situation at the club got even uglier. An intruder infiltrated Billingsley's upstairs rooms, overturning the furniture and rifling the drawers of papers, sweeping them into a pile, and setting them on fire. Someone even broke into his seventh-floor quarters and left a skull and crossbones — not, Billingsley noticed chillingly, a *picture* of a skull and crossbones, but a *real* skull and real bones. And this happened twice. He kept the incidents quiet. If news like that got out, who would dare to come to the Stork Club?

He got a tip that Vito Genovese was on the union side against him. Genovese was considered one of the most fearsome of the Mafia bosses, but Billingsley remembered him as a young whiskey salesman he had employed in his drugstore bootlegging days. He wanted to make sure he would be able to recognize Genovese if they did cross paths, so he got a friend at one of the papers to pass along some news pictures of Genovese. Billingsley stuck them under the glass of a night table so he could study them.

Shermane couldn't understand why the picture of a criminal was at her father's bedside. "Is he after you?" she asked.

"Don't believe everything you read in the papers," he said, trying to calm her down.

As the club became a war zone, Gregory, too, became increasingly disillusioned and distraught. He had been intensely loyal to Billingsley since the Stork's speakeasy beginnings in 1929, even if his conservative tastes had often been offended by his boss's flagrant promiscuities. When Billingsley twitted him, "Do as I tell you, I'm God!" Gregory failed to see the humor and rejoined, "You're not God!" To which Billingsley would retort definitively, and truthfully enough, "In these four walls I am."

Gregory had put up with jealous fits, too, Billingsley sometimes accusing him of forgetting who was the boss and who was the shadow. Having to testify for Billingsley in all kinds of lawsuits, even at times stretching the truth, deepened his ambivalence, and he sank into a depression. When Billingsley innoculously asked him one day about a tip he had pocketed, Gregory snapped: "A dollar. Why? You want part of it?" In fact, even as maître d', Gregory actually pooled tips with the waiters and busboys — to the dismay of his wife.

The ugly confrontations on the picket line and the ever looming threat of violence worsened his gloom. Some days he rushed home shouting, "Hide the kids!" terrifying his wife, who didn't know whether the threat was real or — perhaps more horrible — only in his haunted mind. There were times he mused about writing a book, then shook his head ruefully. "If I did," he told his daughters darkly, "you girls would never collect."

Suffering a bad case of war nerves, like a combat veteran after too many savage battles, Gregory finally told Billingsley that he had to resign. Then, further torn by his departure, he suffered a nervous breakdown. Billingsley rushed to his hospital bedside, wondering who would be struck down next.

THIRTY-SEVEN

WHEN DON BADER WAS APPROACHED at the Albion Hotel's Rainbow Room in Asbury Park in 1957 and asked if he wanted to bring his band to the Stork Club, he had no idea of how desperate Billingsley was, musically or otherwise. As far as Bader knew, it had been the brilliance of their playing.

When his Jersey band churlishly refused to follow him to the Stork Club, Bader, then twenty and already a little Woody Allen–ish looking with thick-rimmed spectacles, a fleshy nose, and a fashionable crew cut, came alone, joining the Latin combo headed by the bandleader at the time, a guitarist who turned out to be the one who had recruited him at the Rainbow Room. Bader was grateful for the break, but it didn't take him long to see that the bandleader wasn't doing much of a job. When three players quit in frustration, Bader was the one who went to the union hall and, strike or no strike, found three replacements. When the trumpet player turned out to be lousy, Bader was the one to fire him. Finally Bader sought out Billingsley and aired his grievances.

"The bandleader's not doing anything. I'm the guy doing all the work."

Billingsley listened and didn't say much. A few days later he called Bader over. "You think you can take over the whole band?"

"Yup."

"Okay." Billingsley fired the guitarist and installed a stunned Bader as bandleader. Crossing the picket line didn't bother Bader much. Hey, it was a small price to pay for being bandleader at the Stork Club.

Billingsley quickly lay down the rules. The way he wanted things done was they way they were done. No mustaches on the musicians — Billingsley despised "germ catchers." No stealing. "If you want a drink," Billingsley said, "don't ask the bartender. Ask me. I don't care what it costs, I'll give it to you." There were quirkier rules, too, Bader found. No playing

DON BADER (AT PIANO) LEADS THE STORK CLUB BAND.

the song "This Could Be the Start of Something Big," because of its lyric "You're lunching at '21' . . ." But Bader subversively managed to sneak it in occasionally, and sometimes the whole room joyously sang out the words together.

But Billingsley was clearly the boss. He fired a captain for taking a tip to show a customer to a table. It would have been fine if the captain had accepted the tip afterward, as a reward for good service. But guests didn't buy their way into the Stork Club.

Another captain was taking an order when he was handed a telegram. Ashen, he tore it open.

HEREAFTER MAKE SURE CHAMPAGNE
IS PROPERLY CHILLED BEFORE SERVING.

He didn't have to think twice about who sent it.

"Next time he won't make that mistake," said Billingsley, watching with amusement. "People always remember telegrams."

Bader was happy with the new piano Billingsley bought him, although he didn't like the way it was jammed in so close to the wall that he hit his elbow when he played. Bader pulled it out a few inches. The next day Billingsley had shoved it back.

Bader pulled it out again, only to find it back by the wall the next day.

He pulled it out once more, and once more it ended up back where it was. The next day when he went to pull it out, he couldn't. Billingsley had nailed it to the floor.

One day a customer buttonholed Bader during a break. "Is it true Billingsley is an anti-Semite?"

Bader couldn't have been more surprised. "No!" he said loyally, refusing to believe it.

Little escaped Billingsley, and he had noticed the furtive exchange. "Don, what did that guy ask you?"

Bader paused. Why lie? "He wanted to know if you're a Jew-hater."

Billingsley pondered that. He didn't seem upset. "How could I be a Jew-hater if my bandleader is Jewish? My lawyer is Jewish. The guy who put me on the map is Jewish." (Bader figured he meant Winchell.) "My bookkeeper is a guy named Cohen."

That cinched it, Bader concluded. If you were an anti-Semite, would you hire a Jew to count your money?

"C'mere," Billingsley said, beckoning Bader upstairs. Remember the bandleader he had fired to give Bader the job? Well, Billingsley said, the man had sent him a letter warning that Bader was not to be trusted, that he was only trying to load up the band with fellow Jews. Billingsley handed Bader the letter.

Bader was indignant, yet amazed that Billingsley would actually show him the letter. Still, he had to admit, Billingsley was hardly a great humanitarian. He was always making cracks about Italians, about the Irish. And you didn't see many blacks in the Stork Club except maybe for some U.N. diplomats. Basically, he thought, Billingsley prized the white *goyische* look.

When the Jewish holidays came around, Bader felt peculiar about taking the days off. He wanted to, but he didn't want to call attention to his Jewishness.

On Rosh Hashanah, during a break, Billingsley came over. "So how come you didn't take off?"

"I . . . I . . . don't know. I didn't think I should."

"You take it off," Billingsley ordered. "It's your holiday. I'll respect you more."

Bader felt truly small.

Eventually, Bader was called before his musicians local in Asbury Park to face charges for crossing the picket line. They ordered him to quit the job.

"You want me to give up the Stork Club? Are you nuts?" He stalked out.

A delegate called after him, "By the way Bader, you better run fast for your subway every night, our boys don't fool around."

Shaken, Bader returned to the club to recount the threat to Billings-ley, who led him into the Cub Room. "See that guy over there?"

Bader gaped. "Is he who I think he is?"

"Uh-huh. Frank Costello. Tell your boys I got friends, too."

Bader believed him. He saw Billingsley one night walk out of the club arm in arm with Costello, and he heard Billingsley say, "C'mon, Frank, I'll take you home." He saw them get into Billingsley's Cadillac. The one with the X.

THIRTY-EIGHT

THE NEW YEAR OF 1958 BEGAN DISMALLY.

A Stork Club regular, Howard Rushmore, the former *Daily Worker* reporter and crusading ex-Communist who had been so helpful to Billingsley and Winchell in their battle with Josephine Baker, had been feuding with his second wife, Frances, a former model, who had recently moved out of their Upper East Side apartment. A few days after New Year's they had another fight. She jumped into a taxi and he forced his way in beside her. She yelled for the driver to take her to a police station. Rushmore pulled out a pistol, shot her dead, and then turned the gun on himself.

Sherman's brother Fred, too, had died recently in Miami, but Billingsley had shunned the funeral. They had never reconciled, and hadn't spoken for years. Passing each other one day on the street near Fred's restaurant, Billingsley's — a name Sherman could never countenance — the brothers had instinctively tipped their hats to each other. Shermane, walking beside her father, looked up in surprise. "Who was that man, Daddy?"

"Oh," he replied casually, "that was your uncle."

Fred had left a typically enigmatic legacy. If anything happened to him, he had instructed his wife, Carolyn, she mustn't sell the furniture. She took it as a signal that valuables had been hidden there. After his death she methodically and then with increasing ferocity tore apart the tables and chairs and bureaus and finally the walls, searching for some chimerical treasure, which never materialized.

On the labor front, there was, however, some encouraging news for Billingsley.

The unions had gone to the New York State Labor Relations Board complaining of unfair labor practices by the Stork Club. The board spent six months hearing more than thirty witnesses whose testimony filled two thousand pages, and decided for the union. But in mid-January the trial examiner for the labor relations board recommended dismissal of the case, arguing that the state panel had no jurisdiction, for the club was engaged in interstate commerce. The ruling was based on voluminous records submitted by Roy Cohn showing that the Stork bought an astonishing 83 percent of its food and liquor from out of state — lobsters from Maine, clams and oysters from Maryland, crabmeat from Florida, turkeys from Colorado, Utah, and Washington, guinea hens from Missouri, and canned goods from China, Italy, and Spain. Of its 3,500 charge accounts, nearly a third were billed to customers in forty states and Canada. The examiner was clearly impressed. "The record establishes a situation hardly with parallel among restaurants in the State of New York."

An exultant Billingsley appeared outside the Stork with trays of brandy for the picketers, a sly move that caught the fancy of the press.

The unions were outraged. Who, after all, wasn't involved in some interstate commerce? Governor Averell Harriman, Mayor Wagner, and other public officials were swamped with angry telegrams. The picketing continued.

Finally even the club-shy Hazel was summoned to help out, her vigilant presence shaping up the staff. She usually showed up in the late morning and had lunch at the Stork, leaving well before the evening's social crush began. She had never been one for late nights, while Billingsley plainly was happier on his own once the sun went down. She knew well enough what he was up to and consoled herself that what she didn't see didn't hurt her — not as much, anyway.

At the club one noontime she suddenly collapsed. Barbara, standing nearby, rushed over, followed by a patron who said he was a doctor. He diagnosed a heart attack, and called an ambulance. Hazel was rushed to Roosevelt Hospital.

Billingsley guiltily and obsessively monitored her care. In a meeting with her cardiologist, he drew a childish picture of a valentine heart and demanded to know everything about how the organ functioned. He spent long hours at Hazel's bedside, issuing orders. Deciding she needed to eat to gain strength, he chose her menus and had Barbara or Shermane ferry over a giant lobster, a double prime rib, and sides of baked potato and vegetables from the Stork Club. It made Hazel sick to see so much food, and she waved it away. Barbara instructed the Stork Club chef to prepare her mother hors d'oeuvres instead. To keep her father happy, she still delivered the lobsters and steak but dropped them off at the nurses' station for the staff. Everyone was happy.

When Hazel was well enough to return home, Barbara and Shermane ministered to her needs. Barbara had by now separated from her husband and, with her daughter Pam, moved back to East Sixty-ninth Street. The house was lively again. But maintaining it was proving to be a huge burden. Soon, falling behind in his bills and seeing no end in sight for his labor troubles, Billingsley came to a painful decision: he would have to sell the mansion. He soon found a buyer for $750,000 and moved the family into a rental apartment on East Seventy-sixth Street.

Sabotage continued to plague the Stork. The air-conditioning failed. Once, with Billingsley inside, the elevator plunged four floors until he hit the emergency brake. Water pipes broke, crumbling the plaster and soaking carpets. Staff lockers were vandalized. Tablecloths and napkins were sliced with razors. Three times Billingsley came upon smoldering refuse, which implied a sinister message: next time it could be a real blaze.

The Harwyn's success nettled him all the more. After Stork Club regular Walter Annenberg was spotted in there, Billingsley returned his two-hundred-dollar charge account deposit. His business was no longer wanted at the Stork.

Annenberg shrugged it off, for Billingsley meant little to him. "I don't scuffle with people like that," he remarked. But he did decide that it might be time to feature a newspaper series on New York nightclubs. His managing editor soon hit on the perfect writer.

Burt Boyar wrote a column for the *Morning Telegraph* that was syndicated in the chain's other turf daily, the *Daily Racing Form,* as well as the prestigious *Philadelphia Inquirer.* Boyar and his friend Sammy Davis Jr., whose biography Boyar was preparing to write, had themselves encountered some shabby treatment at the Stork Club, where they felt they were invariably consigned to Siberia. They received a genuine welcome at the Harwyn, however, where Boyar offered a receptive ear to stories spun by Yetta Golove and other Stork Club defectors.

It took an entire year but finally in January 1959 the New York State Labor Relations Board backed the finding of its trial examiner. It agreed that the Stork Club was beyond the panel's purview and dismissed the union complaint, including the strikers' claims for back pay.

Billingsley quickly went on the offensive, seeking and winning an injunction in the state supreme court barring further picketing. He took added comfort from the Landrum-Griffin Act, which was making its way toward passage in Congress and promised to curb union picketing as an organizational tactic.

Billingsley's gratification, however, was short-lived. A month later the appellate division reversed the no-picketing injunction, and allowed the unions to continue marching outside the club. Not that they had ever stopped.

Another stinging legal setback swiftly followed. His insurance company had reached agreement with Toots Shor's lawyers to settle Shor's four-year-old defamation lawsuit stemming from Billingsley's malicious TV quip about Shor's debts. Billingsley was furious. To make matters worse, the judgment approving the state supreme court settlement established a crucial new legal principle: allegedly defamatory statements on television were to be judged under laws of libel rather than those covering slander. That is, they were to be considered "written" rather than merely "spoken" words — a strong testimony to the new medium's power to cause harm. With his reckless insult, Billingsley had done more than buy himself trouble. He had made — from the media's perspective, anyway — bad law.

THIRTY-NINE

SHRUGGING OFF THE STRIKE, Tommy Wendelken was having the time of his life and making lots of money. One day Billingsley sounded off about some jerk's Cadillac taking up his favorite parking spot across the street.

"That's mine," Tommy said quietly.

"You son of a bitch! That car is *yours?*"

Tommy nodded proudly.

"C'mon," Billingsley said, pulling him out of the door, "I'll race you for fifty dollars."

They shot down the street. Tommy stopped for a red light. Billingsley flew though it and came back exhilarated. "You're a good driver," he assured Tommy. "I want you to teach Shermane how to drive."

Tommy still couldn't believe the things that happened at the Stork Club. One night a customer leaned over his drink and asked a bartender, "You got a car?"

The bartender said no.

The customer reached across the bar. "Here," he said, handing over keys to a vehicle parked outside.

On another night a guest led his girlfriend outside and told her to close her eyes. She opened them to find, waiting at the curb, a pea-green Rolls-Royce, with a chauffeur in matching livery. To go with her eyes, he said.

Billingsley remained a hard boss, one of the toughest men Tommy had ever met. But, Tommy thought, he was also fair, and loyal to those he liked. Clearly he liked Tommy.

Although everyone seemed to freeze when Billingsley walked in, Tommy stayed cool. "Great scarf, Mr. B," he commented one day. Billingsley took it off and looped it around Tommy's neck.

When Billingsley needed money, he simply said, "Get me a hundred," and Tommy would retrieve it from the office. If Billingsley wanted to change into another suit among the hundred hanging in a closet upstairs, Tommy picked it out. When Billingsley's family decided he needed a stylish new hat, Tommy was sent to Cavanagh's to pick one out. And when Billingsley wanted his pistol, Tommy willingly fetched that, too.

One day Tommy got a subpoena to appear before a grand jury. Nervous, he took it to the Stork Club's accountant, J. J. Farrell, having remembered that some time ago J. J. had asked him to sign some papers. "What's this all about?"

"If you have to know," Farrell said, "go see Mr. B."

"You're president of the Shermane Corporation," Billingsley said when presented the document.

Tommy had never heard of the Shermane Corporation. Why would he be president of it? He knew Shermane was Mr. B's youngest daughter, and guessed that the corporation had to be some sort of dodge. And now it was under investigation.

"Is there any extra money in it?"

"No, there isn't," Billingsley said. It was all minor stuff about violations, he explained, and would soon blow over, and sure enough it did.

As he came up on his second anniversary at the club, bandleader Don Bader felt more at home than ever. Billingsley had by now even begun to confide in him. "Y'know," he told Bader one day, "I once screwed a king's wife."

Bader was thoroughly impressed. "Who was it?" he asked.

"I can't tell you."

"What was it like?"

"Just like any other girl," Billingsley said.

Bader was standing at the door during a break one night when a customer walked in and said, "Hi, my name is Kelly."

Bader recognized him; it was the dancer Gene Kelly.

The two stood there awkwardly staring at each other. Finally Kelly asked, "Can you show me to my table?"

Bader realized that his tux had led to the mistake. "I'm not the maître d'," he explained. "I'm the orchestra leader." But nearly everybody who worked at the Stork Club wore a tux, and if Gene Kelly couldn't recognize him as the orchestra leader there was something wrong.

The next day Bader went to a Johnston & Murphy shoes and haberdasher's shop and picked out five fire engine–red jackets for himself and his band at forty dollars apiece. That night they put them on in the back. The maître d' took one look and blanched. "You're nuts," he said, anticipating Billingsley's reaction. "You're lucky if you don't get beat up with those Harlem jackets on."

Bader wasn't intimidated. "Worst," he said, "we take them off."

They took the bandstand with a flourish. The patrons laughed and cheered.

Before closing, Billingsley ambled over. "For the money I pay you each week, Bader," he said approvingly, "it's about time you sprang for some new clothes."

Billingsley told him one night to learn numbers from *Gypsy*. Bader knew the musical was opening on Broadway with Ethel Merman; it was likely she would be celebrating at the Stork Club afterward. He and the group rehearsed the music, but there was one song, no matter how much he tried to like it, he couldn't stand. "It stinks," he told the band.

Several nights later Merman and the cast did sweep in, giddy from the tumultuous ovations. Primed, Bader and the band segued into the score, playing everything but the one song he hated. Perhaps no one else noticed the omission of "Everything's Coming Up Roses," but Bader suspected it hadn't escaped Merman. "You play very well," she told him, but there was something in her voice. "She's giving me a *zetz*," he decided.

In August 1959 Walter Annenberg got satisfaction. In a three-thousand-word article starting on the front page of the *Philadelphia Inquirer*, star columnist Burt Boyar unveiled the seventh part of his series billed as "New York Celebrity Spots." This was his dissection of the Stork Club, which, he wrote, now exemplified "Cafeteria Society." Life at the Stork had changed, he observed:

> *The laughter doesn't ring as gaily. The "deb" has fewer friends, and her looks, which were once fresh and exciting, now seem even trite. Her personality, which once seemed so beguiling, now seems transparent — and through it all you can watch the Decline and Fall of the Billingsley Empire. The E. 53d St. club is now less like a debutante than a movie star of the 1930's who once was aloof but now is eager to chat with anyone who recognizes her. She has aged but not gracefully. She reminds you of a movie star about whom someone speaks, and your first reaction is: "Oh? I thought she had died."*

Boyar conceded that even Billingsley's enemies considered him one of the world's most brilliant nightclub promoters. He related how the "Generalissimo" courted celebrities and wooed the press "like Santa Claus visiting Boys Town" and how he had turned the humble ashtray into his most dependable and effective press agent. But then he charged that the Balloon Nights were essentially fixed, with Billingsley alone holding the key to the prize numbers in the balloons and therefore able to manipulate the results. "At these moments, the Wizard Merlin himself would have gasped with admiration at Sherman's ability to change 'a French poodle' into 'a carton of cigarettes.'"

Without naming Annenberg, he told how Billingsley allowed customers the choice of the Stork or the Harwyn "but not both" and canceled the charge accounts of transgressors.

> The Stork had the only tables we've heard of with built-in microphones. Billingsley's list of accomplishments includes becoming one of the world's great eavesdroppers. This is neither easy nor inexpensive. But, with the help of some electronics engineers the B.B.C. (Billingsley Broadcasting Company) was established. . . . Its microphones have carried the voices of more stars than NBC and CBS combined.

One of the first to discover the bugging, Boyar went on, was an unnamed magazine editor who grew suspicious of a flower arrangement in the Cub Room. She tore it apart to expose a microphone and furiously shouted "Testing — 1 — 2 — 3," so startling Billingsley upstairs, "that he almost dropped his tape recorder."

Billingsley was apoplectic and could plainly see Annenberg's hand in the attack. He also guessed that Yetta had fed Boyar some of his information. Who else would know so much? He ordered Roy Cohn to draw up a libel suit against the publisher, the *Inquirer,* and Boyar.

Bader was on break one night when Winchell walked in. Although Bader had never seen the columnist, who hadn't set foot in the Stork Club since Bader had started working there, he had no doubt who the man was. Everybody knew that sharp profile, that fedora.

"Sherm here?" Winchell asked nonchalantly.

"Upstairs," said Bader. He watched Winchell climb the stairs. Whatever the argument had been about, it was obviously over. Or maybe, Bader thought, Winchell had run out of places to go. Without the Stork he had to be bored to death.

Winchell's return sent a hot current of whispers through the club. *Winchell's back! . . . He's back. . . . Who's back? . . . Winchell! . . . He came in! . . . Winchell's back? . . .* Bader, overcome with emotion, led the band in

"The Walter Winchell Rhumba." *"If I could only go back to the seashore and tell the guys,"* he thought.

Billingsley brought Bader back to earth. "Don," he said, "you can't impress that man. Presidents invite him to dinner."

With Winchell back at table 50, some customers who had been scared off by the strike began trickling in again, although, as Billingsley's loyalists assured him, those who had been kept away by the picket line clearly were not his kind of people anyway.

Within a few months Gregory, rejuvenated by his time away from the club, had also returned. Billingsley, hungry for reinforcements, gave him an effusive welcome.

He also tried to repair his rupture with Hoover. In November 1960 two FBI agents on an investigation stopped into the Stork Club to interview an employee. Billingsley rushed downstairs to greet them. Knowing that his comments were certain to be reported back, he made a point of extravagantly praising Hoover and Tolson, going so far as to say that Hoover, rather than Kennedy or Nixon, should be running for president. He assured the agents that any time he could be of assistance to the Bureau, he stood ready to serve.

A month later, with the police department's licensing division continuing to review the Stork Club's operating license in the fallout from the Billingsley gun case, Billingsley was in the office of a deputy commissioner and former FBI supervisor Edward J. McCabe when he noticed a photo of Hoover on McCabe's desk. "Your old boss has been a patron of the Stork Club," Billingsley said.

As he had hoped, the remark was dutifully reported back to the FBI. But Hoover's reaction was sour. He underlined the word *has* and wrote: "Right. I haven't been there for at least 10 years."

FORTY

A S THE NEW DECADE OF THE SIXTIES DAWNED, the picketing of the Stork Club was entering its fourth year. An exasperated Billingsley filed charges of unfair labor practices against the kitchen and dining room unions. He petitioned the National Labor Relations Board for an injunction against the picketing and brought a $4 million lawsuit against the unions, charging them with abusing and intimidating staff and patrons and threatening him and his family.

One afternoon lunch customers were felled by salmonella. It was traced to the mayonnaise. Had the refrigerator been out again? Or had someone poisoned the food? Billingsley's nerves were shot. He was drinking more coffee, not just the watered-down mix he usually sipped but up to twenty strong cups a day, and smoking two packs of cigarettes daily. He had never been much of a smoker, but the stress and his tobacco sponsorships had finally hooked him. By the time he closed the club after dawn, he was usually too overstimulated to sleep and had to sedate himself with the Nembutal he kept in the men's room.

One morning after taking his dosage, he collapsed again. Gregory and Beautiful Mary, photographer Mary Gillen, called an ambulance and rode with him to Roosevelt Hospital. Because Hazel was herself still too weak from her heart attack, it was Shermane who rushed over to meet them.

Now fifteen, the onetime chubby sprite in corkscrew curls who had handed out puppies on the *Stork Club* television show had turned into a slim-figured teen with lustrous brown hair worn in a long pageboy cut, mischievous green eyes, and a Natalie Wood profile that was drawing growing attention from boys.

When Shermane arrived, her father was being examined behind closed doors. Gregory took her across the street to an all-night coffee shop to wait. He seemed to want to talk.

"Your daddy and I have been together a long time, honey. Sometimes we fight but we always make up. We always love each other." He had something else to tell her. "A long time ago, your father said to me, 'Gregory, when I die, you put me in the middle of the dance floor and you tell the band keep playing. That's where I want to be — but don't let nobody cry.'"

Shermane was stricken. Was Gregory preparing her for something? She realized how little she knew, really knew, about her father. Did he even believe in God? Maybe, in his way. Once, when she was little, she remembered, they were together, just the two of them, at the Atlantic Beach Club, and he stopped to show her an ant on the sand. "Did you ever think how beautifully made this ant is?" he asked. She didn't understand what he was getting at. "It proves," he said, "there's something greater out there than what we are."

When they got back to the hospital, they found Billingsley sitting on an examining table, dressed and wearing his hat, puffing a cigarette. He glared at them. "It's a shame they got you out of bed and dragged you down here in the middle of the night," he complained. "Nothing's the matter with me. Just a little fall." He didn't tell them what he actually suspected — that some union bastard had slipped a knockout drug into his capsules.

The doctors hadn't found anything wrong but suggested rest. Billingsley wanted to rush back to the club to prove that he was all right, and maybe catch some son of a bitch running off with the silverware, but Shermane convinced him that Hazel would be worried sick until he showed up safe at home. He allowed himself to be steered back to the ambulance, but as they got out in front of their building on Seventy-sixth Street, Shermane saw that his hands were shaking. Tellingly, she noticed, he didn't press fifty-dollar bills into the hands of the ambulance attendants and policemen, as he surely would have done in the old days.

Later she asked him gingerly about what Gregory had said. Did he really want to be laid out on the dance floor?

Billingsley looked stunned. "Oh, for God's sake!" he shouted. "That crazy Greek took me seriously!" He burst out laughing.

In February 1960, a month after Billingsley had petitioned the National Labor Relations Board for relief, a federal judge ruled that the Stork Club was indeed being picketed illegally, citing the Landrum-Griffin Act of the year before, which barred picketing for organizational purposes. Although the unions insisted that they were picketing for "informational" reasons, their signs made their purpose clear: they were after a contract. And they were still interfering with the club's deliveries and customers. The court found that the Stork Club was in a bind.

Since the unions did not yet represent the majority of the workers, the club could not recognize the unions as bargaining agents. The unions were therefore in effect holding Billingsley hostage for something he was forbidden to grant. To break the stalemate, the judge ordered an end to the picketing.

Billingsley celebrated in the Stork Club with Sally Dawson, Roy Cohn and his partner Tom Bolan, and Shermane, who sat with them at table 1, feeling very grown-up and sipping her first glass of champagne.

The unions appealed. Within days, meanwhile, a trial examiner from the NRLB began separate hearings on the Stork Club's broader complaint against the unions.

Billingsley had traditionally hosted an April cocktail party at the Stork Club for Broadway's Tony Awards, and the fourteenth annual ceremony of the American Theatre Wing's prizes in 1960 would be no exception, he resolved. He sent out engraved invitations to the eighty-nine nominees and to previous prize winners. The responses, in gratifying numbers, encouraged him to order the food, drink, and decorations.

The day before the event, however, the Actors' Equity Association, the leading stage union, countered with a blitz of telegrams to the invitees.

> WISH TO MAKE YOU AWARE OF LABOR CONTROVERSY AT
> STORK CLUB. PRESTIGE OF THEATER WILL SUFFER IF
> OUR ALLEGIANCE TO LABOR MOVEMENT IS OPEN TO
> QUESTION. URGE YOU TO WEIGH STORK CLUB INVITA-
> TION MOST CAREFULLY.

Only two guests showed up, Lee Tracy of *The Best Man* and Juliet Mills of *Five Finger Exercise* — and then only because, as they said, they hadn't received the Equity telegram. Others by way of explanation sent their Actors' Equity telegrams to Billingsley with apologies scribbled in the margins. *Sorry, Sherm, but our careers come first.* Among those who joined the boycott were Mary Martin, Harry Belafonte, Melvyn Douglas, Walter Pidgeon, and perhaps most woundingly, Ethel Merman. Billingsley suffered additional embarrassments. His party, he learned, had never been *officially* authorized by the American Theatre Wing. And the Tony Awards' publicity director, Michael Sean O'Shea, was discovered to be an employee of Billingsley's perfume company.

A week later came another blow. The labor relations board's trial examiner ruled that picket signs claiming the Stork Club did not have a contract with the dining room union didn't mean the union was necessarily trying to organize the Stork. The union had *not* run afoul of the Landrum-Griffin Act, after all. To take away the union's right to picket, the examiner decided, would be to prevent the workers from presenting their case to the public, their only available forum.

CABARET AND PUBLIC DANCE HALL
EMPLOYEE'S IDENTIFICATION CARD
Division of Licenses, 156 Greenwich St., N. Y. 6, N. Y.

MURRAY HILL STATION

(RIGHT THUMB PRINT)

(SIGNATURE)

ISSUED BY

DEPUTY COMMISSIONER

Happy New Year

SHERMAN'S CABARET CARD, WHICH HE USED
AS A NEW YEAR'S GREETING

The union was delighted, but Billingsley was dumbfounded. The ruling seemed to contradict everything previously decided. Now *he* would appeal.

Citing the ruling, the U.S. Court of Appeals threw out most of the lower court's judgment against picketing, deciding that it was informational, after all, and could go on except for during the hours when it might disrupt deliveries to the club by other unions.

The flip-flopping decisions were becoming a joke, and the *World Telegram and Sun's* editorial page called them "legalistic hocus-pocus." Now the lower court, retailoring its order at the behest of the appeals panel, ruled that the pickets could be barred only between 1:00 and 3:00 P.M. and 7:00 and 8:00 P.M.

That did him a lot of good, Billingsley reflected bitterly. Hoping to win a better decision, Roy Cohn and Tom Bolan continued presenting their case to the NRLB in Washington.

But labor was out to make Billingsley a pariah. When the Newspaper Guild on West Forty-fourth Street lent its Heywood Broun Room for an exhibition of paintings on India by artist Roy MacNicol, who worked for the *Herald Tribune* syndicate, Billingsley joined Eleanor Roosevelt, A & P heir Huntington Hartford, and other benefactors as a sponsor of the show, dedicated to "the universal diplomacy of art" as a symbol of "peace through understanding." The invitations arrived, however, with Billingsley's name crudely blacked out.

Maybe better press relations would help, Billingsley thought. He had long envied a small bistro a few doors east of the Stork Club, Café St. Denis. With all his efforts over the years to cultivate newspaper writers, it irked Billingsley to see how often the little French restaurant got mentioned in the columns. Its success, he figured, was a result of its press agents, and he proceeded to track them down.

Sy Presten, a Glen Ford lookalike who ran his own small publicity agency handling a few choice hotel and restaurant clients, was out of the office the day in mid-June 1960 that Billingsley called. He was with his wife and business partner, Meredith Anderson, a blond and blue-eyed one-time Miss California contestant, who was in New York Hospital about to give birth to their second child.

Billingsley managed to get a call through to Presten. "Can you get over here right away?"

Presten explained the situation, but Billingsley was insistent.

"Okay," Presten finally capitulated, "I can come."

"No, I need to see both of you."

Preston said his wife was probably at that very moment delivering their baby.

Billingsley relented and agreed to give them a few days. "But I'm not waiting until after this week."

As Meredith lay in the hospital, a lavish offering arrived from Billingsley, a tall wooden stork and a Stork Club gift basket filled with bottles of Sortilege perfume and cologne, powders and bath oils, and a Stork Club ashtray.

She had scarcely given birth to their second son, Chip, when Billingsley stepped up his entreaties. What was taking so long? When were they coming?

Days later a wobbly Meredith, accompanied by Sy, showed up at the Stork to be greeted by the impatient Billingsley.

Meredith had seen Billingsley only in photos, table-hopping and posing with his customers. She had expected a glamorous, debonair rogue. This Billingsley was haggard and emaciated. He needed a shave. His rumpled suit looked slept in. It didn't help that Sally Dawson was hobbling around beside him on crutches after knee surgery from an old skiing accident.

Billingsley insisted on giving the couple a tour through the club — by stairs, to Meredith's agony. "I want you to eat here three times a week," he told Sy. "Order the best. You represent me. I'll take care of the tips."

In the kitchen Meredith glanced at a blackboard with two scrawled messages to the staff.

If you know them, they don't belong in the Stork Club.
Don't BS with customers!

She and Sy exchanged uneasy glances and then shrugged. Business was business.

FORTY-ONE

STRIKE OR NO STRIKE, Don Bader was looking for a raise. It wasn't that he was unhappy; he still loved the club and the celebrities he met there. But he had been playing at the Stork Club for three years, and in that time his pay as bandleader had risen from $150 a week for seven nights' work to just $200. Surely the world-famous nightspot could do better.

Billingsley shook his head. "Don," he said, "you don't know what it's like to run a nightclub."

Bader had recently begun to notice Billingsley sipping an occasional scotch. He didn't look well and was paranoid and testy. Some of Bader's mail at the club reached him already opened and retaped with the scrawled message "opened by mistake."

One night Billingsley informed the musicians that he was no longer feeding them dinner. The band played five nights without their accustomed meals. The sixth night Bader ducked out to the lobby pay phone and made a call. Within an hour a man in a white deli apron stood arguing at the Stork Club door. Incredulous, a captain came running back to Bader. "You ordered a delivery from the Stage Deli?" Bader nodded. Soon the unfamiliar fragrance of kosher pastrami, hot corned beef, and half sour pickles filled the Stork Club. The next day they were back on meals.

One night before closing, Bader treated the staff to his imitation of the boss. He jammed a hand into a jacket pocket and crooked his neck. *"Cocksuckers! The cocksuckers are gonna ruin me!"* Waiters and busboys doubled over. Then the laughter trailed off. Bader turned in time to see Billingsley behind him, watching.

Bader wilted. "Uh, hi . . . boss . . ."

Billingsley glared and stalked off.

After waiting for any fallout to settle, Bader went to Billingsley and told him the time had come: the band absolutely needed a raise.

"How much?"

"Ten percent."

Billingsley smiled wanly. "You know what, Don? Business hasn't been that good lately. Not only can't I give you a ten percent raise, I'm giving you a ten percent decrease."

Bader was floored. Sure enough, the next pay envelopes were 10 percent short. The players cursed.

Three weeks later Billingsley called Bader upstairs for a chat. "You know, Don, I've been thinking. You remember that raise you asked me for?"

Bader nodded eagerly.

"I've decided to give you that ten percent raise."

Sure enough, the next week's pay envelopes were 10 percent fatter. Now they were back to where they started. *Cute,* Bader thought.

The players had no written contract but worked on three-month renewal options, agreed upon by handshake. As each period expired, Billingsley had ten days to renew. The next time the contract ran out, they went through their familiar dance. Bader asked for a raise. This time when Billingsley turned him down, the band was ready.

"All right, fellas?" Bader said, looking around. They nodded. "We quit!" Bader said. They started packing up their instruments.

Now Billingsley was stupefied. He summoned Sally Dawson, who rushed down to meet with the band. What was the problem?

No problem, Bader said. There was no contract. They were leaving for El Morocco.

Dawson went back upstairs to type up a contract, and Bader got his raise.

For Shermane's birthday that year, Billingsley decided to throw her a sweet sixteen party at home. To show there were no hard feelings, he asked Bader to play the piano.

Sure, Bader said. "I'll just charge you twenty-five dollars."

Billingsley gave him a long, hard look. "Don, you're playing for a guy named Billingsley."

Now Bader felt insulted, but he countered, "All right, then, give me a bottle of whiskey."

Bader performed, and when the party was over and Bader was packing up, Billingsley still hadn't said anything about the bottle. Should he bring it up? Bader wondered. He decided to forget it.

He was leaving the club a few days later when the doorman stopped him. "Here," he said, handing Bader a heavy case of scotch, "from Mr. B."

Musically, Billingsley knew what he wanted, Bader realized anew. A new dance craze from Latin America, la Pachanga, had invaded the city's nightclubs, including El Morocco, but Billingsley banned it at the Stork.

"When the dance floor becomes a jungle, that's when I'll close my place," he vowed.

In February 1961 the National Labor Relations Board issued a series of long-awaited decisions applying the Landrum-Griffin Act. It ordered the two striking unions at the Stork Club to end their four-year picket line. Overruling the finding of its trial examiner the year before, the panel decided that the picketing was organizational after all and therefore illegal. Not that it stopped the unions. A lone picket continued a vigil under the awning.

Still, Billingsley celebrated, circulating among the club's tables distributing Sortilege and cologne to all. He vowed to press his $4 million lawsuit against the unions and promised a bigger party to come. And after that, he said, "I'm going to take a six-month sleep."

FORTY-TWO

O
N NICE DAYS AFTER SCHOOL, Shermane liked to stroll down Madison Avenue, past their new apartment on Seventy-sixth Street, to the Stork Club, basking in the admiring glances of passing young men. She had gotten her love of walking from her father, and after-school drop-ins for dessert at the Stork Club had long been a family tradition, begun with Jacqueline and carried on with Barbara and now Shermane.

Afternoons were quiet at the club. The lunch bunch had filtered out, and the cocktail crowd had yet to appear. Traditionally, when his daughters came in, Billingsley would smile and wave, usher them to a table like movie stars, and have Gregory or one of the waiters bring them banana ice cream or a Shirley Temple with a little umbrella.

Now, in her last weeks of high school at Spence, Shermane was beyond that, though her father seemed to like to treat her like the tot she was when he first brought her into the club to enliven the television show. It was about the only time she saw him, though. He usually didn't come home until she was leaving for school in the morning.

That afternoon in the late spring of 1962 she spotted the usual pickets circling outside the door. In February, almost a year to the day after the NLRB had found the unions guilty of unfair labor practices, it had reaffirmed its ruling, rejecting the union appeals and definitively ruling out any picketing. But that hadn't stopped it. The pickets had been there — or maybe their grandparents, she thought wearily — almost as long as she could remember. Each time she saw them, her stomach clenched with anxiety, although she thought she recognized some of them from the dining room and supposed that they had children, too, and their children probably looked at her father — and maybe her, too, for all she knew — with the same loathing.

Inside the club, Shermane found her father sitting at a table with Sally and Roy Cohn and a wild-haired, rumpled man she had never seen before. "This is Mr. Earl Conrad, Shim," her father said. "He's helping me write a book."

A book? It was the first she had ever heard of it. She looked the stranger over. Had he come in that cowboy hat? He didn't look like someone his father would let into the club, let alone confide his secrets to. But she kept her dismay to herself and just nodded politely.

Conrad had met Billingsley four years earlier, when he was at work with Errol Flynn on his autobiography, *My Wicked, Wicked Ways*. Flynn, a Stork Club regular, introduced Conrad to the club, and eventually he and Billingsley got to talking about writing Billingsley's own story. Billingsley then had walked him to the bar, cleared a place for him, and with a simple crook of his finger, instructed the bartender to pour Conrad free drinks. Suddenly everyone looked at him with new respect, and Conrad himself was impressed. After Flynn's book was published in 1960, Conrad and Billingsley continued their conversations, and in the summer of 1962 Conrad signed on as Billingsley's biographer.

Week after week the two of them sat with a stenographer in Billingsley's seventh-floor apartment, where one day Conrad peeked through an open door and caught sight of a panel, bristling with wires, built into a wall. He asked Billingsley about it. "I had my kitchen wired, and it helped me to know what was going on down there," Billingsley said. He added that he had shut it off some time ago, explaining, "It was taking too much of my time listening to what was being said."

From time to time Conrad showed Billingsley drafts of what he had written. Billingsley wasn't happy; he found some of the writing primitive. And did he really want all those things he had said to appear in print after all? "I may pay *not* to have this story published," he told Conrad. Five months into their collaboration, Billingsley pulled out.

In the fall of 1962 eighteen-year-old Shermane entered Finch College, a small and socially impeccable women's school in the East Seventies that her father had picked out for its proximity to home. He was determined to keep a close eye on his youngest daughter, who would not be allowed to betray him the way her sisters had.

But it may have been a forlorn hope. Shermane often got into scrapes. Her father had designated Barbara her guardian, but Barbara herself had divided loyalties. She agreed to cover for her younger sister, as long as Shermane was honest about what she was up to. One New Year's Eve Shermane missed her 1:30 A.M. curfew. Billingsley, calling from the club, was in a fury.

She finally strolled in at 3:30, with no ready excuse. Barbara, fearing her father's wrath, suddenly tore off Shermane's pearl necklace. "Shim," she confided with sisterly solicitude, "the story is that your pearls broke, and you worked for two hours in the snow to recover them. Got it? Now call Dad, quick quick quick!"

She was at home one night when a caller phoned at her father's request. He was Cecil Scott, an editor at Macmillan, and suggested they meet over lunch.

Scott was polishing off a martini and she was gingerly sipping a glass of white wine when he announced, "Your father wants *you* to do it."

"Do what?" The little bit of wine was making her light-headed.

"Do the book with him."

Shermane asked about Conrad, and Scott shook his head. "It didn't work out," he said.

Soon her father started peppering her with scraps of paper.

> *Shimmy, hate to clutter you up so take it easy and just use whatever you want too and don't try too hard or think too hard and don't try to put too much time in on this work. I don't want to kill you with overwork and still I want to inform you as to all I can think of. You can figure out if it fits or not. I love you. Daddy.*

FORTY-THREE

S Y AND MEREDITH PRESTEN STRUGGLED to get the Stork Club's name into the papers. The relentless picketing, illegal as it was, coupled with Billingsley's growing public irascibility, was fast undermining the Stork Club's famous aura of glamour. Something forlorn had crept in, a taint of defeat, and by the mysterious currents that guide fashion, it was quickly sensed by the people who had so long clamored to be seen there. Winchell may have come back, but by now, who really cared?

Hemingway's shotgun suicide in Idaho in the summer of 1961 thrust the club briefly into the news again. The image of the white-maned author partying with successive wives at the Stork had been such an indelible image that every newspaper and magazine photo editor sought Billingsley's pictures for their obituaries. The Prestens rushed over to the club to sort through the archives. But however much the Hemingway memorials recalled the glory nights of the Stork Club, they were finally another dismal signpost of the passing of an era.

Allies in adversity, Meredith and Billingsley drew close. He confided one of his prized culinary secrets: the Stork Club's chicken salad was actually made with turkey. She was also shown which tables were wired for microphones and where Billingsley had sat upstairs listening to conversations.

Meredith, in turn, confided that, with Sy away on business so much, the marriage was under strain.

"You need a project," Billingsley said. "When I broke up with Ethel Merman, that's when I built the Cub Room. Now, I've never told that to anyone."

He remained proud and tenacious, Meredith noticed. He had lured back his old driver, George Amodio, and some other Stork exiles from the Harwyn, which had also begun to fade. One night Gregory buttonholed the boss with good news: someone was calling to reserve a table for sixteen.

"You know him?" Billingsley asked.

"No."

"Tell him we're filled up."

In August 1963 Logan died, his second and third wives, Hattie Mae and Frances, grief-stricken. Although he and Hattie Mae had parted acrimoniously, she had never gotten over him. He had been suffering from a multitude of illnesses, including diabetes and heart disease, and had been hospitalized for several weeks when the doctors said he was rallying. Then, suddenly, he died.

He left instructions that he wanted to be buried in the Indian country of Anadarko, next to his brother Robert, who had died so young, and his father, who was also laid to rest there in the family plot.

In his later years Logan had become a benefactor of Native American causes. In 1952, as a wealthy Westchester developer, he and Oklahoma governor Johnston Murray had founded the National Hall of Fame for Famous American Indians, a long-overdue tribute, they said, to "a noble race." Logan donated the first memorial bust on the ten-acre tract adjacent to the Southern Plains Indian Museum in Anadarko — not far from where he had killed Chloe Wheatley's father nearly fifty years before.

Frances and their three boys — Jerry, Bob, and Frank — held a wake for him in Westchester, where Logan's Midas touch was evident in the booming new tracts of homes and office parks carved out of farmland. Sherman and Logan had long been estranged, but Sherman showed up at the funeral home, along with his sole surviving brother, Ora.

Pausing before the open coffin to stare at Logan's emaciated body, Sherman remarked, "I wouldn't have recognized him."

A second blow soon followed. Long after his World War II service, Jacqueline's husband, Alex Rorke, had remained active in intelligence work and unofficial clandestine operations, particularly the secret war against Fidel Castro leading up to the catastrophic Bay of Pigs invasion of 1961. On this subject, at least, Billingsley and his son-in-law saw eye to eye. Billingsley, too, loathed Castro as a typical Communist double-crosser. One day he had asked senior bartender Joe Moran, "How many Cubans we got here?"

Moran made a quick count. "Eight or nine."

"Get rid of them," Billingsley ordered impulsively. But there was no mass firing.

In 1960 Rorke, expelled from Cuba, founded an anticommunist group called United States Freedom Fighters. It sponsored leafleting missions and, after the Bay of Pigs, an attempted bombing raid of a Havana-area oil refinery. He then moved Jacqueline and their three children — nine-year-old Alex Jr. and eight-year-old Hazel had been followed by three-year-old

Brian — to Fort Lauderdale to be closer to the Florida center of anti-Castro operations.

In late September 1963 Rorke, then thirty-seven, and Geoffrey Sullivan, a twenty-eight-year-old pilot from New York, accompanied by a third mysterious passenger, took off from the Opalaca airfield in a light plane ostensibly bound for Honduras. Alex had previously flown a bomber, Jacqueline knew, but somehow it had been withdrawn, and he and Sullivan had rented the lighter plane. Begging him not to go, she saw them off with foreboding. They stopped to refuel on Cozumel in Mexico's Yucatán, took off again — and disappeared.

Grief-stricken, Jacqueline frantically called government offices, but no one knew — or admitted knowing — anything about the affair.

Sherman's way of comforting his shattered daughter was to finally acknowledge the depth of her feelings for her husband. "Oh, my God, you really loved him!" he remarked, trying to think of who, of all his Stork Club clients, had the most pull in the government.

FORTY-FOUR

DON BADER WAS AT THE PIANO when he spotted Billingsley across the room crisscrossing his hands over his head — his signal for "Cut!" Bader checked the clock. It was only 1:00 A.M., and he usually played until 3:00. Stopping the music, he walked over to Billingsley to find out what was going on. The music would end earlier from now on, Billingsley said curtly. Bader figured he was trying to save money.

Billingsley had already dismissed the other two bands that alternated with Bader's. There weren't many customers around that late in the night anymore. And the ones who did show up, well, it wasn't the same, Bader reflected. He was playing one night to a largely empty room when his eye caught some movement from a nearby table. He watched closely and noticed a well-dressed couple sitting close together. Below the tabletop, the tablecloth was shuttling rythmically back and forth. Jeez, Bader realized, she was jerking him off. *And to his music!* A captain finally interrupted the tender moment with an "Excuse me, you can't do that here." Bader was too embarrassed to mention it to Billingsley. Had they sunk that close to the bottom?

Billingsley knew well what he was up against. Upstairs one day he showed Bader a sheaf of bills. "I owe fifteen thousand to Cohn," he said, adding with bravura, "I could go downstairs now and get a check from someone for three hundred thousand dollars to keep the place going, but I won't do that. I'll sell hot dogs first."

Bader marveled at him. The place could be going to hell, but he still assembled the waiters together to ream them out over something or other, while the food for their tables grew cold. Some things didn't change. There was even occasion now and then for a good old-time fight. Someone knocked down a table, waiters came running, and suddenly a guest was on the floor, blood staining his white sport jacket. Just like the old days.

But when Bader picked up the *New York Times* and saw the Stork

Club ad offering a hamburger and french fries for $1.95, it looked like the kiss of death. He clipped the ad and brought it in to the band.

"Guys, look at this. It's all over."

Tommy Wendelken, too, noticed the air of desperation. Billingsley took Tommy outside one day to point out all the office buildings springing up around the Stork Club. "You know, Tommy," he said, "all these buildings, all these corporations, we don't know who they are." He had Tommy distribute circulars for Stork Club credit cards throughout the neighborhood, but the time for that to have been an effective maneuver was long past, Tommy thought sadly. And the staff knew it, too. The employee lockers smelled of steaks. Workers were smuggling expensive cuts of meat out of the kitchen.

"Tommy," Billingsley said one day in late 1964, "you ever hear of something called a discotheque?"

When Tommy said he hadn't, Billingsley told him that people were saying he should put one in the club, whatever it was. Billingsley said he would ask someone he knew at Magnavox.

The next thing Tommy knew, the Shermane Suite was getting wired up. Suddenly there was music — loud *recorded* music. The bands were gone; Don Bader was gone.

Although few people came to dance to it, Billingsley remained enthusiastic. "We have to keep up with the times," he said, conveniently forgetting his strong stand against la Pachanga. "Ninety percent of our customers want it. If you get a demand for certain food or liquor, you put it on the menu." So, he said, if his customers wanted to do the Frug, the Twist, the Monkey, the Fish, the Hitchhiker, or the Watusi, they could now do them at the Stork Club.

Tommy glimpsed the future in other small ways. One night the checkroom girls were clustered around a *TV Guide,* trying to figure out who had just come into the club. That wouldn't have happened in the old days, Tommy thought. Everyone knew the stars then. But now there were so many new celebrities, you couldn't keep up.

And the doorman couldn't park limos with their wheels on the sidewalk anymore. Cars used to be double-parked down the block, Tommy remembered. The doorman got a couple of bucks, and everybody was happy. Now traffic regulations were being enforced. *We lost another way of life,* Tommy thought. When had it changed? There may not have been an exact point, but one day stood out. It was the day President Kennedy was shot. There were no checks for anyone in the club that lunchtime. Dorothy Kilgallen stopped by to find Billingsley and Winchell riveted to the TV. And then the club was shuttered in mourning. Tommy still remembered the sound of the bells. All you heard was churchbells. And it was never the same after that.

FORTY-FIVE

GARY STEVENS WAS HOME ONE AFTERNOON when he got a call from Billy Reardon, whom he remembered from the Stork Club. Reardon was an elegant dancer who partnered extra women for romantic turns around the dance floor. He also greeted guests at the club as a kind of surrogate host for Billingsley.

"Come by," Reardon urged Stevens. "Say hello."

Stevens hadn't gone much to the club after the television show folded, but he promised to stop by that evening.

He regretted it the minute he walked in. The Stork looked like a decaying museum, dingy and musty and somehow frighteningly out of focus. The place was empty except for Reardon and two other figures.

One of the two stood up and mumbled something, and a shocked Stevens now saw that it was Billingsley. He looked gaunt and frail. Stevens watched him walk to the door, gesture, and pump his hand. But when Stevens craned his neck to see whom Billingsley was greeting, he discovered that there was no one there. Billingsley was talking to himself. This was a wake, Stevens decided. A wake for a man not quite dead yet. Another image came to mind. *Sunset Boulevard*.

"Can I get you something?"

Stevens jumped at the voice behind him, which belonged to someone he didn't know. He shook his head. "Thanks," he said. Who could eat anything in this crypt? He made himself smile, and counted the minutes until he could leave politely.

One night around this time Ethel Merman was passing by the Stork Club with Russell Nype, her costar in *Call Me Madam*. She hadn't been there in years but for old times' sake decided to look in.

No one greeted her at the door. Inside there were only three people. One of them, a stooped, gray-haired man with his back to her, got up as she entered. She didn't recognize Billingsley until he spoke. He looked awful — old and scrawny. It was awkward. What could she say?

She noticed that the Cub Room was closed.

Yes, he said, he had closed it after she stopped coming. "I only opened it so that you'd have a place to go," he said with attempted suavity. Perhaps he forgot he had told Meredith Presten he had opened it to take his mind *off* Ethel.

Anyway, as Merman suspected but didn't say, he hadn't closed it on account of her. He had closed it because people had stopped coming.

FORTY-SIX

I N THE SPRING OF 1965 Billingsley moved into the Stork Club. The lease on Seventy-sixth Street had expired, and though Hazel had found a new apartment on the second floor of a large tower going up on York Avenue at Eighty-third Street, it wasn't yet finished. In the meantime, she went down to Florida to be with the stricken Jackie and her three fatherless children.

Nothing had been heard from Alex since his disappearance a year and a half earlier. Billingsley had held a press conference at the Stork Club to announce a $25,000 reward put up by Alex's uncle, a retired hotel manager, for the safe return of the missing fliers. But no trace of them had been found.

Barbara, meanwhile, had divorced John Rogers, remarried, and moved to Greenwich, Connecticut.

As for Shermane, when college let out for the summer after her junior year, she got a job at *Harper's Bazaar* as an editorial assistant and decided to join her father living at the Stork Club.

After her first year at Finch in New York, Shermane had persuaded her father to allow her to attend Connecticut College for Women in New London, about two hours' drive east along the coast. The *women* part of the name satisfied Billingsley, who wasn't aware of its proximity to the U.S. Coast Guard Academy. Like Barbara before her, Shermane was supposed to be in her dorm room at night when her father called. But she quickly learned that by stuffing a tissue in her mouth, holding her nose, and pronouncing her name as *Char-mane,* she could sound like an operator putting though a collect call from Shermane Billingsley in her room in New London, Connecticut, when she was anywhere but there.

Shermane had other secrets. One weekend in her sophomore year she had slipped away to Princeton to experience for herself the parties that her Connecticut College classmates were raving about. She attended a performance of the Princeton Glee Club, and afterward a student escorted her to a house party. She was walking through a corridor from the library when she saw him — a towering young man in a dark green shirt. He looked about six foot five. She was mesmerized. They talked and they danced, and then she had to run off back to school. He took down her phone number but never called.

A year later the student who had escorted her to the Princeton party called to invite her out in New York. On the way they stopped to pick up one of his friends at the Waldorf-Astoria. It was, fatefully, the man in the green shirt! She was in shock — and in love.

A t the Stork Club, Billingsley fixed up quarters for Shermane in his seventh-floor aerie, boarding shut the windows against any intruders from the fire escape. (He thoughtfully left a hammer on the air conditioner so she could smash her way out in case of fire.) It was just the two of them now. Sally Dawson, who had been at Billingsley's side since the early television days of 1951, had packed up and gone home to Texas.

It was suffocating in the city. The streets looked desolate and forlorn. The club was empty, deserted by customers repelled by the air of neglect and Billingsley's fulminations as he cursed the unions and politicians. His familiar world continued to crumble. He heard that in Hot Springs, Arkansas, Owney Madden, the last of his onetime gangster partners, had died of emphysema. Owney the Killer had made it to seventy-three.

Day after day, night after night that summer, Billingsley roamed the club's darkened rooms, leaving the building only once, to take Shermane to Reuben's for cheesecake. He had run through all their money and had even sent her to some of her college friends to borrow a thousand dollars here, five hundred there, to meet his payroll. It was humiliating, but she did it, because he asked. She wasn't aware yet how bad their situation really was — that he had drained the girls' trust funds of nearly $10 million in the struggle to keep the club afloat.

One night in August, taking coffee with her in their apartment, he said, "Shim, you know I've always done the best I could for you."

She looked up sharply, alarmed at what might be coming next.

"And I wanted to do a lot more," he continued. "But, Jesus Christ! I never dreamed things would turn out like this. Everything gone to pot. Now I've just got to ask you to do a little something for me."

She lowered her eyes, nodding, steeling herself.

"I'm selling Three East Fifty-third Street."

She tried to nod, look nonchalant, but her expression betrayed her.

He must have noticed, because he added quickly, "Not the Stork Club name. Just the building. Maybe we'll find a smaller place farther uptown, nearer apartment houses."

He pretended to busy himself with his coffee.

"There's going to be a lot of work, and I'll need you here. I'll want you to keep an eye on your mother now that Jackie and Barbara are gone." Hazel had recently suffered a second, milder heart attack.

"You know," he said, trying to smile, "if we don't watch her, she'll be down here supervising everyone, trying to move boxes herself, and God knows what else. She'll be right back in the hospital if we're not careful."

His tone turned pained again. "Shim," he began uncertainly, "I've always preached education and I want you to have a college degree more than anything in the world. . . ."

"I know," she said, prepared to promise that yes, whatever happened, she would finish her last year of school.

"Can we put it off a year?"

She was caught so unexpectedly that she could barely nod. Fighting back tears, she missed the catch in his voice and only realized how close to tears he himself was when he lurched up and said he was going to the bathroom.

He came back dry-eyed and composed. "You and me, baby, we'll come out of this okay." Didn't she remember, he asked, how they used to be known as "T.B.B." and "T.L.B." — the Biggest Billingsley and the Littlest Billingsley?

She remembered.

"Well," he said, "we'll show 'em."

FORTY-SEVEN

HAZEL RETURNED FROM FLORIDA in the late summer of 1965, and she and Shermane moved into their modest new quarters — Apartment 2B — on East Eighty-third Street. Shermane had resigned herself to not returning to college in the fall. Once things got sorted out, she thought, she could always re-register.

Billingsley continued to stay at the Stork Club, meeting with his real estate lawyer, Fred Carusona, and prospective buyers and draining the last of his bank accounts to keep the club going until a sale went through. He had borrowed everywhere, even $6,000 from Logan's widow, Frances. He kept all his dealings quiet. The property, he knew, would be worth far less if they knew how desperate he was.

One night in late September Billingsley unexpectedly showed up at the new apartment, looking pale and tense. Hazel thought he needed to eat and cooked up some steak and string beans. He ate two forkfuls, and his head dropped heavily on the table.

Hazel frantically ran to call Sherman's doctor, Myron C. Patterson. Shermane, fighting her own terror, stayed behind and tried to prop him up, but his head and neck were rigid. His eyes were open, staring unblinkingly, and his lips moved soundlessly.

Suddenly he sat up and pushed the plate away as if nothing had happened.

Hazel came running back in and started to say that she had reached the doctor but stopped in her tracks when she saw him sitting up. She clasped her hands in prayer. "Thank God!"

Billingsley looked at her suspiciously. "What the hell's the matter with you?"

Hazel and Shermane exchanged stupefied glances. "Sherm," Hazel said gently, as if talking to a child, "you passed out while you were eating. Don't you remember? I called Patterson, and he's coming right over."

He grumbled his protestations and, when the doctor arrived, refused to be examined. It was Mother's health they should be worried about, he mumbled. The doctor advised them to bring him in for an examination in the morning.

After he left, Billingsley went into a tirade. "Never should have come up here. I come here to get a little rest, and you crazy dames make me miserable. Go away! Get out of here!"

That night Shermane and Hazel stood vigil in shifts, snatching twenty-minute naps and sitting in the bathroom outside Sherman's room, where they could monitor him. They heard him repeatedly picking up the telephone receiver and dropping it. Hazel went in and asked who he was trying to reach.

"The front door," he snapped. "Get me Gregory!"

Hazel looked at her watch. "It's after four A.M., Sherman," she said softly. "Only the night watchmen are on now."

"Okay. Thank you," he said, dismissing her like a stranger.

From outside the door they heard him dialing again and then speaking. "Greg, how are we doing? Good. Good. Give me the readings. Okay, set up an extra table when the Curleys come in. . . ."

Curious, they peeked in. He was speaking into the wrong end of the receiver.

In the morning he kept insisting he had to go to the club, but he could hardly walk and was in such a sweat that he repeatedly soaked his pajamas through. He kept greeting imaginary people, giving orders and signing nonexistent checks. While they waited for the doctor, Hazel called a nursing service to arrange for private care. Shermane introduced the nurse as one of her school friends, and the pretty young woman got Sherman to calm down. Soon he was regaling her with yarns of unions and gangsters. But then he said he had to go; he was late for the Stork Club. When Dr. Patterson returned, he ordered an ambulance to take Sherman to Roosevelt Hospital to see if he had suffered a stroke.

Barbara, who was expecting her second child, promised to come from Connecticut as soon as possible. Jacqueline, in Florida, was trying to arrange for someone to watch her three children so she could fly up to New York.

When Shermane saw him later in his hospital room, he was asleep. The bedside nurse said he thought he was in the Stork Club. He had ordered her to take someone's picture and distribute perfume.

Worried what might be going on at the club in his absence, Shermane called there to say that her father wanted to know who was in and what the readings were. Hazel followed up with her own call to say that Mr. B had a sore throat and wanted the chef to send some vegetable soup and ground sirloin to the apartment.

But as Billingsley's stay at the hospital stretched on, it was hard to keep up the pretense. Gregory and Tommy were particularly difficult to fool, as it simply wasn't like Mr. B to be away so long.

Shermane took to stopping by the club in the afternoon and planting herself at table 1 to keep an eye on things. She caught the day manager regularly helping himself to a large glass of gin or vodka. Indignant, she rebuked him. "You wouldn't do this if Mr. B were here, would you?"

"Well," he slurred, "who am I supposed to take orders from?"

Looking in the large mirrors that her father had put up to reflect everything going on, she could see workers slipping out early, many of them clutching brown paper bags. God only knew what they were taking out with them.

She came to rely on Tommy, now the day head captain. Dear, sweet Tommy. He had taught her how to drive, and she never forgot his patience, good humor, and kindness. He was barely ten years older than she, and by far the youngest of the senior staff. She would need his help now more than ever.

After a week in intensive care Billingsley made a remarkable recovery and was moved into a sunny private room high up in a new pavilion. He had no memory of his blackout, but his spindly arms and legs were testimony enough to his breakdown.

He never found out that for a brief time his neighbor across the hall was Winchell, there to undergo dental surgery.

As news of his hospitalization spread, good wishes poured in. Circusmaster John Ringling North cabled, HOPE YOU WILL SOON BE WELL AND STRONG AGAIN.

From his hospital room Billingsley finally gave Tommy the word: let the kitchen help go. He had sold the building to CBS's William Paley.

A few nights later a familiar figure with a trademark fedora and a rat-a-tat-tat voice came through the Stork Club's door.

"I want to take one more walk through the place," he announced.

"Okay Mr. Winchell," Tommy said.

So many of Winchell's memories had been bound up in the Stork Club. In October 1963 he had gotten a telegram. He didn't know whether to laugh or to cry.

> JOSEPHINE BAKER IS INVITING YOU TO HER BENEFIT PERFORMANCE THIS SATURDAY OCTOBER 12 AT CARNEGIE HALL. SHE HOLDS NO ANIMOSITY; HOPES YOU DON'T EITHER, AND FEELS THAT PERHAPS HER PAST VIEWS WERE PREMATURE.
>
> MAX EISEN PRESS REPRESENTATIVE

He scribbled in the margin: *After all the LIES she told! WOW.*

"I know the reputation was that Winchell made the Stork Club," Winchell said. "But I'd come to the Stork Club and spend a few hours here and I could fill up a book, never mind a column." How much came from the club's hidden mikes, he never said.

FORTY-EIGHT

O N MONDAY NIGHT, October 4, 1965, Gregory was at the door as usual, lifting the gold chain for faces he still recognized. With forced exuberance, bartenders shook drinks to the beat of recorded music pounding in from the Shermane Suite. At a table just outside the main room, Shermane sat with her father's lawyer, Fred Carusona, and a tall young navy ensign in officer candidate school, Craig Drill, the man in the green shirt who had been her love since the party in Princeton. Now he was in sailor's whites.

Shermane was intently quiet, trying to imprint the scene on her memory forever. *The last night at the Stork Club.* She kept thinking of her father in Roosevelt Hospital. He of all people should be presiding tonight. As the last customers filtered out, Shermane walked upstairs to the ladies' room to say good night to Nora, the attendant. She wanted to tell her there'd be no more secrets whispered at the vanity tables, no more mischievous little girls to slide under the cubicles, lock them from the inside and then slide out again. . . .

"Miss Shermane, Mr. Craig's waiting."

Gregory interrupted her reverie. He linked his arm in hers and escorted her out to the gold chain. Shermane half imagined she could see her father sitting at his usual table 1, not as he looked now, frail and skeletal, but as she remembered him — tall and commanding, his sharp eyes sweeping his domain, missing nothing.

Suddenly she broke loose from Gregory and rushed back inside to Carusona.

"You'll remember the sign, won't you?" she asked.

"I won't forget it," he promised.

The next day it hung in the window, just as Billingsley had ordered.

STORK CLUB CLOSED

WILL RELOCATE

The newspapers quickly picked up the news, another sign of chang-ing times. THE STORK CLUB FOLDS ITS WINGS, headlined Billingsley's old nemesis, the *New York Post*. Jimmy Breslin of the *Herald Tribune* also weighed in. "So New York changed, and the Stork Club became silly and old. Places like Arthur, which is silly and new, draw the people."

Writing now in Hearst's *Journal-American*, Winchell offered his own poignant obituary to the club.

> *The Stork Club closing is no reason for sad songs. . . . The Stork was dedicated to the excitement of the town. . . . For its guests the Stork was the palace of night clubs. . . . For its host Sherman Billingsley it was his home. . . . Sherman liked to believe that the people who came to his club were more than customers. . . . They were his guests and he was their friend. . . . The fact is Sherman liked nearly everybody and nearly everybody liked him. . . . His generosity and friendship are well known. . . . The mistake Sherman made — if you call it a mistake — was to believe that he could gain and retain friendship by giving it. . . . As we once observed about Jimmy Walker: He was always a friend to the many who were only a pal to him.*

Letters from friends and colleagues poured in.

> *Just a note to let you know how appreciative we are to you for helping us further our career in this business.*
> *We will never forget you for it.*
> *If ever we can be of service to you, please feel free to call upon us. It would only be a pleasure to try to re-ciprocate in some small way for all you have done for us.*
> *Sy Presten*

From the road, where she was touring with *Kismet*, Anne Jeffreys, who with her husband, Robert Sterling, had made a radiant pair at the Stork Club, wrote in sadness that "my home away from home is no more. I truly grieve."

> *Time changes everything, but you . . . will never be forgotten by the many people you befriended. There will never be another equal to the old Stork Club.*

From Gracie Mansion, which they were soon to vacate for incoming tenant John V. Lindsay, Barbara Wagner, the mayor's wife and a former Stork Club employee, wished Billingsley "all good luck in the future in whatever new Stork Clubs open up."

Another began:

> *Sherman, Dear . . .*
>
> *When I read in W.W.'s column Friday night that you had closed "our Stork Club," I have been trying to find the proper words to write to you , but they just do not seem to come to me . . . it was like reading about the death of an old and valued friend. I have no idea what your reasons were for making the great decision, but whatever they were, I am sure you were right. It could have been the way this crazy world is getting crazier — and it is almost frightening. . . . I still re-member what you did for me many years ago — I will not and CANnot ever forget it — So, should the idea of a new Stork Club strike you at anytime, I will be at your beck and call. . . .*

It was signed "Dorothea." The letterhead read: DOROTHY LAMOUR, TOWSON, MARYLAND.

Strangers, too, deluged the hospital with mail.

> *Some time ago I had the pleasure of visiting your Stork Club and needless to say I had a most enjoyable evening. Since then I have married and now have twin sons 13 years old, so you can see it was a long time ago since my evening at the Stork Club.*
>
> *Mainly I just wanted to let you know there are people, even if plain people like myself, who do wish you well.*
>
> *Should you be coming down to the Jersey Shore after you are feeling better, please feel free to stop in for a visit.*

Many shared their memories.

> *. . . once I peeked into the Cub Room. You were there and stood up as if to come over. I ducked back.*
>
> *We now have two children and it is rarely that we get out together . . .*

*Just as there will always be a Statue of Liberty in
New York, there must always be a Stork Club . . .
We were far from being your steadiest patrons.
But — we loved the place.*

From Mount Mercy Convent in Mount Washington, Maryland, Sister Mary Susanna sent her prayers and those of her third-grade pupils for Billingsley's quick recovery and "though far from a celebrity" recalled happy occasions with her parents in the Stork Club.

*You, while a great man, with much to do, took a
few moments to greet us. Your generous kindness will
long remain a happy memory. . . .*

Tommy helped clear out the club. Billingsley told him to offer Oscar Tucci of Delmonico's a chance to buy the furnishings.

Tucci wanted to know how much Billingsley was asking.

"Tell him," Billingsley said, "to make out a check for whatever he thinks is fair."

Emptying the club, Tommy found a locked closet for which no one had a key. He ended up taking a fire axe to the door.

What he found inside amazed him: large dusty glass jars and snaking coils of brittle rubber tubing. It looked like stuff from an old still, bootlegging apparatus. When had Billingsley stopped making his own booze?

FORTY-NINE

O N   A   C O L D ,   O V E R C A S T   M O R N I N G   in late November 1965, Billingsley was finally discharged from the hospital. When Shermane arrived to take him home, he was already dressed and waiting impatiently. As they prepared to leave, a nurse appeared with a wheelchair.

He stared at it with distaste. "Do I have to get in that thing?"

"Just to the front door," she said. "Then you're on your own."

In the taxi he sank back on the seat and clutched the leather handstrap unsteadily. Billingsley saw from his hack license that the cabbie was Greek. *"Sigga-sigga,"* he said, the same way he used to caution "easy, easy" to the Greek busboys who charged through the kitchen's swinging doors with heavy trays.

Walking into the apartment, he clutched Shermane's arm tightly. "I feel a little dizzy," he admitted and then looked around, puzzled. "Isn't there another room?"

Hazel shook her head, driven to tears by his disorientation.

"I could have sworn there was a big, big room like in the club," he said.

Over the next few weeks he settled down at home, taking his pills, resting and eating five meals a day to regain his weight. The doctors had suggested a fortifying beer before lunch and dinner, but beer made Billingsley gassy. Hazel came up with carbohydrate-rich alternatives, including vichyssoise fortified with wild rice.

She watched out for him, and he watched out for her. With her heart condition and high cholesterol, she wasn't supposed to have candy, but she still sneaked out regularly to the five-and-ten for jellybeans, her favorite. Even in the days when Billingsley brought home fancy chocolate bonbons from the Stork Club, she had preferred her penny candy. It so exasperated him that she had to hide her supply, which he would inevitably discover when looking for something in the closet.

As he regained strength, he took to the telephone, calling his lawyers incessantly. At night he called Gregory, who was working at Bill's Gay Nineties; Beautiful Mary, who had gone to work for columnist Jack O'Brian at the unpromisingly hybrid *World-Journal-Tribune*; and other members of his old Stork Club family. They all told him they were waiting for him to reopen so they could come back to work.

When he felt well enough to get dressed, Shermane went to Saks to pick out some new clothes that would fit him. She gave a salesman his collar size, and was directed to the boys department. A tailor came to the house to take in his suits.

Each morning after breakfasting on Sanka and oatmeal, he sat in the living room and watched the pigeons on the sill outside the window. He had never felt at home in the new apartment on the far East Side and kept asking which way Fifth Avenue was, and which way downtown. After a while he would go into his room to think about the book, which he was still intent on writing, until lunchtime. Sometimes Gregory or a few old customers came by, but he discouraged visits. He didn't want people to see him until he gained another twenty pounds.

One afternoon when they were alone, Shermane announced that she had something on her mind, something she had put off saying because of his condition. But it was now time to tell him.

"What?" he asked distractedly.

"Craig asked me to marry him, and I have accepted."

She didn't give him a chance to respond before quickly adding: "We would like your blessing more than anything."

She waited, staring at his curiously blank face for a sign of his reaction.

"Come out to the kitchen," he finally ordered.

He reached into the liquor cabinet and, taking down a bottle of scotch, poured a measure into two glasses. Shermane had never seen him take a drink of hard liquor before, and was strangely gripped by the spectacle, almost more riveted by that than anything he might say. He raised his glass.

"To you and Craig."

Overcome with joy, she was surprised later to overhear him talking to her mother. "We'll be two sick old people trying to take care of each other. They all run off and leave you when you can't do any more for them."

Despite herself, she smiled. Same old daddy.

Now that Shermane was safely provided for, Billingsley was consumed with guilt over Jacqueline's ordeal. There still had been no word about the fate of Alex Rorke since his disappearance more than two years before. Reaching out in desperation to his circle of friends, he wrote Hearst president Richard E. Berlin, begging him to intercede with the FBI for any information on Rorke. There had a been a time when Billingsley would have thought nothing of calling Hoover directly, but those days were long past.

Berlin passed on the plea to Assistant Director Cartha "Deke" De-Loach. A search of Bureau files revealed that Rorke had been a clerical employee in the FBI's New York office in 1951 before leaving for college. After Castro's rise to power, Rorke operated as a freelance photographer while working on an anti-Castro air campaign that dropped leaflets over Cuba and purchased bombers to attack the island. For a time he was being "counseled" by the Central Intelligence Agency, but in June 1962 the Agency told the FBI that it was dropping him as too much of a "loose talker."

After Rorke publicly announced in April 1963 that he had bombed Cuba, the FBI, at Attorney General Bobby Kennedy's behest, conducted an extensive investigation, reporting its findings to the Justice Department. Prosecution was passed up, and the case closed. As far as the FBI knew, Rorke was dead.

Bureau supervisors suggested that DeLoach inform Berlin of this "in confidence" and say they could not be of help to Billingsley.

Hoover strenuously disagreed. "No," he wrote in an internal memo, "I do not want in any way to get involved in this." Berlin, he said, might advise Billingsley, and it could all become public.

Besides, Hoover added, recalling Barbara's elopement, "Billingsley & I broke many years ago. . . ."

As they set the wedding plans for January, Craig was accepted as part of the family. He and Billingsley were playing checkers one night when Craig asked his future father-in-law a question. Billingsley seemed befuddled.

"Son, I don't know anything anymore."

It was a simple family affair in their East Eighty-third Street apartment. No lavish nightclub ballroom reception. No society orchestra. No news photographers. Afterward the couple decamped for Norfolk, Virginia, where Craig was serving his navy duty.

They spoke often on the phone. Billingsley reported proudly that he was gaining weight, thirty-five pounds since leaving the hospital. The tailor had to come back to let out his suits. He told Shermane that he and Mother had even looked at some restaurants for sale. The only place he wouldn't go, he said — *couldn't bear to go* — was the cleared site of the Stork Club, where William Paley of CBS was building his vest-pocket park in honor of his father.

FIFTY

A YEAR HAD PASSED — exactly — since the last night at the Stork Club. Billingsley spent the afternoon of October 4, 1966, on the phone with Tom Bolan in Roy Cohn's office, sorting out the tangle of litigation that had survived the club's closing. The cases included a final charge of discrimination, this one brought by two executives of the Scoville Manufacturing Company, one black and one from India, who claimed they had been refused service the previous year. Their complaint had been upheld by the city's Commission on Human Rights, and they were suing Billingsley, the club, and one of his captains for nearly half a million dollars.

As usual when he talked to lawyers, Billingsley had worked himself into a rage. By dinner he had calmed down but didn't feel well.

At 11:00 P.M. he made Hazel a cup of tea and brought it into her room. After watching the news, Billingsley said he still felt awful and had a terrible pain in his jaw. She said it was probably a head cold and told him to take two aspirin. He nodded agreement and went back to his room to read the papers. After so many years of staying up all night, he usually couldn't get to sleep before dawn.

Hazel was about to turn off the light when he walked in again. As he reached the foot of her bed, he crumpled heavily against it. The mattress slipped, exposing a bag of candy that spilled all over the floor.

"Hazel," he murmured, "are you still hiding jellybeans under the mattress?" He made a rattling sound in his throat, as if to dislodge a bone, fell to the floor, and was dead.

Shermane was awakened by the phone in Norfolk at 5:00 A.M. Hazel's voice sounded strangely controlled.

"Shimmy," she said, "I have some bad news. We lost Daddy this morning. Dr. Patterson said it was his heart."

Shermane rushed to pack. At 7:00 their next-door neighbor, a school-teacher, called in shock: the news was already on the radio. In New York Peter Lind Hayes and Mary Healy, hosts of a morning radio show on WOR, broke in with a personal note of condolence to the Billingsley family. "Sherman passed away this morning, and he was very kind to us for a number of years," Peter said, recalling the television show "from the fabulous Stork Club."

"He was a very simple, kind, and gentle man," Hayes went on. "He had a lot of people that didn't agree with that particular side of Sherman, but we were there, Charlie, and he was a dear fellow. He was very nice to us."

It was kind of strange to think of the club now as a park, he said, but Mary said it was a nice way to remember their friend Sherman.

Peter agreed. "A fellow that did many kindnesses without getting recognition for them."

By 10:00 Shermane was on a plane to New York. Looking out of the window at the clouds, she imagined she saw her father in his maroon-and-green-striped robe sitting at table 1 with a cup of coffee and then striding down Fifth Avenue chomping an apple. She heard him singing his off-key version of "Jimmy Crack Corn." She imagined she was ten again, and on the TV show with Burl Ives. And she imagined hearing her father say, "Two sick people trying to take care of each other . . ."

She arrived at the apartment in a daze. It was filled with people coming and going. For a long time she stood outside the closed door to his room, afraid to enter. Finally she asked someone if he was in there, and was told no.

She slipped in. The bed was made and the room tidied up. The ashtray was sparkling clean. She dropped into the red leather chair facing the bed and just sat there.

The papers the next day were filled with obituaries and farewell columns from Billingsley's longtime newspaper cronies. Nobody got his age of seventy right. Jack O'Brian — whose tribute was headlined SHERM DIED WHEN THE STORK DID — came closest with sixty-eight. The *Times* took him at his word and made him sixty-six. Winchell defended his pal for "the celebs he barred from his Stork Club. . . . Most were obnoxious drunx. . . . Others included ingrates who accepted his gifts (and no tab) and then panned him to competitors et al. . . ."

A letter came in from Texas to Hazel and the girls.

> *I believe this is the most difficult letter I will ever have to write. As you know, through the years, Mr. B was truly my friend — I should say my very good friend — and I like to think I was his good friend. Through all the channels of business we had a rela-*

tionship which was bound by loyalty and friendship and when I heard the TODAY show yesterday and learned of his death, my heart simply sank to the lowest possible depth. Suddenly all of the good times and hard times flashed through my mind. I know there is not one thing that I can say or do, but I just had to let you all know that, although we have lost a husband, father and friend, I really believe that his final reward will be that of a very special kind. Perhaps he didn't always do exactly the right thing, but one thing for sure, he certainly did many more good things than bad. He was a far better person underneath that hard crust than most of us will ever be and whatever follows this life on earth — if it is based on our lives on earth — I believe we can all know that he has a happiness and peace which he really never did know here. . . .

My best love to you all, Sally.

Shermane and Craig were the first to arrive at the Frank E. Campbell Funeral Home on Madison Avenue at Eighty-first Street. Shermane was spooked by the black-clad figures tiptoeing about in squeaky shoes.

"We just brought the body up," the funeral director said, escorting her into a viewing room.

She was suffocated by the smell of flowers. Her father would have hated this. She wanted to throw the windows open, let in air.

"We tried to copy the hair from a photograph," the director said, "but there was less to work with than when the picture was taken."

Shermane usually felt it coming, like a sneeze impossible to stifle. This time, however, she had no warning. A cry of pain tore through her, and she wept uncontrollably. The director hurried from the room.

She stared at the pale, gaunt figure in the coffin. That wasn't her father, she kept telling herself. It looked nothing like the warm, strong man she adored.

"How are you, dear?"

She looked up to see Gregory. He took his hands in hers, hugged her, then left her to genuflect at the coffin.

The funeral home began to fill up. There were society matrons and judges, politicians, newsmen, actors, and one toothless old man who said he worked at the club in the speakeasy days.

Some men she barely recognized congregated at the door. They said they were waiting for Frank Harris and Ed Wynne, names that made her

recoil. "I'm sorry," she said, "you'll have to wait outside. You weren't men enough to face him when he was alive. You're not going to see him now."

She noticed for the first time a huge bouquet of dozens of red roses closest to the coffin and reached to turn over the card.

Costello.

When she looked up, Gregory was working the room, shaking hands and slapping backs. "How are you, Mr. Farley? Nice of you to come. Mr. Lahr, let me take your coat. Mrs. Wagner, won't you come this way? Jimmy! How you doing, boy? Where you working these days?"

Tommy Wendelken watched Gregory for a while. Then he went over and whispered in his ear: "Gregory, forget it. It's all over."

AFTERWARD

I T STARTED, LIKE SO MANY OTHER STORIES, with an unexpected phone call and a voice you could never make up or ever forget.

"Ahh, mon ami, unbelieeeevable, of course — excuse me — zey wair eftair eem lak zey wair eftair air, but Zhosephine, she staaht eet, but of course, ahh, you know zaat . . ."

I knew nothing, including the identity of the Gallic typhoon on the other end of the line.

"Oooooooo pardon, mon ami, ees Jean-Claude Bak-air. Ah ad to call youuuuu, ma fren. Hav you heerd what ahm telling youuuu? Eee bug ze Stork Cluuub. Excuse me sir! Whaat you theeenk?"

I didn't think anything. "Look, suppose you tell me . . ."

"Ooooo, allo, you wrote today ze storee about Lennee Bernstein?"

The New York Times had indeed that day in July 1994 front-paged my story about Leonard Bernstein's FBI file. Obtained by a civil liberties group, it detailed decades of investigation into the late conductor's leftist causes and associates.

"So, zair you air, mon ami . . ."

I still didn't know what he was talking about. But two words jumped out. Stork Club. Three, counting Zhosephine.

When I finally sorted it out, it came down to this: my caller was Jean-Claude Baker, an adopted son and biographer of the quixotic Josephine Baker, whose luscious nude likeness enlivened the walls of Chez Josephine, an atmospheric bistro of his on West Forty-second Street's Theater Row. That Hoover's FBI had shadowed Baker as well as Bernstein and countless other cultural icons deemed subversive did not surprise me. I remembered, too, that she and the Stork Club had been entangled in a celebrated imbroglio over racism in the fifties. But I had never heard that she had somehow instigated it, or that the Stork Club had been bugged. Now *that* sounded interesting.

The Stork Club existed in some Valhalla of forties glamour and black-and-white *Life* photo spreads, but how many actually still remembered the place? When I mentioned it to a young investment banker I knew, he looked blank for a moment and repeated, "The store club . . . ?" I did some research and found, to my surprise, that the *Times* story nearly thirty years earlier about the tearing down of the Stork Club to make a pocket park had been written by . . . *me.* I had totally forgotten the piece — the closest I had ever come to the Stork Club.

But as a longtime investigative reporter, I was tantalized by the mention of electronic eavesdropping at the club. Had that been known? I didn't think so. I was also captivated by the romance of the Stork Club era, which I was too young to have really shared. Still, as a threshold baby-boomer (my parents, who had emigrated to New York from pre-Nazi Berlin, didn't wait for the end of the war to have me), I experienced enough of the heroic forties and flighty fifties to kindle ardent interest in a return visit via interviews and archives.

Sherman Billingsley was long dead, but I tracked down his youngest daughter, Shermane, in suburban Ridgewood, New Jersey, a world apart from the stylish Manhattan of the Stork Club. The divorced mother of two grown sons, she lived in a handsome modern house surprisingly devoid, it seemed, of Stork Club memorabilia, with one exception: over the mantle hung a gaudy painting of Balloon Night at the Stork in the fifties, an Albert Dorne original reproduced on Stork Club menus and postcards. Against a background of joyous guests grasping for prizes were the identifiable faces of Winchell and Arthur Godfrey, Dorothy Kilgallen, Morton Downey, Tallulah Bankhead, and, in the center, Billingsley himself in a tuxedo, escorting a fur-clad, diamond-bedecked ingenue to her table.

Another portrait of Billingsley hung in the living room, a hypnotic, lustrous black-and-white photograph from the forties showing him in a dark suit and white shirt and tie and no jewelry but for a platinum ring with a cabochon sapphire on his left pinky, the gift of Steve Hannagan.

Other than that, I saw no sign of the signature black-and-white Stork Club ashtrays, pitchers, matchbooks, lipsticks, Sortilege perfume, suspenders, neckties, wooden storks, or other souvenirs that Billingsley had given away or patrons had helped themselves to over the decades, and that now graced the dusty shelves of collectibles shops from SoHo to San Francisco. I didn't know yet that Billingsley had pretty much died broke, a sad and raging Lear with nothing left to bequeath Shermane and her two sisters — worse than nothing, actually, since he had drained their trust funds of what today would be nearly $50 million in a desperate effort to keep the Stork Club going in the face of a ruinous battle with the unions.

Her father had been making notes for a book, Shermane said. She had tried to write it with him and then again after his death, but it had never come together. In fact, I found, stories about Billingsley's book had circulated for years during his lifetime. One of his more colorful patrons, the bon vivant playwright and confidence man Wilson Mizner, had reacted with mock horror. "Write a book?" he shrieked. "He could start another Civil War!" The attempted collaboration with author Earl Conrad had ended badly. Tony Butrico, who served Billingsley for twenty-seven years as a cashier, bartender, and maître d', had also been reported to be working on a book called *The Stork Was a Dirty Old Bird,* but it never appeared, and Butrico had since died. Just after the war the publisher Stanley M. Rinehart Jr. had approached Billingsley about writing at least an introduction for a Stork Club cocktail book, but it emerged as Lucius Beebe's bar book. A former Stork Club maître d', Mearl L. Allen, offered a dyspeptic and purportedly verbatim view of Billingsley in a 1980 memoir, *Welcome to the Stork Club.* Runyon died before he could finish his own planned book, and Hemingway, who had told Billingsley he wanted to write about him, or so Billingsley claimed, never carried out the idea.

I asked if I could see her father's writings. At the least, they might make an interesting feature for the *Times* and could resurrect interest in a book. Shermane pondered it, and agreed. I soon found myself struggling through Billingsley's scrawlings in pencil and pen in ten small notebooks and several hundred sheets of yellow and white legal pads. They encompassed a rich jumble of autobiography, rationalizations, gossip, and history on a broad American canvas stretching from covered-wagon days through Prohibition to the Vietnam era. Clearly, by his own account, the Stork Club had started off as a gangster front, a fact that had long been suspected but never before substantiated. I spent almost two years on and off deciphering and digesting Billingsley's memoir, getting it transcribed and fleshing it out with interviews and other research, and in July 1996 the *Times* ran my piece with some atmospheric photos and an old Stork Club postcard. There was indeed interest in a book.

In time, I augmented Billingsley's accounts with a pioneer memoir by his brother Fred, generously provided by his granddaughter Gail Michaelsen, and with equally rich remembrances by Shermane and her sisters, Barbara and Jacqueline. (Jackie died some months after I interviewed her). At ninety-five and going strong, Blanche Risk, the sister of Billingsley's first wife, Dee Dee, offered a trove of early family photos and extraordinary recollections of Billingsley as a young blade in Oklahoma and New York. Generously — and, I would add, courageously — Logan's three sons, Jerome, Robert, and Francis, and Logan's third wife, Frances, also provided invaluable documents of family history, including many spanning the infamous bootlegging years. Logan's second wife, Hattie Mae, left tape-recorded recollections of her life with Logan, and Glen Billingsley's wife, Barbara (the actress who played June on *Leave It to*

Beaver), confirmed Hemingway's role in quashing their spurious Stork Club in Key West. Tom Bolan made available his and Roy Cohn's dusty files on Stork Club litigation. And the irrepressible Jean-Claude Baker provided invaluable guidance and exhaustive new material from his voluminous archives on the Josephine Baker affair, including many papers from Winchell's private files.

I owe considerable debts, too, to Stella Pavlides, for accounts of her father Gregory's epic service at the Stork Club and her generosity in sharing in her own extensive photo collection, to Yetta Golove for the narration of her checkered career as Billingsley's longtime gal Friday, and to Don Bader, Tommy Wendelken, Frank Carro, George Amodio, and Albino Garlasco Jr. for their stories of life under Billingsley. Bartender Joe Moran, no longer with us, was the first ex-staffer steered to me by Jean-Claude Baker. He led me to others, including Beautiful Mary, photographer Mary Gillen. I called her, but by the time I was ready to interview her, she had died. Sally Dawson graciously discussed many aspects of her difficult years at the strike-crippled club. Gary Stevens was a crucial participant and witness through the notorious television years. Emmy Lou Shelton shared her all-too-brief fairy tale of life as a Stork Club coatcheck girl, and Eleanor Dana O'Connell, one of the last of the *Follies* dancers (and also going strong, at ninety-two) could still recall Billingsley's courting of the girls outside the New Amsterdam Theatre.

Many people filled in details of the Stork Club years. Master researcher Jeff Roth at the *Times* mined the morgues of lamentably dead New York newspapers for chronicles of the gangster era. Faigi Rosenthal at the *Daily News* and other librarians at the *New York Post* offered generous access to their morgues, as did Howard Mandelbaum at Photofest and Laura Giammarco at Time-Life. Ken Cobb and Lenora A. Gidlund were expert guides through the treasures of the New York City municipal archives. The Museum of Television and Radio made available the few Stork Club television shows that have survived, the Public Library of the Performing Arts at Lincoln Center had playbills and photos of Hazel as a *Follies* dancer, the New York Society Library proved an invaluable resource, and Susan Baxter turned over her extensive personal library on the nightclub era. I am also greatly indebted to Eddie Jaffe, the last of the old-time Broadway press agents (before the profession gentrified into public relations *consultants*), Sy Presten and Meredith Anderson, Burt Boyar, John Lahr, Liz Smith, Eartha Kitt, Peggy Sobol, Paula Lawrence, Judy Green, William Alexander (Sandy) McLanahan, Lillian Camp, Lena Horne, Lee Williams, Arthur Christie, William Dufty, Jean Bach, Bill Harbach, David Nasaw, Susan and Judge Stanley Billingsley, Tex McCrary, George A. Polychromopoulos, Mary Healy and the late Peter Lind Hayes, Tom Corbally, Sylvia Lyons, H. Peter Kriendler, John Springer, Michael and Deborah Conrad, Hal Layer, Erna

Charleton, Phil Manos, Fred Robson, Aaron Maltin, Bob Burchett, Martin Hyman, Catherine Tamis, John Kaiser, Sheldon Abend, Laura Billingsley, Neal Gabler, Sherman Mohler, and Robert Mosley, a diehard fan of the Stork Club who, after me and Shermane, was perhaps the most eager person in the world to see this book completed. My deepest thanks, too, go to my agent, Gloria Loomis; her assistant, Katherine Fausset; my editors, Rick Kot and Judy Clain; their associate, Michael Liss; and senior copyeditor Stephen H. Lamont.

My greatest and most inexpressible debt, as always, is to my family — my daughters Anna and Sophie, who endured countless karmic visits to East Fifty-third Street, and my best friend and loving wife, Deborah. If they have forgotten all their sacrifices, I haven't.

Ralph Blumenthal
New York March 1999

POSTSCRIPT

THROW YOUR OWN

STORK CLUB PARTY

BY SHERMANE BILLINGSLEY

DEAR FRIENDS,

S O MANY OF YOU HAVE WRITTEN such wonderful letters to me over the years, sharing your memories of the Stork Club. "I had my 'Sweet Sixteen' party at the Stork!" "Dad proposed to Mom while dancing in the Shermane Suite!" "My father's first stop in New York after returning from World War II was the Cub Room!" "My sister and I still remember the scent of our mother's perfume as she kissed us good night before leaving for the Stork Club!" Still others wrote that they never had the opportunity to visit the Stork Club but collected the original black-and-white Stork ashtrays and other memorabilia because it helped them feel a part of it.

Most of your letters ended with a request: Would I please help you create a Stork Club party for a special occasion? Birthday? (Celeste Holm always celebrated hers there!) Engagement? (Grace Kelly and Prince Rainier announced their engagement in the Cub Room.) Easter? (Burt Lahr, Irving Berlin, Bing Crosby, and John Jacob Astor all brought their children to the Stork Club.) New Year's Eve? (Picture J. Edgar Hoover, Mary Martin, Fred Astaire, and Ginger Rogers, dressed in their finest, donning paper party hats!) This book has given me the perfect opportunity to help you plan your dream event at your very own Stork Club, whether it's a specially designated part of your home or a banquet hall booked for the night.

I learned from the best by watching and listening as my father, Sherman, personally took charge of every detail involved in planning his fabulous events. Some children learn at their father's knee; in my case, I was perched on top of Table 50 in the Cub Room as soon as I could sit up! In fact, I still cherish a photo taken of me when I was about nine months old, seated on Table 50 with my father and Walter Winchell nervously flanking me to make sure that I didn't tumble off!

Table 50 was in the entrance corner of the Cub Room and seated up to ten people. It afforded a view of all who came and went. It was the first choice of everyone, from Marilyn Monroe and Joe DiMaggio to J. Edgar Hoover. But it was also the family table. No matter which celebrities were expected, Table 50 was reserved for my mother, my sisters, and me every Thanksgiving, Christmas, and Easter. It is where my memories of growing up at the Stork Club begin and end. Over the years, it was where pictures were taken of me with my childhood heroes: Hopalong Cassidy, Roy Rogers, the Cisco Kid, and even Rin-Tin-Tin!

One special photograph was taken of me with James Arness when he was starring as Marshall Matt Dillon on *Gunsmoke*. I was a big fan of *Gunsmoke* and had a huge crush on James Arness. But one year, it was on opposite my father's *Stork Club* television show and my mother forbade me to watch any other program when my father's show was on. Now, I dearly loved my father and, as you know, often appeared on *The Stork Club* show. But I really preferred to watch *Gunsmoke*! Mother was horrified, and we had quite a row about it; she considered it traitorous to choose anything that competed with the Stork Club — on any level!

Until I was six or seven years old, my nanny, Nellie Fitzgerald, would take me to the Stork Club every afternoon around 4 P.M. to visit my father. Sometimes my father would order a plate of stew or a bowl of rice pudding. More often, he would opt for his usual ⅓ coffee, ⅓ milk, and ⅓ hot water, while Nanny had tea and pastry and I ordered banana ice cream in a tall glass of ginger ale.

I was never bored. As my father kept a stash of gifts for his guests' children, I was often surprised with a new coloring book and crayons, a Trudy doll (a knob turned the head and changed the facial expression), or some other toy. Between lunch and dinner the club was usually not busy, so my father would go up to his seventh-floor suite and bring down one of the pets that my mother would not allow in our home: my guinea pig, parrot, or rhesus monkey.

I have always related to Eloise of the Plaza because when I could escape from my nanny, I would rush upstairs to the ladies' room, lock all the cubicles from the inside, and crawl out. That meant having to find the skinniest busboy to go up and unlock them when Dorothy Kilgallen and her mother stopped by one afternoon after shopping.

By the time I was ten, my father would pick me up every day after school at 3 P.M. Together we would walk from the school on East Ninety-first Street to the Stork Club on East Fifty-third Street. I treasured those walks because I had my father's undivided attention, and we talked about what we had done during the day. Once at the Stork Club, we sat at my father's table. I had graduated from banana ice cream in ginger ale to Steak

Diane (recipe to follow) and a Coke, but my father's afternoon snacks remained unchanged. By 4 P.M. we were often joined by his associates and friends, stopping by for early cocktails with perhaps a touch of business mixed in. I still remember sitting there as Roy Cohn and my father discussed legal strategies. Sometimes the visitors joining us were more glamorous: Clare Boothe Luce, the senior editors of *Vogue*, or the top executives from Elizabeth Arden's Red Door Salon, to name a few.

On my first date, around age fifteen, my father insisted that I bring the young man to the Stork Club and seated us at Table 50. As we were preparing to leave, he said, in easy earshot of my date: "Now, you know what to do if he tries to kiss you. You punch him in the stomach, and when he doubles over, you sock him in the jaw!" Needless to say, I received not the slightest suggestion of a kiss; but amazingly, the young man continued to call for many years and, as with a number of other men that I dated, grew quite fond of my father.

For over twenty years I watched in awe as my father went about planning and hosting fabulous events. I have distilled all that he taught me into three basic principles: prepare, make your guests feel special, and relax! If you follow these fundamental rules, each of you can be your own Sherman Billingsley and throw a memorable Stork Club party in your home, a restaurant, or a banquet hall.

Sherman's Rule #1: Prepare!

My father put in at least sixteen hours every day making sure that the food was made from the finest ingredients, the silver polished, the salt and pepper shakers filled, the flowers fresh, and the staff respectful and ready for anything. You must begin by determining the size of the Stork Club party you want to have. Is it an intimate dinner party for a group of eight to ten (the Cub Room)? A fun-filled baby shower for twenty-five to thirty (the Blessed Event Room)? A New Year's Eve gala for fifty to sixty (the Shermane Suite)? Once you have a sense of the size of your party, consider the location. Can you host the event in your home? If not, find a restaurant or banquet hall that you can work with to re-create the ambience of the original Stork Club.

You will be fine using plain white tablecloths. Sometimes the Stork Club tablecloths had a green border. If that's your preference, just use a dark green Magic Marker to draw the border on the skirt. To be authentic, make sure that each table has a bowl of iced olives, radishes, scallions, and celery hearts, as well as a basket of French rolls. The wooden stork bud-vase holders have become collectors' items, but a bowl of red roses as a centerpiece is right out of the original Stork Club. The black-and-white ashtrays are also scarce, but if you don't personally own one, someone you know probably has one to lend you.

As for glasses and flatware, keep it simple. Shortly after the club closed (the family and "steadies" always called it "the club"), I had a call from a restaurateur saying that the then "junior" Rockefellers, Hearsts, and Astors wanted to open a new Stork Club. They asked me for some advice, as well as my endorsement. When I heard their ideas about Baccarat glasses and sterling flatware, I suggested they lie down until the feeling passed. When you are feeding two thousand patrons a day, you keep everything sparkling but sturdy and do not create the temptation for theft — unless it's good advertising for you.

Sherman's Rule #2: Make Your Guests Feel Special!

Start with the concept of the gold chain. Create your own Stork Club gold chain by hooking together two or three gold-plated link belts and stringing it across the entry to the party room. As your guests arrive, they have to be "cleared."

One of the most exciting things about going to the Stork Club was knowing that you were sure to see celebrities! It was not unusual to see Cary Grant and Greer Garson sweeping past the gold chain after her final curtain call in Broadway's *Destry Rides Again.* Or to bump into Frank Sinatra on the dance floor of the Shermane Suite as Walter Winchell called in notes for his column. Few of us can include contemporary celebrities on our guest lists, but you can invite your guests to come as their favorite movie star or recording artist. Pick an era. If you are hosting a seventy-fifth birthday party for your father, set the party in the decade he was born and ask your guests to come as their favorite celebrity couple: the Duke and Duchess of Windsor, Humphrey Bogart and Lauren Bacall, Lucille Ball and Desi Arnaz, or Katharine Hepburn and Spencer Tracy, to name a few. Or make someone a celebrity for the night. Write a press release about the guest or guests of honor (college graduate, engaged couple, etc.). Depending on where you live and the scope of your party, the social editor of your local daily or weekly newspaper may find it worth covering!

Flashbulbs were always popping at the Stork Club. Have someone take pictures dressed like Beautiful Mary, with rhinestone barrettes in her hair and wearing a white blouse and short black skirt. For a vintage feel, use black-and-white film. Take pictures of each guest or couple. After developing the film, place a photograph of each guest in a white paper frame on which you have written "Stork Club" and the date. When they receive your gift, it will always remind them of you and the unforgettable party you threw.

Sherman's Rule #3: Relax!

My father used to tell his staff: "Once the party starts, don't get nervous about foul-ups. They'll happen. Stay calm and smile, unless someone drops dead!" Was he remembering the day my pet monkey got loose and ran through the dining room in the midst of lunch hour? Or was he still laughing about the night Tallulah Bankhead beckoned him over and said, "Sherman, darling, this is the best steak I've ever eaten in a restaurant. It tastes . . . well . . . charbroiled." My father never let on that it was indeed charbroiled: the kitchen had just caught fire and all the meat had burned up!

Remember: Expect the unexpected, but don't let your guests know when something goes wrong.

Now that you've learned my father's approach to creating a memorable experience at the Stork Club, let's pick the right room for your event.

CUB ROOM

Your special dinner party for eight to ten guests should take place at Table 50, the most exclusive table in the Stork Club's most exclusive room. Leather banquettes and molded wood paneling lent an air of intimacy. Illustrated portraits of the Beautiful Girls (the models, actresses, and socialites who graced the covers of *Cosmopolitan, Good Housekeeping,* and *Redbook*) hung on the walls. An evening in the Cub Room meant gaiety, glamour, and gossip!

Wedding Anniversary / Engagement Dinner / Birthday
An intimate celebration for 8–10 guests

Invitations:

- Announce that you have reserved Table 50, the most famous table at the Stork Club
- Design your invitation as a speakeasy membership card, or include a password
- Ask guests to come as a celebrity whom they might have run into at the Stork Club
- Enclose a press release on your guest(s) of honor

Props:

- Gold chain (hook together two or three gold-plated link belts)
- Blowup portrait of guest(s) of honor
- 72-inch round table
- White tablecloth (dark green border optional)
- Solid white napkins, folded to stand
- Black ceramic ashtray (authentic Stork Club or plain black)
- Black ceramic water pitcher (authentic Stork Club or plain black)
- Stork figurine
- Centerpiece of red roses
- Champagne stand

Menu:

All food recipes are taken from the Stork Club chef's original notes. In many cases, there are no indications as to the size of the portions or cooking time, so you should do at least one run-through before your event.

All cocktail recipes are from *The Stork Club Bar Book*, by Lucius Beebe, Rinehart & Company, Inc., New York, 1946. The book is out of print, but your library may have a copy of it.

Cocktails:

Stork Club Cocktail

dash of lime juice
juice of half an orange
dash of triple sec
1½ oz. gin
dash of Angostura bitters
Shake well and strain in a chilled 4-oz. glass.

Honeymoon

1½ oz. applejack
1½ oz. Benedictine
juice of half a lemon
3 dashes of curaçao
Shake and serve in a 3-oz. glass.

- Scotch and soda, with glass swizzle sticks
- Martinis
- Old-fashioneds

Wines and Champagnes:

Lucius Beebe observed that:

- Taste in table wines at the Stork Club ran almost exclusively to claret and Burgundy, as well as German wines of the Rhine.
- Ten bottles of champagne were served for every bottle of still wine. The favorites at the Stork Club were Bollinger, Veuve Clicquot, Mumm, and Dom Pérignon.

Canapés:

- Pigs-in-a-blanket (miniature franks), with frilly toothpicks
- Pâté

Appetizer:

- Shrimp, lobster, or crabmeat cocktail
(*Iced bowl of olives, radishes, scallions, and celery hearts, and a basket of French rolls on the table*)

Entrées:

Chicken à la Chesterfield
(*a favorite of Walter Winchell's*)

Alternate slices of roast turkey (Surprise! It wasn't made with chicken!) and baked ham on a broiler pan. Top with broccoli. Spoon sauce over meat and broccoli and broil.

Sauce (makes 2 cups):

- Melt 1½ tbs. butter or margarine in saucepan.
- Stir in 1½ tbs. flour.
- Heat and gradually add 1½ cups light cream combined with ½ cup milk. Stir over low heat until mixture thickens. Simmer 5 minutes.
- Stir some of mixture into 2 beaten egg yolks.

- Return egg mixture to saucepan and heat a few minutes longer.
- Stir in 1 tbs. hollandaise sauce (homemade or bottled), 1½ tbs. prepared mustard, ¾ tsp. salt, dash of pepper, 2 tbs. heavy whipping cream.

Roast of Veal with Cub Sauce
(a favorite of Sonja Henie's)

5-to-6-lb. boned loin of veal
⅔ cup vegetable oil
5 tbs. unsalted butter
salt and pepper
diced celery and carrots
½ cup port wine
½ cup stock
1 bouquet garni (celery, thyme, bay leaf, parsley — tied in a bunch)

Preheat oven to 400 degrees. Heat oil and butter in a roasting pan over medium-high heat. Season veal with salt and pepper and brown lightly on all sides. Remove the veal and stir in the diced celery and carrots. Add ¼ cup port, ¼ cup stock, and the bouquet garni.

Return veal to pan and roast in oven, covered, for 35 minutes. Add remaining port and stock and continue cooking for an additional 20 minutes. Remove veal from oven and let stand for 10 minutes, covered in aluminum foil, while preparing sauce.

Serve with snow peas and wild rice.

Sauce (makes 1 cup):

- In a small saucepan, combine ¼ cup melted currant jelly, ¼ cup pan juices, ½ cup port wine.
- Bring to a boil and simmer 5 minutes.
- Add 2 tsp. ground ginger, 2 tsp. dry mustard, ⅛ tsp. salt.
- Cook a few minutes longer; stir in juice from 1 lemon.

Dessert:

Pineapple à la Stork

Quarter a pineapple lengthwise, including the leaves. Hull and slice fruit and return to shell. For each portion, serve one quarter of pineapple with a few sections of grapefruit and orange. Place a scoop of lemon sorbet in the center and top with a maraschino cherry. Sprinkle with Cointreau. (For a birthday party, place a candle in the sorbet.)

BLESSED EVENT ROOM

This large private room on the second floor of the Stork Club had its own bar and service kitchen. It accommodated approximately one hundred guests but could be partitioned for smaller gatherings. It was where I celebrated my preadolescent birthdays, when little girls wore velvet dresses with touches of lace, little boys donned bow ties with short pants and knee socks, and patent leather was on every foot. There was plenty of room for musical chairs and Pin the Hat on the Stork. No one shushed us. My father loved children and he wanted the Stork Club to be a place where you could feel comfortable bringing the entire family.

Baby Shower / Child's Birthday / Milestone Birthday
A youthful occasion for 25–50 guests

Invitations:

- Buy boxed invitations with a stork motif
- Purchase diaper pins (kilt pins will work, too) and fasten to a handwritten memo providing details about the event

Props:

- White and gold helium balloons
- Poster board of a stork with separate cutout of top hat (used for Pin the Hat on the Stork)

Entertainment:

- Rent a VCR and select an age-appropriate movie for your guest of honor.

Children:

> *Little Miss Marker* (Shirley Temple)
> *National Velvet* (Elizabeth Taylor)
> *The Secret Garden* (Margaret O'Brien)

All of these child stars grew up at the Stork Club!

Adults:

The Stork Club (Betty Hutton and Barry Fitzgerald)

- Teach your children or grandchildren the Bunny Hop, Lindy, or Charleston!

Menu:

All food recipes are taken from the Stork Club chef's original notes. In many cases, there are no indications as to the size of the portions or cooking time, so you should do at least one run-through before your event.

All cocktail recipes are from *The Stork Club Bar Book,* by Lucius Beebe, Rinehart & Company, Inc., New York, 1946. The book is out of print, but your library may have a copy of it.

Cocktails:

Blessed Event

juice of half a lime
dash of curaçao
2 oz. Benedictine
2 oz. applejack
Shake and strain. Serve in a cocktail glass.

Champagne Cocktail

chilled champagne
1 lump of sugar, saturated with Angostura bitters
1 cube of ice
twist of lemon peel
Serve in champagne glass.

Shirley Temple (nonalcoholic)

ginger ale
maraschino cherry
Serve in a champagne glass.

Canapés:

- Children:
  - Pretzels
  - Popcorn
  - Cubes of cheese

- Adults:
  - Cheese platter
  - Smoked salmon and cucumber on pumpernickel triangles

(Iced bowl of olives, radishes, scallions, and celery hearts, and a basket of French rolls on every table)

Entrées:

Chicken Burger à la Stork
(a favorite of Irving Berlin's)

- Finely grind the meat from a 5-lb. chicken.
- Mix in a dash each of salt, pepper, and nutmeg.
- Add 1 oz. soft butter.
- Add ½ pint heavy cream.
- Mix well.
- Shape into patties.
- Dip each patty quickly in melted butter, sprinkle with fresh bread crumbs, and broil about 10 minutes, turning and coloring both sides.

Serve with a hot tomato sauce, French-fried sweet potatoes, and fresh peas.

Billingsley Chop Suey

(created especially for Margaret O'Brien)

- Melt 1 tbs. butter or margarine in a Dutch oven.
- Stir in 1 cup washed, drained wild rice; heat for 5 minutes.
- Add:

    3 beef bouillon cubes dissolved in 3 cups boiling water
    1 cup sliced celery hearts
    1 cup coarsely chopped lettuce
    1 cup coarsely chopped raw spinach
    ¾ tsp. salt
    speck of pepper

- Simmer, covered, for 20 minutes, then turn heat very low and cook about 30 minutes, or until liquid has been absorbed.
- Meanwhile, pan-broil until medium done two 10-oz. boneless rib steaks.
- Cut into 1-inch pieces; toss with rice mixture. Serve hot.

Makes 4 servings

Dessert:

Stork Snowballs

- Individual scoops of vanilla ice cream covered with
    coconut flakes
    chocolate sauce
    colored sprinkles

For a child's party, put a candle in each scoop of ice cream and present them all on a platter as you would a cake. Let the birthday celebrant blow out all the candles and then present individual servings.

For a baby shower, alternate pink and blue candles in each scoop of ice cream. Let all of the guests blow out their candles to celebrate the impending arrival.

SHERMANE SUITE

The consummate party space, the Shermane Suite was the largest room in the Stork Club. Square in shape, it was swathed in aquamarine drapery. Gold braid festooned the fabric to frame arched mirror panels. Here, the music never stopped, with two bands alternating until closing time at 3 P.M. Couples crushed onto the dance floor, ice cubes clinked, and flames from Cherries Jubilee, Crêpes Suzette, and Baked Alaska competed with Elizabeth Taylor's diamonds.

My father liked up-tempo and never allowed a slow waltz, except for the Duke and Duchess of Windsor. Choose either the big band sound or Broadway show tunes from the forties and fifties. End your party with a conga line as your guests pick up their coats.

Balloon Night and New Year's Eve
A romantic night of dining and dancing for 50 or more guests

Invitations:

- Shiny white invitations printed in gold, or shiny black invitations printed in white, each with burgundy or dark green tassels
- Balloons printed with party information

Props:

- Gold chain (hook together two or three gold-plated link belts)
- Party hats and horns
- Red bow ties for gents
- White cotton gloves for ladies
- Netting for ceiling (use fish or tennis netting)
- Balloons in assorted colors

Entertainment:

Make this a Balloon Night! At the Stork Club, my father would hang a fishnet over the dance floor filled with hundreds of gaily colored balloons. Some balloons contained crisp hundred-dollar bills; some round-trip tickets to Hollywood; others held slips of paper to be redeemed for a Cadillac, a thousand-dollar bottle of perfume, or a pedigreed puppy. The balloons were released at midnight, and captains hurried around the dance floor with hat pins while the most sophisticated people in the world waited with childlike anticipation.

Your prizes need not be expensive or outrageous. Go for whimsy: a gift certificate for a shoe shine, a hansom ride through the park, a small telescope to watch "the stars." It's not about the cost, but rather caring about how much your friends enjoy the evening.

Menu:

All food recipes are taken from the Stork Club chef's original notes. In many cases, there are no indications as to the size of the portions or cooking time, so you should do at least one run-through before your event.

All cocktail recipes are from *The Stork Club Bar Book,* by Lucius Beebe, Rinehart & Company, Inc., New York, 1946. The book is out of print, but your library may have a copy of it.

Cocktails:

Dry Martini

⅔ oz. London or dry gin
⅓ oz. French vermouth
Stir, decorate with an olive, and serve in a 3-oz. cocktail glass.

Orchid Cocktail

dash of Crème Yvette
white of one egg
2 oz. gin
Shake hard and strain. Serve in a chilled 4-oz. wineglass. (Use only a dash of Crème Yvette. It will produce a delightful violet flavor, with a color as nice as an orchid flower.)

Romance Cocktail

½ oz. brandy (cognac) and curaçao mixed in equal parts
½ oz. Amer Picon
½ oz. French vermouth
½ oz. Italian vermouth
Add cracked ice and shake. Serve in a cocktail glass.

Champagne Punch (makes 1 gallon)

2 qt. champagne
1 pony maraschino
3 ponies brandy
1 pony curaçao
dash yellow chartreuse
juice of 4 lemons
2 qt. sparkling water
sugar to taste
fresh berries
Place a block of ice (or lots of ice cubes) in punch bowl, pour punch over, and serve.

Wines and Champagnes:

Lucius Beebe observed that:

- Taste in table wines at the Stork Club ran almost exclusively to claret and Burgundy, as well as German wines of the Rhine.
- Ten bottles of champagne were served for every bottle of still wine. The favorites at the Stork Club were Bollinger, Veuve Clicquot, Mumm, and Dom Pérignon.

Canapés:

- Quail eggs topped with caviar
- Thinly sliced beef rolled around scallions
- Asparagus tips rolled in smoked ham

Appetizer:

- Endive salad with blue cheese, walnuts, and sliced orange

Serve with:

Chutney Dressing

¼ cup chopped chutney
½ cup salad oil
2 tbs. vinegar
1 tsp. salt
½ tsp. pepper
1 clove garlic

Mix ingredients together and mariante 1 to 2 hours. Remove clove of garlic. Shake and serve with endive salad.

(Iced bowl of olives, radishes, scallions, and celery hearts, and a basket of French rolls on every table)

Entrées:

Steak Diane
(a favorite of Dorothy Lamour's)

thinly pounded slices of steak
lightly toasted slices of white bread
thinly sliced onion
thinly sliced tomato
pickle relish

The secret to the success of Steak Diane is to keep everything thinly sliced and flattened!

Quickly sauté meat and place on top of bread. Top with onion, tomato, and relish. Cut in quarters and serve with Spooner Steak Sauce.

Spooner Steak Sauce

- Sauté ½ cup finely chopped onions in ⅛ lb. butter until onions are golden.
- Add 1 bottle A.1 steak sauce.
- Add 1 pint heavy cream.
- Add 1 tsp. English mustard.
- Stir.
- Add ¼ cup chopped chives.
- Add 1 tsp. oregano.
- Bring ingredients to a boil and then simmer 5 minutes.
- Add juice of 1 lemon and a few drops Tabasco.

Beef Bourgeoisie
(a favorite of John Wayne's)

4-lb. rump of beef
diced onions and carrots
1 cup flour
3 quarts boiling stock or water
1 pint red wine
3 cups canned stewed tomatoes
2 crushed cloves of garlic
1 bouquet garni (celery, thyme, bay leaf, parsley — tied in a bunch)
salt and pepper
1 glass Madeira wine

In a sauté pan with a little fat, brown the beef. When brown, remove the meat from the pan.

Using the same pan, fry diced onions and carrots until slightly brown. Add flour and fry just a little. Add boiling stock of water, red wine, and stewed tomatoes. Stir well and let boil a few minutes. Add garlic, bouquet garni, salt, and pepper.

Place the beef in the sauce and cook on low heat for 3 hours or so, depending upon the tenderness of the meat. When done, remove the beef and strain the sauce. Remove all the grease that appears on top of the sauce. Test for seasoning. Pour in Madeira wine. Put meat back in the sauce and let it boil a few minutes.

Slice the meat against the grain and serve with garnish of cooked carrots, small braised white onions, new peas, and Madeira sauce.

Madeira Sauce

Reduce 1 glass of Madeira wine with a little sugar. Add pan juices and let boil a few minutes.

Desserts:

Crêpes Suzette à la Stork

The crêpes are prepared in advance; the rest is showmanship!

    6 sugar lumps
    1 orange
    1 lemon
    ⅓ cup orange juice
    ½ cup butter or margarine
    2 tbs. granulated sugar
    ¼ cup Cointreau or curaçao
    2 tbs. rum or Benedictine
    ⅓ cup brandy or Grand Marnier

Rub lump sugar on rinds of orange and lemon; add lumps to orange juice; crush until dissolved.

Melt butter or margarine in chafing dish and add orange juice mixture and granulated sugar; heat. Place crêpes, folded in quarters, in sauce; ladle sauce over crêpes until they are saturated. Mix Cointreau or curaçao and rum or Benedictine and pour over crêpes. Pour on brandy or Grand Marnier but do not stir.

When mixture is heated, tilt pan to flame so sauce catches fire. Spoon flaming sauce over crêpes. Serve crêpes and sauce on heated plates.

Sorbet

If you are intimidated by fireworks, there is nothing more classic and elegant than an assortment of sorbets garnished with mint leaves and raspberries. Serve with petit fours.

So there you have it. If you follow the three basic principles that my father practiced — prepare, make your guests feel special, and relax — and select a room that is appropriate to the occasion, you are ready to host your own Stork Club party!

Writing this has given me an opportunity to relive some priceless childhood memories. In fact, I can't wait to host my next Stork Club party! Now whose birthday is coming up . . . ?

CHEERFULLY,

SHERMANE

New York City
October 2001

PHOTOGRAPHIC CREDITS

BIBLIOGRAPHY

Allen, Mearle L. *Welcome to the Stork Club*. San Diego: A. S. Barnes & Company, 1980.

Amory, Cleveland. *Who Killed Society?* New York: Cardinal, 1962.

Baker, Jean-Claude, and Chris Chase. *Josephine: The Hungry Heart*. New York: Random House, 1993.

Batterberry, Michael and Ariane. *On the Town in New York: A History of Eating, Drinking and Entertainments from 1776 to the Present*. New York: Charles Scribner's Sons, 1973.

Beebe, Lucius. *The Stork Club Bar Book*. New York: Rinehart & Company, 1946.

Behr, Edward. *Prohibition: Thirteen Years That Changed America*. New York: Arcade Publishing, 1996.

Billingsley, Fred. Unpublished memoir. Courtesy of Gail Michaelsen.

Billingsley, Sherman. Unpublished memoir. Courtesy of Shermane Billingsley.

Brown, Eve. *Champagne Cholly: The Life and Times of Maury Paul*. New York: E. P. Dutton & Company, 1947.

Conrad, Earl. *Club*. San Francisco: West-Lewis Publishing Company, 1974.

Davis, Harry Alexander. *The Billingsley Family in America*. Rutland, Vt.: Tuttle Publishing Company, 1936.

Derks, Scott (editor), Gale Research Inc. *The Value of a Dollar: Prices and Incomes in the U.S. 1869–1989*. Detroit: A Manly Inc., Book, 1994.

Diliberto, Gioia. *Debutante: The Story of Brenda Frazier*. New York: Alfred A. Knopf, 1987.

Douglas, Ann. *Terrible Honesty: Mongrel Manhattan in the 1920s*. New York: Farrar, Straus and Giroux, 1995.

Eder, Shirley. *Not This Time, Cary Grant! And Other Stories About Hollywood*. Garden City, N.Y.: Doubleday, 1973.

Einstein, Izzy. *Prohibition Agent No. 1*. New York: Frederick A. Stokes Company, 1932.

Engelmann, Larry. *Intemperance: The Lost War Against Liquor*. New York: The Free Press, 1979.

Erenberg, Lewis A. *Steppin' Out: New York Nightlife and the Transformation of American Culture, 1890–1930*. Chicago: University of Chicago Press, 1981.

Flynn, Edward J. *You're the Boss*. New York: Viking Press, 1947.

Fowler, Gene. *Beau James: The Life and Times of Jimmy Walker*. New York: Viking Press, 1949.

Gabler, Neal. *Winchell: Gossip, Power and the Culture of Celebrity*. New York: Alfred A. Knopf, 1994.

Gavin, James. *Intimate Nights: The Golden Age of New York Cabaret*. New York: Grove Weidenfeld, 1961.

Gill, Brendon, and Jerome Zerbe. *Happy Times*. New York: Harcourt Brace Jovanovich, 1973.

Gray, Barry. *My Night People: 10,001 Nights in Broadcasting*. New York: Simon and Schuster, 1975.

Hanfstaengl, Ernst. *Unheard Witness*. Philadelphia: J. B. Lippincott Company, 1957.

Harris, Michael. *Always on Sunday: Ed Sullivan: An Inside View*. New York: Meredith Press, 1968.

Israel, Lee. *Kilgallen*. New York: Dell, 1979.

Klurfeld, Herman. *Winchell: His Life and Times*. New York: Praeger Publishers, 1976.

Kriendler, Peter H., with H. Paul Jeffers. *"21": Every Day Was New Year's Eve*. Dallas: Taylor Publishing, 1999.

Leider, Emily. *Becoming Mae West*. New York: Farrar, Straus and Giroux, 1997.

Machlin, Milt. *The Gossip Wars: An Exposé of the Scandal Era*. New York: Tower Books, 1981.

Mason, Philip P. *Rumrunning and the Roaring Twenties: Prohibition on the Michigan-Ontario Waterway*. Detroit: Wayne State University Press, 1995.

Merman, Ethel, with George Eells. *Merman—An Autobiography*. New York: Simon and Schuster, 1978.

Mohler, Barbara Billingsley. Unpublished memoir. Courtesy of Barbara Billingsley Mohler.

Morris, Lloyd. *Incredible New York: High and Low Life from 1850 to 1950*. Syracuse, N.Y.: Syracuse University Press, 1996.

Mosdale, John. *The Men Who Invented Broadway*. New York: Richard Marek Publishers, 1981.

Nasaw, David. *Going Out: The Rise and Fall of Public Amusements*. New York: Basic Books, 1993.

O'Connor, Richard. *Heywood Broun: A Biography*. New York: G. P. Putnam's Sons, 1975.

Parish, James Robert. *The George Raft File*. New York: Drake Publishers, 1973.

Runyon, Damon. *The Saga of "Mr. B." of the Stork Club*. Unpublished fragment. Courtesy of Shermane Billingsley.

Russell, Francis. *The Shadow of Blooming Grove: Warren G. Harding in His Times*. New York: McGraw-Hill, 1968.

Sann, Paul. *The Lawless Decade*. New York: Crown Publishers, 1957.

Still, Bayrd. *Mirror for Gotham: New York as Seen by Contemporaries from Dutch Days to the Present*. New York: Fordham University Press, 1994.

Sylvester, Robert. *No Cover Charge: A Backward Look at the Night Clubs*. New York: Dial Press, 1956.

Sylvester, Robert. *Notes of a Guilty Bystander*. Englewood Cliffs, N.J.: Prentice-Hall, 1970.

Thomas, Bob. *Winchell*. Garden City, N.Y.: Doubleday & Company, 1971.

Walker, Stanley. *The Night Club Era*. New York: Frederick A. Stokes Company, 1933.

Walsh, George. *Gentleman Jimmy Walker*. New York: Praeger Publishers, 1974.

Wilson, Edmund. *The American Earthquake*. New York: Da Capo Press, 1996.

Winchell, Walter. *Winchell Exclusive*. Englewood Cliffs, N.J.: Prentice-Hall, 1975.

Wolf, George, with Joseph DiMona. *Frank Costello: Prime Minister of the Underworld*. New York: William Morrow & Company, 1974.

Yablonsky, Lewis. *George Raft*. San Francisco: Mercury House, 1974.

INDEX